# Lecture Notes in Computer Science

T0237991

*Commenced Publication in 1973*
Founding and Former Series Editors:
Gerhard Goos, Juris Hartmanis, and Jan van Leeuwen

## Editorial Board

Roland T. Mittermeir (Ed.)

# From Computer Literacy to Informatics Fundamentals

International Conference on Informatics in Secondary Schools –
Evolution and Perspectives, ISSEP 2005
Klagenfurt, Austria, March 30 - April 1, 2005
Proceedings

 Springer

Volume Editor

Roland T. Mittermeir
Universität Klagenfurt
Institut für Informatik-Systeme
Universitätsstr. 65-67, 9020 Klagenfurt, Austria
E-mail: roland@ifi.uni-klu.ac.at

Library of Congress Control Number: 2005922177

CR Subject Classification (1998): K.3, K.4, K.8

ISSN 0302-9743
ISBN 3-540-25336-X Springer Berlin Heidelberg New York

Springer is a part of Springer Science+Business Media

springeronline.com

© Springer-Verlag Berlin Heidelberg 2005
Printed in Germany

Typesetting: Camera-ready by author, data conversion by Scientific Publishing Services, Chennai, India
Printed on acid-free paper     SPIN: 11407003     06/3142     5 4 3 2 1 0

# Preface

Twenty years ago, informatics was introduced as a compulsory subject in Austrian secondary schools. During this period informatics has experienced drastic evolutions and even some shifts of paradigms. This applies to an even larger extent to the didactics of informatics.

*ISSEP - Informatics in Secondary Schools, Evolution and Perspectives* - takes stock of how the developments in the field are reflected in school throughout Europe. Teachers of informatics at secondary schools as well as educators of such teachers propose innovative methods of instruction, discuss the scope of overall informatics instruction, and discuss how innovative concepts can be disseminated to students in education as well as to active informatics teachers.

Due to the penetration of information technology into society at large and into schools in particular, the relationship between informatics and education leading to general computer literacy or to the use of IT-based approaches in conventional subjects, e-learning in school, is an evident focus of many contributions.

According to the broad scope of the conference its proceedings are split into two volumes. This volume, From Computer Literacy to Informatics Fundamentals, covers papers reporting on national strategies of informatics instruction and their evolution in accordance with the penetration of information processing equipment in our daily life. In one way or another, these strategies strive to accommodate the needs of basic skills in information and communication technology (ICT) with educational principles that can be conveyed by informatics instruction in a traditional sense. Hence, the papers on national strategies are complemented in two ways: firstly, by contributions that strive to identify fundamental issues, informatics can contribute to the general education process of the youth; and, secondly, by papers presenting approaches on how to link or even to combine instruction about such informatics fundamentals with the need to introduce pupils to the productive use of ICT. The other ISSEP volume, subtitled Innovative Concepts for Teaching Informatics, addresses specific didactical models for teaching informatics as well as models of teaching using ICT [1]. Its scope ranges from teacher education via ethics and self-controlled learning to various facets of e-learning.

Out of 51 submissions from 10 countries the program committee selected 16 contributions for publication in this volume. Each paper was reviewed by at least three members of the program committee. The reviewing process and the ensuing discussion were fully electronic.

Thus, this volume, though consisting mainly of contributed papers, is nevertheless the result of an arrangement of papers that aimed in their final versions to specifically contribute to the facet of the program for which they were accepted. The editorial introduction shows how they contribute to the various facets of the conference.

A conference like this is not possible without many hands and brains working for it and without the financial support of gracious donors. Hence, I'd like to thank particularly the members of the program committee, notably those who were keen to review late arrivals or to provide additional help in conflicting situations. Special thanks are also due to the organizing committee led by Peter Micheuz, to Annette Lippitsch for editorial support and administration, as well as to Karin Hodnigg for operating the electronic support of the conference.

The conference was made possible due to the support of several sponsors whose help is gratefully acknowledged. Printing and wide distribution of the two volumes of proceedings was particularly made possible due to a substantial contribution by the Austrian Federal Ministry of Education, Science, and Culture; I'd like to single out particularly Dr. Anton Reiter for his dedicated efforts and creative inputs.

Finally, hosting of the conference by Universität Klagenfurt is gratefully acknowledged. Its facilities and the beautiful surroundings of Carinthia provide the proper setting for a successful event.

January, 2005                                                  Roland Mittermeir

1. Micheuz P., Antonitsch P., Mittermeir R.: Informatics in Secondary Schools – Evolution and Perspectives: Innovative Concepts for Teaching Informatics, Ueberreuter Verlag, Wien, March 2005.

# Organization

ISSEP 2005 was organized by the Institute of Informatics-Systems, Alps-Adria University Klagenfurt, Austria.

## ISSEP Program Committee

| | |
|---|---|
| Mittermeir, Roland (Chair) | Universität Klagenfurt, Austria |
| Adam, Hans | BORG Graz, Austria |
| Böszörmenyi, Laszlo | Universität Klagenfurt, Austria |
| Breier, Norbert | Universität Hamburg, Germany |
| Clark, Martyn | University of Leeds, UK |
| Dagiene, Valentina | Vilniaus Universitetas, Lithuania |
| Dorninger, Christian | Bundesministerium für Bildung, Wissenschaft und Kultur, Wien, Austria |
| Friedrich, Steffen | Technische Universität Dresden, Germany |
| Fuchs, Karl | Universität Salzburg, Austria |
| Fullick, Patrick | University of Southampton, UK |
| Futschek, Gerald | Technische Universität Wien, Austria |
| Garzotto, Franca | Politecnico di Milano, Italy |
| Hartmann, Werner | ETH Zürich, Switzerland |
| Hitz, Martin | Universität Klagenfurt, Austria |
| Holzinger, Andreas | Medizinische Universität Graz, Austria |
| Hopfenwieser, Lisbeth | Technische Universität Wien, Austria |
| Hubwieser, Peter | Technische Universität München, Germany |
| Knierzinger, Anton | Pädagogische Akademie der Diözese Linz, Austria |
| Królikowski, Zbyszko | Politechnika Poznanska, Poland |
| Moreaux, Patrice | Université de Reims, France |
| Mühlbacher, Jörg | Universität Linz, Austria |
| Neuwirth, Erich | Universität Wien, Austria |
| Reiter, Anton | Bundesministerium für Bildung, Wissenschaft und Kultur, Wien, Austria |
| Schubert, Sigrid | Universität Siegen, Germany |
| Schauer, Helmut | Universität Zürich, Switzerland |
| Scheidl, Gerhard | Pädagogisches Institut des Bundes in Wien, Austria |

Spirin, Oleg                    Zhytomyr State Pedagogical University,
                                 Ukraine
Waldner, Walter                 HTBLA Klagenfurt, Austria
Weissenböck, Martin             HTBLA Rennweg, Wien, Austria

## ISSEP Local Organization

Micheuz, Peter (Chair)          Universität Klagenfurt and Gymnasium
                                 Völkermarkt, Austria
Antonitsch, Peter               Universität Klagenfurt and HTL
                                 Mössingerstr., Klagenfurt, Austria
Hodnigg, Karin                  Universität Klagenfurt, Austria
Lippitsch, Annette              Universität Klagenfurt, Austria

## Main Sponsor

ISSEP 2005 and the publication of its proceedings was supported by bm:bwk, the Austrian Federal Ministry for Education, Science, and Research.

# Table of Contents

## Fundamentals Versus ICT

# Introduction

Roland T. Mittermeir

Institut für Informatik-Systeme
Universität Klagenfurt
9020 Klagenfurt, AUSTRIA
roland@isys.uni-klu.ac.at

The external motivation to organize a conference on Informatics in Secondary Schools with specific focus on the Evolution and Perspective of School Informatics was an anniversary. 1985 informatics instruction was introduced in secondary academic schools (*AHS*) in Austria as an independent subject. It encompassed two credit hours of basic informatics instruction in the $5^{th}$ form (age group 14 – 15 years old) and possible electives thereafter. A few years later, electives in informatics could be chosen even at lower grades.

To account for this fact, the opening keynote is given by three pioneers who have been instrumental in the formation of school informatics and who helped to shape the subject in its initial twenty years. *Anton Reiters* contribution tells from a ministerial perspective how this came all about. *Peter Micheuz'* very personal contribution shows how these developments are perceived from the perspective of a practicing teacher. The differentiating nuances between the perceptions reported in these contributions are probably not too specific for a particular country.

Since Austria's secondary school systems is structured into two huge blocks, the (general, humanistic) academic secondary schools (*AHS*, i.e. *Allgemeinbildende Höhere Schulen*) and vocational secondary schools (*BHS*, i.e. *Berufsbildende Höhere Schulen*), Micheuz' contribution is complemented by *Martin Weissenböck's* paper explaining the details of the highly structured and, therefore, relatively inhomogeneous block of *BHS's*. This highly structured system of vocational secondary schools is a distinct characteristic of the Austrian school system. As the system of vocational schools covers a broad spectrum, the role of informatics in these schools varies accordingly. It ranges from special engineering curricula in informatics which have already a substantial tradition to rather non-technical curricula, where informatics is rather seen as data processing or as web design.

The next block of papers gives an account of various national perspectives on informatics instruction and its introduction into curricula of secondary schools. In light of the current enlargement of the European Union towards the East, special focus is laid on countries which joined the union recently or which are even a step further to the East. This block is opened by *Martyn Clark* and *Roger Boyles* investigation, whether and what kind prior informatics instruction would help students to succeed in entry level exams to British universities. Next, *Ewa Gurbiel* and her colleagues report on a reform of the Polish school system. It led to the introduction of informatics related content, ranging from informatics proper via ICT to computer support in traditional subjects. The paper explains how informatics related education is spread over the various levels of the educational system. Remaining in northeastern Europe,

R.T. Mittermeir (Ed.): ISSEP 2005, LNCS 3422, pp. 1–3, 2005.
© Springer-Verlag Berlin Heidelberg 2005

*Valentina Dagiene* describes the contents of Informatics instruction in Lithuania. There, from the 9th to the 12th form students get a rather rich spectrum of compulsory ICT and informatics instruction with optional extensions in the two uppermost grades.

The tension between application oriented ICT and the aim of conveying fundamental principles of informatics to students is further highlighted by *Christian Dorninger's* arguments calling for standardization. It is certainly up for debate, to which extent general schools should apply company-specific standards as their yardstick. Critics should admit though, that in spite of currently popular instances, educational standards might in principle be established for contents of exclusively fundamental nature as well. Establishing such standards would just require agreement on a list encompassing such fundamentals. Dorninger's recommendations attempt the range from basic skills to technical specialties taught at the university level. This implies already that the standards mentioned have to be methodologically much richer than what comes to mind when thinking about ECDL.

*Aleksandr Kuznetsov* and *Sergey Beshenkov* allow a glimpse at Russian informatics instruction from basic up to university levels. Derived from theoretical principles, a list of topics and related instructional processes is presented.

Two Ukrainian papers complete this section. *Oleg Spirin* shows how hardware constraints influence the curricula of Ukrainian schools and how they can be overcome at least to a certain extent. The paper also informs about the actualization of informatics competences of teachers, an aspect relevant all over the world. Another paper showing how to cope with limitations is *Yuri Ramsky* and *Olga Rezina's* account of introducing Ukrainian students to internet search. The West-European perspective of the internet as an infinite world-wide library has to be at least slightly adjusted, when realizing that these pupils native language is written in a different script. Realizing these limitations might, on the other hand, remind us that the west-centric perspective on Latin script and English language provides also only a very truncated view of the world. Further, we rather don't imagine creating a search system to simulate internet search in order to prepare even those pupils for modern information retrieval where scarcity of resources prohibits interconnection to the real web.

Summarizing these national perspectives one witnesses that the penetration of personal computing and the (almost) ubiquitous presence of certain types of application software had substantial effects on the shape of what was introduced as informatics instruction. Principles of abstraction and algorithmization gave way to intellectually less rewarding topics such as using a text processing system to write a letter or using spreadsheets to perform some calculations which were never meant to be done by such tools when the tool was invented.

The dispute centers quite often on the role of programming in informatics instruction. The arguments supporting programming changed over the years. Algorithmization, the necessity to formulate extremely precise, the capability of modeling, the need to anticipate consequences of commands and the need to think in alternative branches is just an incomplete list of arguments. Nevertheless, programming is undoubtedly a distinctive characteristic of computing and informatics as argued by *Jürg Nievergelt* in his keynote opening the discussion about *Fundamentals*. Programming must not capture all of the attention of informatics instruction though.

How broad the discussion about fundamentals can be conducted is shown by *Laszlo Böszörmenyis* paper. Certainly in agreement with the mainstream of informatics educators about the final goals of informatics instruction, he argues to give plasticity to the current body of knowledge deemed appropriate for school by teaching from a historical perspective. This should allow pupils to share part of the excitement created by the inventions once made by the masters of the discipline. In comparison, *Susanne Loidl*, *Jörg Mühlbacher* and *Helmut Schauer* approach fundamental topics in a less controversial way. The distinctive feature of this paper is the simplicity of examples the authors are proposing in order to demonstrate pupils highly complex fundamentals of the discipline. Using e-learning supportas mentioned might allow engraining these concepts so that they are also retained by students.

The next set of papers presents approaches to avoid what sometimes is mentioned as conflicting goals: basic ICT training and informatics-instruction proper. *Karin Hodnigg* presents spreadsheets beyond the tool aspect. Her focus is not on tips and tricks relating to the individual cell but on the perspective of the sheet as a huge computing space with scoping and data-flows, hence on a programming plane. Her projection-screen model seems intuitive and overcomes some inconsistencies one runs into when explaining spreadsheets with the broadly known semantic models of programming. *Markus Schneider* dwells also on the perspective that filling in spreadsheets is programming. To do this in a methodological way, he proposes functional data flow modeling. This not only combines ICT-aspects with software engineering concepts. It also proposes a methodology for systematic spreadsheet development that leads to a relationship between layout and semantics. *Siglinde Voss* shows how to introduce object-orientation based on word processing software. Taken together, these three papers show how multifaceted programming can be and how different the approaches to teach its discipline are. The spectrum opened by these papers is further widened by *Bruria Haberman* and *Zahava Scherz's* contribution. Building on already existing programming knowledge, their approach introduces component based software development with the full spectrum from specification comprehension and specification writing to black box and white box reuse of ADT's. Their approach conveys the declarative and procedural aspects of logic programming. It puts apparently also substantial emphasis on code reading, an aspect neglected in most approaches.

The papers by *Peter Micheuz* and by *Maciej Syslo* et al come back to the issue of the transition from ICT to informatics from the vantage point of two different educational systems. While *Peter Micheuz* argues to subsume ICT in a broad framework of informatics related instruction, *Maciej Syslo* and *Beata Kwiatowska* explain why the various IT-related facets of education are kept separate in Poland. They also report on principles of peer-guided, self-organized training of fellow teachers to raise their competences in integrating information technology in their teaching activity. *Peter Antonitsch*, on the other hand, addresses a procedural didactical issue when discussing the pros and cons of using either highly specialized instructional environments or micro-worlds when teaching programming. It might be surprising that he resolves the dispute by finally proposing an ICT solution to solve the problem.

The volume concludes with a contribution of *Werner Wiedermann*, reporting on developments in the telecommunication industry and their impact on learning in mobile contexts. His keynote leads the way to eLearning and mLearning, topics beyond informatics instruction, and therefore discussed in the accompanying volume. But nevertheless, currently, these topics are still to a large extent within the scope of informatics teachers or at least in the scope of educational projects where informatics teachers are members of the educational team.

# Incorporation of Informatics in Austrian Education: The Project "Computer-Education-Society" in the School Year 1984/85

Anton Reiter

Federal Ministry of Education, Science and Culture,
Vienna, Austria
Anton.Reiter@bmbwk.gv.at

**Abstract.** Effects of information technology on economy, society and education were discussed already at the beginning of the 1980's. The German computer scientist Klaus Haefner even predicted an educational crisis caused by the penetration of information technology into our lives. When the personal computer became the "machine of the year 1985", politicians and educators in the industrialized countries proclaimed "computer literacy" as an essential part of education and demanded the integration of new technologies into the curriculum.

This paper describes the comprehensive instruction project "Computer-Education-Society" of the school year 1984/85, launched by the Austrian Federal Ministry of Education, Arts and Sports[1] on the background of the author's personal involvement as a permanent speaker at the central teacher seminars in Vienna and as a historical dedication to the 20th anniversary of the implementation of the subject *Informatics* at the compulsory secondary general school (*AHS*).

## 1 Introductory Remarks

The rather frightening predictions in George Orwell's well known book "1984" that our lives would be affected, modified and even governed ("Big Brother") more and more significantly by new information (and communication) technologies[2] (in recent literature usually abbreviated with NICTs), might have had some effects on Austrian policy-makers. They considered it as duty of the government's education system to adequately prepare the young people of the 1980's for a life in the so-called post industrial era, a forthcoming technologically advanced information society.

Within two decades the NICTs have changed the world of work and sciences, daily life and our educational system. Computers accomplish tasks of the human intellect

---

[1] Currently: Federal Ministry of Education, Science and Culture (*Bundesministerium für Bildung, Wissenschaft und Kultur*).

[2] It's a matter of fact that in many (recent) publications the term "new information and communication technology" (NICT) is not precisely defined or explained. In most cases it refers to the use of computers, multimedia and telecommunication as tools for teaching and learning. But it also has relevance to the subject *informatics* or *computer science*. During the early 1980's the communication aspect played a minor role. The PC was predominantly available as stand alone device.

R.T. Mittermeir (Ed.): ISSEP 2005, LNCS 3422, pp. 4–19, 2005.

with high efficiency and reliability and they can be linked together to form extensive electronic systems of information and communication. The world's largest and most famous electronic network - the Internet (WWW) - has got an outstanding relevance not only for the field of education [10, 16] but also for the economy and daily life in the industrialized countries. That's why any educational policy has to meet the challenges of the NICTs and to take them into account when discussing future aspects of teaching and learning.

## 2   The New Education Crisis

The German computer scientist Klaus Haefner[3], speaker at worldwide IFIP[4] conferences, raised doubts about the contemporary educational system. He saw the educational system as moving too slowly towards information technology (IT) in general. In the beginning of the 1980s he stated: "Since more and more information processing is being transferred from human brains into the information technology, the presented role of the educational system will be questioned." [12, p. 525] Education would have to change drastically the way to prepare students of all ages for their future role in society, Haefner demanded.

Looking ahead many activities up to now still performed by humans would be taken over by technology, he argued. Instead of human hands, robots would manipulate materials. The low costs benefit ratio of information technology would make it possible to use automated production. Human activity would then be shifted into control activities. People would prefer technical information processing in professional as well as in private applications because it would be more economic, available around the clock, more reliable, and much faster compared with human information handling. Education would have to be adapted quickly or it would run the risk of misqualifying people, Haefner warned.

But in the beginning of the 1980s, he could justifiably claim that "politicians, administrators and teachers presently behave in a way as if information technology does not exist at all. The overall goals of the public educational system have been basically unmodified for decades. It is still the intention of 99 percent of all curricula to educate the autonomous human brain as the sole source of information storage and information processing." [4, p. 973] The human brain would be challenged by the growth of information technology and subject to competition of information processing systems. Humans as information processors would be in fact often not needed anymore, since there was a growing choice of using information technology instead.

To overcome the crisis mentioned in time, Haefner recommended as invited speaker in the House of the Association of Industrialists in Vienna in 1984 and the following years certain educational goals [14]. His recommendations reached from the necessity to understand the forthcoming changes in society as impact of IT via the demand to bring IT into the class for proper use up to the development and

---

[3] His book "Die neue Bildungskrise" [13] became a bestseller.

[4] International Federation for Information Processing – the IFIP secretariat is in Laxenburg close to Vienna (www.ifip.or.at).

evaluation of new curricula, and to the suggestion of starting of in- and pre-service teacher training.

**Fig. 1.** With reference to his publications and convincing talks and lectures, the German computer scientist. Prof. Dr. Klaus Haefner was consulted when building an IT-related infrastructure within the educational system in Austria

Haefner's "revolutionary" ideas regarding education and society influenced politicians and educational policy makers in Germany and Austria to establish an IT-related infrastructure within the educational system. They became only partly true. Thanks to robots used in production, even skilled workers lost their jobs and had to acquire new qualifications. On the other hand, the amount of working hours per week did not decrease to 30 hours as a direct result of IT as often predicted by Haefner. But as far as information finding and knowledge management is concerned, it became a matter of fact that the quantity of information now available no longer enables individuals to amass encyclopedic knowledge. Instead of memorizing the data it is often more important to find the proper information whenever required, be it by querying data bases or via web quest on the Internet. However, locating information is not enough. At least a higher cognitive process has to be applied in order to construct solutions and to decide then.

Looking back, there is no doubt that 20 years ago the IT-hype did not happen at the advent of the so-called information age just because technology (the microcomputer) was available (the IBM PC XT[5] came on the market in 1981). Rather strong outside forces, coming from computer industry, politics, commerce and so on were pushing it forward. In response to these pressures, most of the developed countries started ambitious and costly programs to introduce computers into schools in the beginning of the 1980s [6, p. 27ff.].

---

[5] See the introductory book of Steven Manus concerning the IBM PC [17].

One main goal of the IT-approaches was to have computer science[6] taught at vocational and upper secondary education. This should develop computer-related skills for the labor market. A second objective was to teach computer literacy to all students at all levels of education in order to provide them with a basic understanding of the way computes work and about the impact of computers on society and on the individual. Well known and often presented and described broad policy approaches were undertaken by the U.K., (Microelectronics Education Program starting in 1980 [7]), France (L'informatique pour tous 1985 [18]), Norway (Program of Action 1984 -1988), the Netherlands (the Dutch NIVO project 1985) and Portugal (the Minverva Plan 1985-1988).

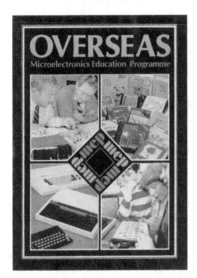 

**Fig. 2.** and **Fig. 3.** Show the booklet-covers of MEP [7] and "informatique pour tous" [18]

# 3  General Principles and Objectives of Informatics Instruction

In an official folder of the Austrian Federal Ministry of Education, Arts and Sport, the *BMUKS,* basic knowledge in informatics was demanded, no matter what level or type of school it concerned. It listed the general principles shown in Fig. 4 [3].

In detail, education in information technology should be conveyed in a differentiated way. Based on concepts originating in the late 1980s [12, p. 5 f.; 21, p. 119 f.] the following three categories were aimed at:

1. basic instruction in information technology for all pupils,
2. advanced instruction in information technology with informatics as distinct subject,
3. job-specific instruction in information technologies.

---

[6] The term "computer science" used in the US and in anglo-american publications corresponds with the term "Electronic Data Processing" (EDP). Nowadays the subject EDP is replaced in Austria even in the curricula of vocational schools, mostly by the new subject "informatics" enriched with so-called socioeconomic themes.

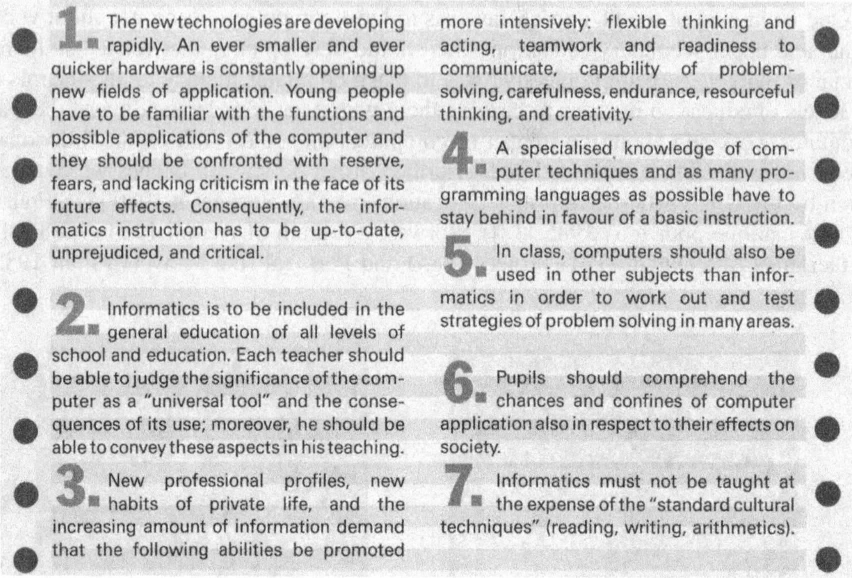

**1.** The new technologies are developing rapidly. An ever smaller and ever quicker hardware is constantly opening up new fields of application. Young people have to be familiar with the functions and possible applications of the computer and they should be confronted with reserve, fears, and lacking criticism in the face of its future effects. Consequently, the informatics instruction has to be up-to-date, unprejudiced, and critical.

**2.** Informatics is to be included in the general education of all levels of school and education. Each teacher should be able to judge the significance of the computer as a "universal tool" and the consequences of its use; moreover, he should be able to convey these aspects in his teaching.

**3.** New professional profiles, new habits of private life, and the increasing amount of information demand that the following abilities be promoted more intensively: flexible thinking and acting, teamwork and readiness to communicate, capability of problem-solving, carefulness, endurance, resourceful thinking, and creativity.

**4.** A specialised knowledge of computer techniques and as many programming languages as possible have to stay behind in favour of a basic instruction.

**5.** In class, computers should also be used in other subjects than informatics in order to work out and test strategies of problem solving in many areas.

**6.** Pupils should comprehend the chances and confines of computer application also in respect to their effects on society.

**7.** Informatics must not be taught at the expense of the "standard cultural techniques" (reading, writing, arithmetics).

**Fig. 4.** Scan-image of page 2 of the *BMUKS*-folder of 1985 [3]

## 3.1 Basic Instruction

Suggested aims of a basic instruction in information technologies were as follows:

- Meaning and impact of the computer: The pupils should get acquainted with a world in which information and communication technologies and, above all, the computer, play a decisive role such that they understand this world. They should get an insight into the vast range of applications and the new facilities generated by the use of these technologies. However, they should also be able to recognize the limitations of these technologies and be aware of problems that arise in connection with social, professional and private spheres. Issues such as economic and social consequences, competition, modifications in the structure of the labor market and jobs, data protection and privacy protection[7] must also be discussed. This approach should give the pupil the fundamentals necessary for independent and objective assessment.
- *Use of the Computer*: Pupils should get acquainted with the responsible use of information and communication technologies, as well as computers in their professional and private lives. They should be motivated and their capability of using the new techniques should be promoted by allowing them to gain practical experience, thus reducing unfounded fears that sometimes go along with these techniques. Computers should be used as tools in performing easy tasks of information logistics based on information processing.

---

[7] These general goals drawn up in the middle of 1980s are still valid and could partly be added into a catalogue of ethical guidelines for pupils concerning the use of the Internet (WWW).

Hence, the curriculum for a basic instruction in information technology comprised four sections:

- to use computers and information systems,
- to deal with the applications and the impact of data processing,
- to solve problems using algorithmic methods,[8]
- to get acquainted with the fundamentals of hardware and software.

## 3.2  Advanced Instruction

For a more profound education in information technology, the subject *informatics* should take into account aspects particular to each type of school. This caused different types of schools to get curricula with different emphasis. The pupils should be motivated trying to understand the problems put before them and to break them down into partial problems, to structure data, to develop procedures for problem solving, to formulate these procedures accurately and completely, and to convert them into a computer language. Furthermore, they should learn to test solution procedures, to correct them and to assess them. The examples of instruction should, as far as possible, be related to problems corresponding to the subjects of the type of school concerned, to the vocations concerned or to everyday life. Instruction in informatics should promote teamwork, perseverance, independence, self-criticism, responsibility and the pleasure in one's creative work.

Advanced instruction in information technologies should take into account the following aspects:

- to deal with the capacity and the limits of performance of a computer,
- to convey methods for problem solving,
- to convey information about programming languages,
- to deal with programming and data structures,
- to use computers for calculations, to draw up graphics and to simulate processes, etc.

## 3.3  Job Specific Instruction

As third aspect, vocation related education in information technology, such as often provided at the company level,[9] was seen as part of training or advanced training. It concerns also nowadays nearly every professional field.

- In the industrial and technical areas it covers for instance measuring and control techniques, computer-aided drawing, computer-aided design (CAD), programming of machines and production processes, simulation of technical processes, industrial automation, etc.
- In the commercial and business fields information technology covers file management, word processing, office communication and office organization, etc.

---

[8] Algorithms were rather considered to be part of a more profound basic instruction in information technology.

[9] E-Learning during breaks and at the working place goes in that direction.

As main goal and as objective for the future the then existing differentiation between informatics which comprises a critical view of computers and the more technical and algorithm-oriented EDP at medium and high vocational schools should be diminished sooner or later. The socio-economic dimension with relation to society should be binding for both types of school in future.

# 4 The Project "Computer-Education-Society"

According to Haefner's proposals, information technology should become part of a basic general education in Austria. That's why in 1984 Austria's Federal Ministry of Education, Arts and Sports (*BMUKS*) launched a specific project on future informatics instruction, the project "Computer-Education-Society" (in German: *Computer-Bildung-Gesellschaft* or *C-B-G*). This initiative, whose organization structure has since changed several times, was started by Minister Dr. Helmut Zilk[10] in cooperation with associations of labor and industry (Federal Board of Economy, Association of Industrialists; Labor Board, Austrian Federation of Trade Unions), pedagogic institutes and leading IT-companies. The project departed from a situation where only a very small part of the Austrian population was informed about the new technologies and related matters. Its operational goal was that "in the future, basic education in information technology is to be seen as integral part of general education." [15, p. 9] Due to the general motto of the C-B-G-project "Prepare the youth and offer a chance of entry to adults" various aspects explained next had to be tackled [4, p. 25f.].

## 4.1 Syllabus Development

In the spring of 1984 the goal to introduce informatics as an obligatory subject at the high-level secondary general school (*Allgemeinbildende Höhere Schulen, AHS*) had made considerable progress. A syllabus working group consisting of AHS-teachers, representatives of both, associations of employers and associations of employed, as well as representatives of universities, of school inspection, and officials of the *BMUKS*, was formed (c.f. [20]). This team drew up a draft of the AHS-syllabus. The foreseen instruction of informatics should convey not only basic EDP-knowledge but also sociological and economic aspects. The latter was a totally new concept. It should raise lots of controversy among future informatics teachers.

The approach was finally approved by representatives of all parties, representatives of employer's as well as of employed, by educational scientists, and by politicians. The demand that the social consequences of modern technologies, their implications on professional life, economy, communication, family-life etc. would have to be dealt with at least on an equal level in the conception of an informatics syllabus was finally advocated by the majority of people engaged in the discussion, notwithstanding that representatives of the Austrian trade union considered it more important than the involved teachers (c.f. [1]).

Under the scenario of *EDP-context* emotional discussions about contents and usability of chapters like *EDP and Society, EDP and the Development of Qualifications,*

---

[10] Prof. Dr. Helmut Zilk was head of the Ministry of Education, Arts and Sports in 1984 and later on mayor of Vienna for a long time [27].

New *Ways of Technological Control, Data Privacy Protection, History and the Development of EDP,* and *Rationalization and Full Employment* took place. But nevertheless, these chapters remained doubtless important issues and as so-called sociopolitical and socioeconomic aspects of informatics part of the informatics syllabus[11].

**Fig. 5.** Minister Dr. Helmut Zilk launched the project "Computer-Education-Society" with engagement in 1984

Further thematic priorities of the syllabus were the strategies of problem solving, technological concerns of hard- and software, work with user software, and of course programming. In the didactic remarks of the syllabus, teamwork was stressed as the primary form of instruction in order to take into account the fact that the instruction in informatics would offer the chance to teach social behavior and modern working techniques.

In June 1985 the Federal Parliament passed the 8th amendment of the school organization law (*Schulorganisations-Gesetz-Novelle, SchOG*) with the votes of all three parties represented in parliament at this time. Thus the introduction of informatics as an obligatory subject in the 5th form of the *AHS* was legally established. With the introduction of the subject informatics into the *AHS* one of the substantial goals of the project *C-B-G* was reached[12].

At the beginning of the 1985/86 school year informatics was introduced as a compulsory subject in the 5th form of all *AHS*, with the option of continuing informatics as an optional subject in the 6th to 8th forms.

---

[11] Some teachers still consider these chapters only as sort of an "appendix" as expressed in an interview of an experienced informatics pioneer and vocational lecturer. [22, p. 400].

[12] I'd like to mention that I was a member of that working group of 5 teachers who published 1985 the first textbook for the new subject informatics [2]. Another book was published by Ueberreuter in 1986 [8].

## 4.2  Teacher Training

Successful establishment of informatics in schools depended on the qualifications of prospective teachers of informatics, thus teacher training and advanced teacher training were essential aspects of the project *C-B-G*. Together with representatives of the IT-industry, of employer's and employee's organizations, the *BMUKS* developed a programme of teacher training[13].

After intensive negotiations with representatives of the Federal Board of Economy (*Bundeswirtschaftskammer*), the Association of Industrialists (*Industriellenvereinigung*), the Labour Board (*Arbeiterkammer*), as well as the Austrian Federation of Trade Unions (*Österreichischer Gewerkschaftsbund*) an agreement was reached that 16,5 out of a total of 80 hours of instruction were to be dedicated to socio-political and socioeconomic themes of informatics. The *C-B-G*-seminars lasted two weeks. They represented a symbiosis of a basic technical course, which offered both an insight into the operation, functioning, and programming of personal computers, with a platform for public discussions about the influence of information-processing technologies on society and economy. Topics treating the social, economic, and political consequences of a computerized world had to be integrative parts of the seminars. From my point of view as an official representative of the *BMUKS* and as speaker in that field they were considered of equal importance[14] to the lectures or exercises dealing with hardware, software, programming etc.

**Fig. 6.** The central teacher seminars lasting 2 weeks took place at IBM and at Philips Data System (PDS). This picture of Dec. 1984 shows me as opening speaker (sitting) and MR Dr. Klaus Satzke representing prevocational schools (standing at right)

---

[13] Since fall 1999 prospective teachers of the subject informatics at higher secondary general and higher vocational schools can study informatics at the universities of Klagenfurt, Salzburg and Vienna. Since 2002 Linz also offers teachers formation in informatics.

[14] As permanent speaker in this field I made an inquiry on the acceptance of the socioeconomic themes. Evaluating statements of about 120 teachers showed that more than 30 percent rejected them. The teachers main interest was rather the development of databases (dBase), calculations with spreadsheets, programming with GWBASIC, and of course, word processing (with Easy writer or Wordstar).

**Fig. 7.** Exercises on the PC at PDS during a seminar for future informatics teachers

From 20th August 1984 to 28th June 1985 a little less than 500 teachers of *AHS*, compulsory junior secondary general schools (*Hauptschulen*), and pre-vocational schools (*Polytechnische Schulen*) were instructed at the central *C-B-G* teacher training seminars at IBM and Philips Data Systems in Vienna. As mentioned, these seminars triggered off a discussion concerning the socioeconomic aspects of informatics. But the teacher's initial reservation gave way to an increasing readiness to accept this form of a modern informatics instruction. These issues became fixed in their minds.

I'd like to add some simple BASIC-program-listings[15] of the *C-B-G*-seminars. Nowadays one would find several alternative and quicker ways for instance by using the pocket calculator. Those who consider these programs too trivial may nevertheless appreciate that at the seminars 20 years ago, some teachers got shiny eyes when an operation succeeded. They could hardly get away from the PC when the course was over.

<u>Sample 1</u>: Find the greatest common divisor (GCD) according to Euklid's algorithm

```
  5 REM ** Greatest common divisor **
 10 PRINT „digit 1"
 20 INPUT A
 30 PRINT „ digit 2"
 40 INPUT B
 50 LET R = A - INT (A/B)*B
 60 LET A = B
 70 LET B = R
 80 IF R = 0 THEN 100
 90 GOTO 50
100 PRINT "GCD"
110 END
```

---

[15] I replaced German identifiers by corresponding English terms. The BASIC-syntax remained.

<u>Sample 2:</u> Find mirrored palindromes (the word can be read in both directions, but has another meaning such as EVIL and LIVE)

```
 5 REM ** mirrored palindromes**
10 PRINT "type a word"
20 INPUT WORD$
30 LET MIRROR $ = " "
40 FOR I = LEN (WORD$) TO STEP -1
50 LET MIRROR$ = MIRROR$ + MID$ (WORD$, I,1)
60 PRINT MIRROR$
70 NEXT I
80 PRINT MIRROR$
90 END
```

<u>Sample 3:</u> At what age someone may be elected?

```
 5 REM **election age**
10 PRINT „How old is the person"
20 INPUT A
30 IF A •   21 THEN 60
40 PRINT "The person cannot be elected"
50 GOTO 70
60 PRINT „The person can be elected"
70 END
```

To complement the central seminars in Vienna further (advanced) training courses took place at the institutes of further training for teachers of compulsory general schools (*Pädagogische Institute*) in the provinces and at schools with adequate equipment. The upgrade courses of the *C-B-G* seminars were transferred to the *Pädagogische Institute* all over the country. These courses were organized as "didactic workshops" to illustrate the possibilities of computer applications in education. Furthermore, the programme of the Austrian Computer Society (OCG)[16] offered special seminars, which effectively supported the advanced training of teachers in the school year 1984/85. At the beginning of the school year 1985/86 about 1600 teachers were basically qualified for teaching the new subject informatics at *AHS* [4].

### 4.3  Supply of Equipment for the *AHS*

The aim to expand education with information technologies necessitated to provide schools with equipment and programmes geared towards the pedagogic objectives. A hard- and software working team consisting of *AHS*-teachers from all over Austria, representatives of school inspection and administration, and experts from the *BMUKS* was set up and new equipment for a total of 169 *AHS* was tested nationwide. In the first effort the call for proposals was published in *Wiener Zeitung*, the official newspaper, in December 1984 according to *Ö-Norm* A-2050. In January 1985 the tender was opened, and already in 1985 the acceptance of the tender was awarded by the *BMUKS*. In total, 1026 IBM compatible microcomputers[17] (MS-DOS 2.0) were purchased at an expense of about ATS 50.000,00 per configuration[18].

---

[16] see www.ocg.at

[17] PCs of Honeywell Bull, Philips Data System, and Toshiba were ordered.

[18] Due to decreased prices for hardware, one would get today at least 2 or even 3 configurations for this price of roughly € 3.600,00.

The call for proposals obliged the companies to supply user software, manuals, and printers. With the help of the delivered integrated software package "Open Access" pupils could understand the principles of data bases and became familiar with word processing and spreadsheet calculation.

Each of the newly equipped 169 public *AHS* was supplied with six XT-compatible microcomputers. The other 69 *AHS* had at least four units each at their disposal. Suitable computer rooms were provided in most cases.

### 4.4  Interactive Videotex (*Bildschirmtext*) for Federal Schools

At this time powerful, but stand-alone personal computers did not guarantee a modern instruction in informatics. Consequently it was imperative to include new trends and technological developments in the instruction. Considerations of educational policy determined the decision to supply each of the 238 public *AHS* with a MUPID (multi-function universal programmable intelligent decoder) computer and an interactive videotex connection. The use of MUPID-2[19]allowed the connection to the videotex, anticipating future perspectives of an all-embracing exchange of communication and information between the schools themselves, and between schools and databases or external systems as nowadays realized by using the Internet.[20]

**Fig. 8.** Prof. Dr. Hermann Maurer participated not only at the development of the MUPID computer. He also created an online videotex-corner (*"Maurers Btx-Ecke"*). In computer magazines he was called "The Btx-pope"

Interactive videotex[21] was a text information- and text communication system, developed on the basis of TV-, telephone-, and computer technologies. User could recall information in form of texts, graphs, pictures, and tele-programmes from the

[19] The well known Austrian Mathematician, computer scientist ant telecommunication expert Hermann Maurer developed the MUPID together with Reinhard Posch.

[20] In the beginning of the 1980s the Internet (interconnected network) was part of the ARPAnet. The Internet started its triumphal and explosive worldwide growth in the middle of the 1990s

[21] The French system Minitel and Prestel in England corresponded to the Austrian" Bildschirmtext" (in Germany called Videotext).

information in form of texts, graphs, pictures, and tele-programmes from the public telephone network and read it on the terminal. MUPID-2 was a microcomputer which could be expanded by externals and used in connection with the nationwide communication network. Its programming facilities and the possibility of file transfer of so-called telesoftware offered a wide range of applications for education and for the home.

To actually take advantage of the new communicative effect of interactive videotex, a teacher training course for informatics was offered. This package, called "Autool", allowed organizing courses without knowledge in programming. The constant control of progress determined the further form of a lesson.

Interactive videotex connection at school did not only offer an interesting area of activity for informatics instruction, it could also promote the integration of informatics into other subjects. Available learning and simulation programs as well as the possibility to recall lexical knowledge and to obtain daily information about recent events could be useful for teachers of all subjects. Notwithstanding the advantages of the medium the pro and contra in public discussions about its effects on social and private life continued [20]. Retrospectively seen, videotex did not gain a basic foothold in the Austrian school system. With the advent of the Internet the operation of videotex was stopped by Telecom Austria.

## 4.5  Installation of Information-, Instruction-, and Training Centres

The *C-B-G*-project's aim to introduce informatics into schools and to offer adults the chance of instruction and continued instruction gave birth to the idea of creating a permanent place of information and training in the field of information processing [4, p. 29 f.; 15, p. 63].

In the spring of 1984 a first concept for a generally accessible centre equipped with personal computers was developed in cooperation with the *Arbeitsgemeinschaft für Datenverarbeitung*[22] (working team for data processing). Moreover, the demand for a central location where it should be possible to test and compare different computers of different producers was voiced in the discussion about advanced teacher training and school-external adult education.

This discussion resulted in the EDP-information-, instruction-, and training centre *Ettenreichgasse* in Vienna. Thanks to the cooperation of various IT-companies and institutions this centre was realized. A concept of equipment was developed together with Austrian EDP-companies, the associations of employers and employed, banking institutions etc. The companies gave their products, which were of considerable financial value, as objects of permanent loan. This form was chosen to avoid getting soon a "museum of technology", as well as to minimize service and repair costs.

The Federal Government supplied several rooms and furniture at the federal teacher training college (*Pädagogische Akademie des Bundes*) in Vienna and paid for electricity and cleaning. It slso provided three tutors looking after visitors and equipment of the centre. All institutions supporting the centre with material or funds, that is to say IT-producing companies etc. were represented as external members.

---

[22] See www.adv.at

The tasks of the information-, instruction-, and training centre were as follows:

- The centre should enable all teachers to test, enlarge, and increase their knowledge of appliances of various producers. The EDP-centre should also be used for school-external adult education. There were regular courses of public adult education centers (*Volkshochschulen*) and working groups.
- Moreover, the institution was opened to a wide public in the form of regular "*Tage der offenen Tür*". This "Open House" was above all attended by pupils who wanted to put into practice the knowledge gained in informatics- and EDP-instruction. As a result of the success of this institution in Vienna an expansion of further EDP-information-, instruction- and training centers to the provinces took place.

From the middle of the 1980ies onwards a number of information centers[23] throughout Austria were offering interested pupils, teachers and parents the opportunity to try and compare various computer models and programs. These centers were also available for training and advance training purposes as part of adult education programs.

## 5  Conclusions

One of the most important outputs of the *C-B-G*-project was according to my opinion the completion of the EDP-curricula of the medium and higher vocational schools with the socio-political and socioeconomic aspects of informatics. *C-B-G* has to be considered as strong motor for the further developments[24] in the complex field of Austrian school-informatics. It was likewise instrumental for integrating new information and communication technologies such as Multimedia and Internet into all levels of Austrian education in the respective curricula of different subjects as demanded by OECD [6], UNESCO [23 to 26], and in recommendations of the EU-commission [9] in recent years. It should be mentioned as well that the comfortable human-computer-interfaces of today, used in connection with E-Learning or mobile communication are products of applied informatics. I'd like to stress that the discipline informatics must defend its per se-position of being an essential part of general education [22, p. 39 ff.] irrespective of the requirements of media literacy or IT-standards at the level of the European Computer Driving Licence also in the future.

## References

1. AK/ÖGB: Technikbewertung EDV. Auswirkungen des EDV-Einsatzes auf Arbeit, Wirtschaft und Gesellschaft, Reihe „Arbeitswelt und Schule", Wien 1985.
2. Anzböck, Friedrich/Mathuber, Alf/Prowaznik, Bruno/Reiter, Anton/Wöhrl, Manfred: Informatik 5. Klasse AHS, Wien (Bohman) 1985.

---

[23] The very successful institution "education highway" in Linz (www.eduhi.at) was a former expansion of the Viennese EDP-information-, instruction- and training centre.

[24] See the contribution of Peter Micheuz in this book that analyses the further developments of informatics at general secondary schools in Austria

3.  BMUKS: Informatics Instruction in Austrian Education. New Information Technologies and School, Folder, Vienna 1985

4.  BMUKS: EDP/Informatics in Austrian Education. An Initiative of the Federal Ministry of Education, Arts and Sports, brochure of the BMUKS, Vienna 1986.

5.  CEO-Forum: Key Building Blocks for Student Achievement in the 21st Century, Washington 2001.

6.  CERI/OECD: New Information Technologies. A Challenge, Paris 1986.

7.  Department of Education and Science of England, Northern Ireland and Wales: The Microelectronics Programme, Newcastle 1981.

8.  Dinauer/Sziruscek/Wurnig: Informatik, Wien (Ueberreuter) 1986.

9.  Erault, Michael (ed.): Education and the Information Society. A Challenge for European Policy, Councel of Europe, 1991.

10. Forsyth, Ian, Teaching and Learning materials and the Internet, 2nd edition, London (Kogan) 1988.

11. Haefner, Klaus: The Concept of an Integrated System for Information Access and Telecommunication (ISIT) and its Impact on Education in the 90s, in: Levington S.H. (ed.): Information Processing 80, Amsterdam (North Holland) 1980, p. 973-978.

12. Haefner, Klaus: Challenge of Information Technology to Education. The New Educational Crisis, in: Lewis, Bob/Tagg, Donovan (eds.): Computers in Education, Proceedings of the IFIP TC-3, 3rd World Conference on Computers in Education – WCCE81, Lausanne, July 27-31, Amsterdam (North Holland) 1981, p. 525-531.

13. Haefner, Klaus: Die neue Bildungskrise. Herausforderung der Informationstechnik an Bildung und Ausbildung, Basel (Birkhäuser) 1982.

14. Haefner, Klaus: Herausforderung der Informationstechnik an Bildung und Ausbildung, in: Vereinigung Österreichischer Industrieller (Hrsg.): Bildungswesen und Informationsgesellschaft. Dokumentation einer Enquete, Wien (Edition Bildung) 1985, S. 39-53.

15. Lehner, Karl/Reiter, Anton (eds.): Informatics in Austrian Education revised and supplemented edition, Vienna (BMUK) 1991.

16. Maier, Pat/Barnet, Liz/Warren, Adam/Brunner, David: Using Technology in Teaching and Learning, London (Kogan) 1998.

17. Manus, Steven: IBM PC. Einführung in System und Betrieb, München (Goldmann) 1984.

18. Ministère de L'Education Nationale: Informatique pour tous, Paris 1985.

19. Neuwirth, Erich/Schauer, Helmut/Tauber, J. Michael (Hrsg.): Kinder, Computer und Bildung, Schriftenreiher der OCG, Band 31, Wien 1985.

20. Österreichische Computer Gesellschaft (OCG): Gesellschaftliche Probleme der Computerisierung in Österreich, Arbeitskreis: Computer und Gesellschaft", Wien 1985.

21. Reiter, Anton: EDV/Informatik im österreichischen Bildungswesen, in: Reiter, Anton/Rieder, Albert (Hrsg.): Didaktik der Informatik. Informations- und kommunikation stechnische Grundbildung, Wien (Jugend und Volk) 1990, S. 118-140.

22. Reiter, Anton: Eine Standortbestimmung der Schulinformatik, in: Reiter, Anton/Scheidl, Gerhard/Strohmer, Heinz/Tittler, Lydia/Weissenböck, Martin (Hrsg.): Schulinformatik in Österreich. Erfahrungen und Beispiele aus dem Unterricht, Wien (Ueberreuter) 2003, S. 33-56.

23. UNESCO: Education and Informatics Worldwide. The State of the Art and Beyond, London 1992.

24. UNESCO: Information and Communication Technologies in Teacher Education. A Planning Guide, Paris 2002.

25. UNESCO: Information and Communication Technologies in Teacher Education. A Curriculum for Schools and Programme of Teacher Development, Paris 2002.
26. UNESCO: Open and Distance Learning. Trends, Policy and Strategy Considerations, Paris 2002.
27. Zilk, Helmut: Humanistisches Bildungsideal bleibt aufrecht, in: Vereinigung Österrei chischer Industrieller (Hrsg.): Bildungswesen und Informationsgesellschaft. Dokumentation einer Enquete, Wien (Edition Bildung) 1985, S. 11-15.

# 20 Years of Computers and Informatics in Austria's Secondary Academic Schools

Peter Micheuz

Alpen-Adria-Gymnasium A-9100 Völkermarkt, Austria
University Klagenfurt, A-9020 Klagenfurt, Austria
micp@gym1.at

**Abstract.** The way in which Austrian schools have reacted to the needs of a growing digital society has been, all things considered, a success story. This is remarkable as schools in general are not necessarily places where excessive progress takes place. Many teachers are rather conservative and not willing to take part in every new promising development unless they are fully convinced of its benefits. This applies especially to teachers who are now confronted with introducing new technologies. Unlike the more or less established subject Informatics, the overall penetration of information technology in education is still at the beginning. We have to remember that the present situation has not appeared from nowhere, but has to be seen as a result of a comparatively short, but all the more turbulent history with roots already in the seventies. The official start for the subject Informatics in the secondary academic schools in Austria (AHS)[1] can be dated back to 1985 when all these schools have been equipped with computers for the first time. „History does nothing; it does not possess immense riches, it does not fight battles. It is men, real, living, who do all this" is a quotation from Karl Marx and can be applied very well to the development of Informatics in Austrian general educating schools. Even if the visible changes in hardware, software and curricula are remarkable enough it should be pointed out that this short history was a history of people behind these developments, enthusiastic teachers as well as responsible policy makers in that field.

*Reminding means choosing.*
*Günther Grass*

## 1 Introduction

The development of Informatics in schools in general and in secondary academic schools of Austria in particular is characterized by permanent changes and improvements in hardware, software and by corresponding didactical approaches as well. Teaching Informatics in the early eighties was understandably a pioneer work

---

[1] Austria has two categories of schools which provide secondary education for the students aged 15 to 18 (19) years ( in [7], p. 20]]. One is AHS (allgemein bildende höhere Schule) aiming at a general education, the other is BHS (berufsbildende höhere Schule) which is a collective term for various types of schools offering vocational education.

R.T. Mittermeir (Ed.): ISSEP 2005, LNCS 3422, pp. 20–31, 2005.
© Springer-Verlag Berlin Heidelberg 2005

for non-typical adventurous teachers who recognized the signs of time and taught a subject with no experience at all but all the more enthusiasm.

In this keynote I want to point at some milestones which have been set by central decisions of the Ministry of Education in form of hardware and software equipment, enactment and organisational measures which have been taken to introduce the subject Informatics nationwide and obligatory for all. Due to lack of empirical data, I will try to attach some personal impressions as I have experienced this exciting time. In retrospective, the last three decades of history of Informatics at the AHS can be classified into five sequential periods, each of them characterized by more ore less big changes.

> *I think there is a world market for maybe five computers.*
> *Thomas Watson, chairman of IBM, 1943*
> *640 KBytes RAM is all that any application will ever need.*
> *Bill Gates*

## 2 The Very Roots and Single Initiatives (1975–1985)

The history of computers in the AHS goes back to the late seventies and early eighties when some teachers started teaching EDP (electronical data processing, in German: EDV – Elektronische Datenverarbeitung) with some home computers of the first generation. It was the time when the computer came into the mind of a broader public and some teachers experimented with the first affordable computers such as Commodore Pet, VC64, Amiga and Apple II and shared their experience with a handful of students.

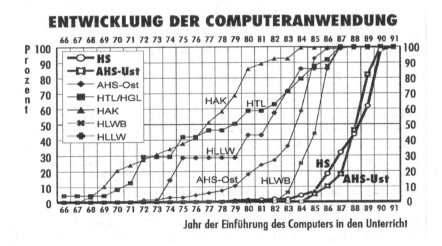

**Fig. 1.** Development of use of computers in all types of schools

This diagram (see [9], p. 20) shows the continually growing curve (AHS-Ost) of the application of computers at the upper level of the secondary academic schools in

Austria from 1970 on. From 1980 to 1985 the number of schools which used computers in a rudimentary and rather unorganized way increased significantly.

Personally, I could not resist the temptation and took part in this development. From 1981 on I jumped into the cold water and taught a subject EDV for three years with 16 to 18 years old students in the form of elective courses. Because of lack of computers in the school (AHS) where I am still teaching we had to use the computers of a vocational school in the same town. From my point of view this adventure turned out to be very successful. Quite a number of Austrian teachers did as well and were encouraged enough that most of them have not given up teaching Informatics till yet.

These days, it is hardly imaginable to teach Informatics with a computer which obviously has no operating system, which is not networked, has no harddisks and floppy drives and, moreover, is equipped with a monitor with an intolerably awful solution. It was at the time when just the unemotional message "OK" appeared on the screen. It was the time when programming in BASIC dominated the lessons (see Fig. 2). At least I successfully passed the era of punchcards ...

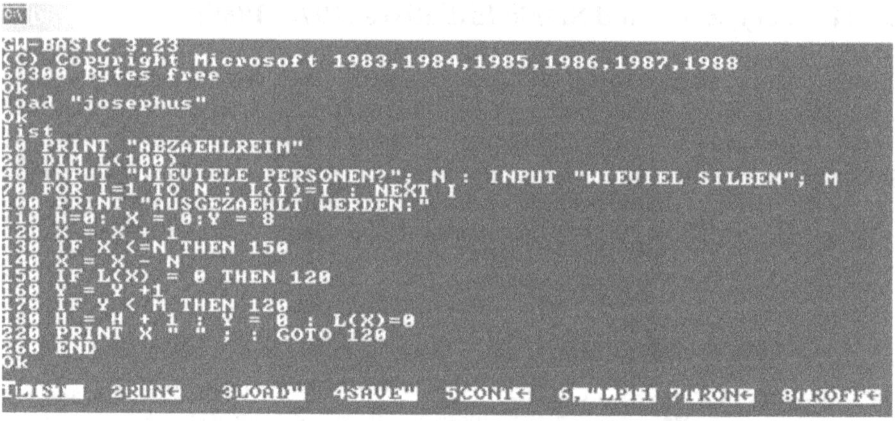

**Fig. 2.** The GW Basic Interpreter and a well known algorithm

At this point the legendary computer courses in Graz, the capital of Styria, have to be mentioned. In these courses, which were held regularly in the first two weeks of the holidays every year, hundreds of interested Austrian teachers got their first computer related lessons. These annual conventions were very popular and served as the very information- and communication centre for its participants. Among the trainers there were many deserved teachers. Most of them are still very active in the field of school Informatics.

I do not exaggerate when asserting that this institution, which is still alive today in a reduced way, has triggered off and influenced the development of school Informatics in Austria extraordinarily.

Inspired by these in-service-trainings and with the experience of already teaching the subject EDV, I was comparatively well prepared when in 1985 the new subject Informatics was introduced nationwide in the 9th grade for 15 year old students. This decision to install Informatics as a regular subject obligatorily for the 9th grade and optionally for the $10^{th}$ - $12^{th}$ grades was made last but not least by the former Minister of Education Dr. Zilk. This change in the organisational structure of the AHS has survived till these days. So has the curriculum, which has nearly remained the same for almost 20 years. But now, for the current schoolyear 2004/05, a new central curriculum for the subject Informatics at the secondary level of the AHS has been enacted ([7]).

> *BASIC - A programming language.*
> *Related to certain social diseases in that those who have it*
> *will not admit it in polite company.*

## 3 The Experimental Stage (1985–1990)

In 1985 all AHSes were equipped with computers, that meant a comparatively big investment. They got six(!) computers for the subject Informatics, IBM-compatibles XT-8086 with 640 kB RAM, two floppy disc drives, running on he DOS operating system and additionally impact printers. Compared to the affluence of software nowadays, there were very little applications available. The programming language GW-Basic, the spreadsheet "Supercalc", an exotic word processing software "Textmaker" and the integrative software "Open Access".

Above all, it meant a big challenge to educate and prepare teachers in a short time in order to reach a veritable return on this investment. The so called C-B-G (Computer Bildung Gesellschaft) courses with 14 days of central instruction in Vienna are legendary in retrospective, because this training formed the formal qualification for teaching Informatics for a long time.

For teachers who had nothing to do with computers before, these two weeks might have been a valuable first contact. As far as I remember the instructions were rather confusing and there was much self education, further study and training necessary to provide the teachers with basic knowledge and skills.

This was the time when many interested students knew a lot more than their teachers. The self image of Informatics teachers has been therefore different from that in traditional subjects. At that time many of them actually represented the rare species of learners, instructors and experimenters who sometimes had to cope with the fact to know little more - if at all – than many students. To tell the truth, it is likely that this phenomenon can also be experienced these days...

Many of the comparatively young teachers of Informatics were autodidacts and enthusiastic programmers, exploring the fascinating potentials of programming in GW-Basic without really knowing the meaning of the letters GW[2]. Actually these early years were dominated by programming because of lack of comfortable application software.

In 1985 every 15-year-old student had to attend the subject Informatics in the $9^{th}$ grade. The problem of the small number of computers was solved by generously splitting classes into small groups.

---

[2] Some say GW-Basic was named after Greg Whitten, an early MicroSoft employee.

Simultaneously with the introduction of the obligatory subject Informatics in the 9th grade, the optional subject Informatics for the grades 10 to 12 was established. The first courses started in the schoolyear 1986/87 with the first final exams ("Matura") in 1989. The acceptance of these elective courses was comparatively high right from the beginning on, that is, about 30% of the all the students attended these courses then. There are unfortunately no exact numbers about current percentages. But informal surveys are anything but encouraging.

The following years were characterized by the emergence of a programming language and environment which should dominate the education in programming for more than ten years: Turbo Pascal. This marked the change from an interpreted language to a native compiler and from "spaghetti code" to structured programming.

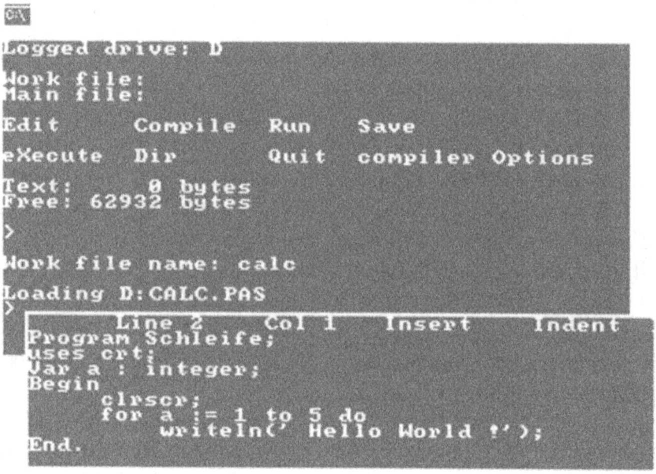

**Fig. 3.** The Turbo Pascal interface with a fullscreen editor

For programming languages, a lean but didactically most valuable roboter system ([12]), developed by a deserving Austrian teacher, further Logo, dBase and the hype of Turbo Prolog should be mentioned. In some cases even batch programming in DOS and assembly programming were taught according to the level of knowledge of the respective teacher.

Application software such as word processing, spreadsheet calculation, and database software underwent a development to integrative software, the ancestor of the later office suites. Open Access and Enable were representatives of that kind of software. The first one was used to some degree. The second one, Enable, was to my knowledge, completely refused. For the first time teachers had to cope with what was considered to be an unnecessary upgrade. Understandably none of the teachers wanted to relearn. Isn't this a well known phenomenon this very day?

In addition to algorithms and programming and the (rudimentary) application software the curriculum also stipulated knowledge about hardware, mathematical and logical basics and naturally some soft topics such as data security and the implications of information technology on society. But as "real programmers" many teachers did not attach as much importance to these topics as the curriculum demanded.

It should also be mentioned that in that period the first viruses appeared and thus revealed the vulnerability of information technology. Since 1987 an apparent change from intellectual exercise to dangerous activity took place. The Vienna Virus written in Austria in 1988 with the falling letters on the screen is still well kept in mind by those who suffered from it.

**Fig. 4.** A MUPID with its almost 10 kg heavy 5 ¼" floppy drive

It is remarkable that the first but still rather ineffective steps to telecommunication in schools in form of MUPID (Multipurpose Universally Programmable Intelligent Decoder or joking: Most Useful Product Invented In this Decade) were taken very early (see Fig. 4). This device was delivered to every AHS and worked - if it has ever been installed and configured - with the unimaginable data transfer rate of 300 byte per second. But the time was not mature for text based telecommunication. It never reached a critical mass. Consequently this undertaking with its roots in Graz, Austria, was doomed to fail as the World Wide Web began its triumphal procession around the world.

In the five years from 1985 to the 1990 the computer continuously became a mass product and at the end of this period almost half of Austrian students declared to have access to computers at home ([9]).

*Change is not merely necessary to life - it is life.*
*Alvin Toffler*

## 4  Networking and the Beginning of the GUI Era (1990–1995)

In 1990 the second wave of hardware equipment heralded the period of integration of the computer into other subjects than Informatics together with the introduction of networked computers. Fifteen computers including a server with the Novell network operating system was installed especially for that purpose in all AHSes. I can remember very well my reverence for the server. For some time, I really thought this was a special sort of hardware and did not know that it was just the software which distinguished a client from a server.

This computer network needed of course maintenance and, therefore, special know-how. System administration in schools was born.

With that equipment also these little animals called mice became an input device and triggered off the era of the point and click generation. It seems a little bit ridiculous, but the Ministry of Education strictly advised that these mice had to be plugged in - without exception - by the company which delivered the computers.

In this context one additional computer classroom was adapted and should be used frequently by the 13- to 14-year old pupils. Enactment by the Ministry of Education was made to foster the use of computers at an earlier age than fifteen.

This period from 1990 on is also characterized by comparatively enormous efforts in organizing in-service-trainings for teachers in order to encourage them to use the computer in the so called key-subjects (Trägerfächer, supporting subjects) German, English, Mathematics and Geometrical Drawing. In retrospective we can state that this integrated approach, called ITG (informationstechnische Grundbildung, information technology based education), did not work very well to say the least. Too few computers equipped with proprietary software and teaching more than thirty pupils on fourteen computers can be mentioned as evident reasons.

Nevertheless, the acquisition of these computers – IBM compatibles AT with harddisks and 1 MB memory - was finally no stranded investment. These computers were widely used not only for the obligatory subject Informatics and the elective courses in the upper secondary level but also for 13 and 14-year-old pupils. There was a special curriculum and even programming was quite usual.

According to the COMPED[3] study ([9]) the applications Supercalc, MS Works, Textmaker, CAD 2D, Word Perfect and Logo can be found in the top ten list.

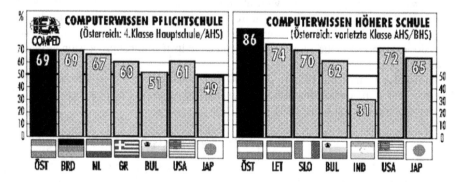

**Fig. 5.** Result of the COMPED-test on computer competence in 1992. Left: lower secondary level. Right: upper secondary level

---

[3] COMPED: Computers in Education Study, initiated by the IEA (International Association for the Evaluation of Educational Achievement). Austria entered this organisation as the last country in 1989. This international study based on a comprehensive test where also many thousands of Austrian pupils were involved. As a result a lot of scientifically proven information about the application of computers in schools at that time is available.

This study reveals – more than 10 years later – astonishing facts. It included the evaluation of the pupils and students IT-competencies in form of basic computer knowledge and skills. Even programming skills were tested. Today it is unthinkable to assign the same elementary programming tasks to pupils at an age of 14 years. Teaching programming at the lower level of the AHS practically does not take place any longer. But you could very well pose the same questions today as standard software related assignments are concerned. What we can learn from this is that most of the problems are still the same, only the tools and products are changing. Old wine in new bottles ...

Fig. 5. impressively shows the excellent performance of Austrian pupils at the age of 14 years concerning computer literacy and programming skills. Unfortunately, since then, no comparably substantial test has been done.

In 1993 8 Intel-PCs 486 (4MB RAM, 40 MB HD), Novell Netware 3.11, a server (8 MB RAM, HD 240 MB) formed the hardware basis for lessons in Informatics the following years in all AHSes. The change from DOS to WINDOWS and, accordingly, the shift from the textual to the graphical user interface was unstoppable and influenced the subject Informatics especially as the application software was concerned. Didactics in Informatics changed in many schools and classes from a programming and algorithm orientation to an application oriented approach. There Microsoft Office began to occupy a superior position and has kept it till today. It is worth mentioning that Excel 5.0 was released in 1993 and has dominated the field of spreadsheet software. As Windows 3.1/3.11 is based on DOS, there were still many applications running on DOS with a textual interface.

At that time a veritable number of schools nationwide decided to enforce their Informatics education at the 7th and 8th grade and in the upper secondary level. This measure of course required appropriate and engaged teachers and a certain amount of belief in progress by the school administration.

*Describing the Internet as the Network of Networks is like*
*calling the Space Shuttle, a thing that flies.*
*John Lester*

## 5  More Autonomy, Consolidated Standardized Application Software and the Kickoff of the Internet Era (1995–2000)

1997 marks the last year of centrally controlled investment of hard- and software. From that time on it was up to the schools to buy hardware from their budget. Due to the shift to more autonomy the schools themselves were made responsible for their hardware equipment. Till now it is up to schools to provide a sufficient infrastructure according to the needs of their profiles in terms of pushing IT. Thus, in 1997 the fourth and the last central wave of hardware and software equipment took place with the first Pentium computers and a Windows NT network. At the same time Austrian secondary academic schools went online. An internet access for one computer with a modem (33 kBit) was established in all AHSes.

With the advent of Windows 95 and Windows NT, object orientation appeared in form of the continuous interaction with graphical user interfaces. Programming and algorithms lost importance at the expense of a rapidly growing offer of Windows software. Windows-based application software and later on integrated development environments such as Visual Basic and Delphi converged in terms of handling and stopped the uncomfortable situation of software with extremely varying user interfaces. In the retrospective - despite many side blows - Microsoft Windows has to be seen rather as a blessing than a curse. The standard, which was set, and the consistency in handling all applications influenced the learning curve of the students positively. This argument doubtlessly applies to the use of application software. But programming, which still played a role in the elective courses, slowly migrated from the popular GW-Basic and Turbo Pascal under DOS to the event driven successors Visual Basic and Delphi. More than ten years of procedural programming under familiar development environments made the shift to event driven, object oriented and graphical development environments rather difficult: An experience I shared with many other teachers.

Didacts still argue that an unreflected use of event driven development environments affect the algorithmic aspect of programming where the user interface and aspects of design distracts from imparting the concepts.

Anyway, with the introduction of the graphical user interface the era of complex software and thus the world of objects arrived. Handling objects in standard software became a matter of course and developing programs in a Windows environment required the save application of at least predefined graphical objects and classes. It became obvious that the facilities an operating system provides and its general design philosophy exert an extremely strong influence on programming style and on the technical cultures that grow up around its host machines.

The increasing penetration of the internet and the number of networked computers in schools consequently made a professional system administration necessary. Many in-service trainings took place in order to qualify the responsible teachers and to guarantee a functioning infrastructure at schools.

The role of the internet was still underdeveloped for the reason of a poor bandwidth. In this time an average secondary academic school in Austria had a single ISDN – connection shared with a lot of computers. A productive integration of the internet even in Informatics lessons was not possible, not to mention using the internet in other subjects. But since 1996 the know-how in schools concerning the internet has rapidly grown despite the mentioned deficits. First homepages were produced and the vision of publishing for the whole world had its impact on the subject Informatics. Webdesign, markup and script languages, the client-server concept and network fundamentals enriched the stagnating education in Informatics and opened a completely new perspective.

Last but not least Linux came into mind of many teachers of Informatics and with it the idea of open source. Although not shown separately in the central curriculum for Informatics, Linux found its ways into many schools at least in form of stable internet servers. It will be interesting to watch the development of Linux as a desktop system.

Until now very little about the education of teachers in the field of Informatics has been mentioned. Central courses, such as the one in Graz, which started in 1980, are are still maintained to a reduced extent, but the main responsibility has been conferred to regional in service centres, the PIs (Pädagogische Institute – pedagogical institutes).

Almost as long as the subject Informatics has existed, there were efforts and preceding debates about installing a full academic study to educate teachers for the subject Informatics. In 2000 this became true at the universities Wien, Salzburg, Klagenfurt and in 2001 also in Linz.

> *Getting information off the Internet is like taking a drink from a fire hydrant.*
> *Mitchell Kapor*

## 6 E-Learning, Standards and Increasing Didactical Issues (2000–2005)

Parallel to the hype of the internet at the beginning of the $3^{rd}$ millennium a new era began when a nationwide initiative provided secondary schools with a predominantly excellent access to the internet. From this time on, the way for an adequate use of the internet has been smoothened as an effective information and communication tool.

A recent survey in 2004 (see [13], p. 87f) revealed the fact that at least almost every pupil of AHSes in Carinthia/Austria has access to a computer at home and almost two thirds have an internet access. Due to autonomous decisions of the schools, the quality of the hardware equipment of the AHSes already differs considerably. About one third of the AHSes is emphasizing IT as part of a school development program. Some of these schools are involved in e-learning and notebooks projects in which computers and the internet should support the learning process. But looking at the latest PISA results for Austrian students, we have to state an urgent call for action to deal with education in a fundamental manner. Till now there has been no proof that the (unreflected) use of computers has a convincingly positive effect on the improvements of learning processes.

In the last years autonomic decisions of schools have led to an enormous diversity in organisational structures, e-learning initiatives and still reinforced informatical education. This process is still going on rapidly and it is not difficult to predict that this development will continue. This is as certain as the fast-paced progress in the hard- and software development.

Another big issue in the political discussion about quality in schools is the shift from input control by open curricula to output measurement and the definition of clearly defined standards. It seems that Informatics respectively ICT leads the way in this context in form of a wide offer of certifications as for instance the ECDL. As an additional qualification since the year 2000 it has also been accepted in secondary academic schools and supported by the Ministry of Education. It will be interesting to watch the further development of certificates in schools in general.

Actually, many didactics experts attach rather little value to the ECDL in terms of its role in general education. In my opinion the argument is two-sided. As long as the offer of this certificate leads to a reliable basic qualification in terms of computer literacy and to improved basic skills in the use of computers, there is no reason to object to it. In case of a mere product training without any conceptual background this absolutely deserving initiative of the ECDL has to be reflected seriously. This applies to all the other certificates which are offered at the secondary academic schools as well. Apprehensions that the ECDL is totally dominating the subject Informatics and thus leaving too little room for other important curricular contents have unfortunately been proven in some cases. Convincing the teachers that this is the wrong way and simultaneously showing concepts to do it better is doubtlessly a big challenge for the young field of Informatics didactics. Unfortunately, there is still an underdeveloped market of schoolbooks which lead in this direction in Austria.

Another important challenge is the demand for assuring the position of Informatics in the canon of all the other obligatory and elective subjects as well. The need for an independent subject Informatics is still alive and beyond question in Austria at the moment. The recent reform of the upper secondary level of the AHS offers students ways for a special education in Informatics in form of elective courses and a reinforced integration of informatical methods in other subjects as well. The new enactment for the final examination at the AHS, called Matura, determines this new option in order to foster the use of the computer and to encourage students to attend elective courses in Informatics. At the moment it is difficult to predict to what extent students will accept this interesting option. A quantitative and qualitative evaluation in this regard would be highly appreciated.

> *I find the great thing in this world is not so much where we stand,*
> *as in what direction we are moving.*
> *Oliver Wendell Holmes, Jr.*

## 7  Conclusion

The twenty years of computers and Informatics at Austrian's secondary academic schools are characterized by a matchless dynamic and the need for teachers who permanently engage themselves in new tools and concepts. Enthusiastic and mainly self-taught teachers who invested a lot of time and money have led the way for a remarkable history of the computer and Informatics in the AHS.

We have experienced the development from rudimentary personal computers with text-based software to worldwide networked multimedia machines which are suitable for almost all purposes. We have experienced various didactical approaches, shifts in the way of programming, and in the intensity of teaching application software. The role of the computer has changed from a rare experimental tool to a ubiquitous object of common utility. But despite this drastic development there are long-term basics and meta-concepts which have survived it.

It is not only the ongoing drastic shift in our society and economy caused by information technology which puts pressure on the educational systems. The schools themselves are involved in a continuously changing process in which informatic systems are strongly involved and still discussed.

Doubtlessly we have experienced already a diversified and rich history of the computer in schools, but the big challenges are still in front of us. This especially applies to the subject Informatics and to the use of ICT in education in general.

Considering the almost unmanageable offers and shifts in contents, methods, and software tools. it is highly advisable to adapt the introductory quotation of Grass "Reminding means choosing" to "Teaching means choosing". To find an appropriate choice is the very challenging task of teaching Informatics.

Concerning the use of ICT, it could be beneficial to confront the reader with a very disputed quotation by Manfred Spitzer, a well known German brain researcher: "If sometimes teaching and learning material has to be purchased, attention should be paid that it is functioning without electricity – in that case you can't be wrong."

Third time is a charme and therefore I conclude these reflections with a quotation worth being considered especially in the context of Informatics.

"Men have become tools of their tools." The author Henry David Thoreau, an American philosopher, lived from 1817 to 1862 ...

# References

1. Anton Reiter-Albert Rieder, Didaktik der Informatik, Jugend und Volk, 1999
2. Schwill A.(Ed.), Informatik und Schule, Springer, 1999
3. Schauer H., Michael Tauber (Eds..), Informatik in der Schule, R.Oldenburg, Wien, 1980
4. Mittermeir R. (Ed.) et al., Informatik in der Schule-Informatik für die Schule, Böhlau, 1992
5. Weinhart K. (Ed.), Informatik im Unterricht, Oldenburg, 1979
6. Koerber B. (Ed.), Informatische Bildung in Deutschland, LOG IN Verlag, Berlin, 1998
7. Reiter A. et al., Schulinformatik in Österreich, Ueberreuter, 2003
8. Hüffel C., Reiter A. (Ed.), Praxis der EDV/Informatik, Jugend&Volk, Wien, 1996
9. Haider G., Schule und Computer, Österreichischer Studienverlag, 1994
10. Reiter A., Anekdoten zur Informatik, Studienverlag, Innsbruck, 2001
11. Menzel K., Basic in 100 Beispielen, Teubner Verlag, Stuttgart, 1981
12. Köck et al., Werkzeug Computer, Schulbuch A. Pichler, Wien, 1986
13. Micheuz P., Informatics at an Early Stage, in Johannes Magenheim, Sigrid Schubert (Eds.), Informatics and Student Assessment, GI-Edition Lecture Notes in Informatics, GI, Bonn, 2004
14. Banville E. et. al., European Linkages in Teaching Computing at Primary and Secondary Level (Sokrates – Comenius Conference CTC Link 97), Dublin, 1997, http://www.ctc.deu.ie

# Informatics Education at
# Vocational Schools and Colleges in Austria

Martin Weissenböck

Höhere technische Bundeslehranstalt Wien 3R,
Rennweg 89b, 1030 Wien, Austria
martin.weissenboeck@htl.rennweg.at

**Abstract.** The contribution offers a survey about vocational schools in Austria (both intermediate and higher education) and the development and position of the informatics education. The main area of the account lies within the "technical and vocational schools and colleges", but also the other forms of vocational schools ("schools of occupations in the business sector", "schools of management and service industries", "schools of social occupations") will be explained[1]. In addition a selection of various special school models will be dealt with. Furthermore the development of the informatics curricula, the present state and the current trends will be described.

## 1 Tasks of Vocational Schools

Amounting to 195,476 pupils, the technical and vocational schools and colleges outstrip those from the grammar schools (189,753 pupils)[2]. Considering that the vocational schools comprise only the forms 9 to 13, the grammar schools on the other hand 5 to 12, it is not surprising that more graduates leave the vocational schools (about 17,000 graduates) than the grammar schools (about 16,000 graduates). Nevertheless the vocational schools rank lower in the public perception.

Figures of graduates from vocational colleges may go to University or take up a job immediately – a model of education which is unique in Europe.

## 2 Systematics

### 2.1 Arrangement According to the Level of Education

The Austrian School system provides for three levels of vocational education.

---

[1] See also http://www.berufsbildendeschulen.at/.

[2] Statistik Austria, http://www.statistik.at/fachbereich_03/bildung_tab10.shtml1. All figures concern the school year 2002/03.

R.T. Mittermeir (Ed.): ISSEP 2005, LNCS 3422, pp. 32–36, 2005.

**Part-time Vocational Schools for Apprentices (Berufsschulen)**
Part-time vocational schools for apprentices[3] are part of the dualistic education of apprentices. As a rule apprentices are trained in school once a week, the rest of the time they work in a company.

**Vocalional Education and Training (VET) Schools (Mittlere Schulen, Fachschulen)**
Vocational education and training schools[4] (Fachschulen) last from three to four years (in a few cases even shorter) and end with a final exam. School-leavers are employed as skilled workers and they might, by attending a Secondary College (Aufbaulehrgang – Kolleg), reach the level of a VET College.

**Vocalional Education and Training (VET) College (Höhere Schulen)**
Vocational education and training colleges[5] provide curricula lasting five years. They end with a "Higher School Certificate and VET Diploma". The expression "Higher School Certificate" refers to the permission to go to University after the exam, the expression "VET Diploma" refers to the professional qualification and chances to take up a job.

### 2.2 Arrangement According to Contents

Both, VET schools[6] and colleges[7], offer subject matters containing technical, commercial, and social fields.

**Schools and Colleges of Engineering, Arts and Crafts**
The schools and colleges of engineering, arts and crafts[8] are probably the best known technical and vocational schools. On more than 80 locations all over Austria the classical branches of the engineering disciplines like civil engineering, mechanical engineering, electrical engineering or electronics are taught. But also the disciplines economics and business engineering, electronic data processing and organisation or information technology are offered. There are also schools specialising for instance in chemistry, food technology, or business management[9]. VET schools are often added to the VET colleges.

---

[3] All legal quotations - if not indicated otherwise - come from the School Organisation Act (Schul organisations gesetz), see also http://www.ris.bka.gv.at. This is not a word-by-word translation. § 46 Assignment of the Berufsschule: It is supposed to convey (parallel to the job) the fun damental theoretical knowledge, to support the education in a company and to enlarge general education.
[4] § 52 Assignment of VET Schools: They are supposed to convey essential specialized knowledge and skills needed in jobs of industrial, technical, artistic, commercial or social branches.
[5] § 65 Assignment of VET Colleges: They are supposed to convey a higher general and specific education which enables school-leavers to take up a higher job of technical, industrial, artistic, commercial branches. It qualifies them to go to University.
[6] Details to be found in: § 54 School Organisation Act.
[7] Details to be found in: § 67 School Organisation Act.
[8] § 72. Schools and Colleges of Engineering, Arts and Crafts. They serve to gain higher technical or commercial education in diverse fields of economy. Lessons in a workshop and practical education convey practical skills.
[9] The curricula can be found at: http://www.bmbwk.gv.at/schulen/bw/bbs/bbmhs/Berufsbildende_Schulen_H1745.xml

**Schools and Colleges of Occupations in the Business Sector**
School-leavers from schools and colleges of occupations in the business sector[10] are often employed in administration or trading. Knowledge in informatics is taken for granted.

**Schools and Colleges for Occupations in the Service Industries**
School-leavers from Colleges for Occupations in the Service Industries[11] have interesting job prospects in tourism, for example. Also in this branch companies expect perfect computer skills.

### 2.3  Examples For Special Forms

**Schools for Employed Persons**
These are generally run in the form of evening classes.

**Secondary Colleges**
Secondary Colleges lead graduates (from grammar schools or other vocational schools) to the goals of a VET college. Therefore, they have to pass only the VET diploma, as they have already got the school-leaving exam ("Higher School Certificate"). Add-on Courses *(Aufbaulehrgänge)* which can be run by Secondary Schools enable school-leavers from VET schools to pass the final exam.

## 3  History and Position of Informatics at Schools and Colleges of Engineering, Arts and Crafts

Informatics has had a long tradition at vocational schools. About 30 years ago the compulsory subject "electronic data processing" (2 lessons per week in the IV. form[12]) was introduced. Then simple programming was in the centre of education. Soon the education was prolonged into twice 2 lessons per week (11th and 12th grade).

In the other forms of vocational schools subjects were included that belong to informatics as well.

With small computers and personal computers coming into fashion sufficient training units could be installed for the first time.
Informatics developed fast:

- on the one hand, it was introduced as part of the technical general knowledge in every branch.
- on the other hand, certain forms of a special informatics education was set up.

### 3.1  Informatics as a Basic Discipline

Understanding for the fundamentals of economic contexts is imparted in all branches of education. Similarly informatics education has continued to develop. The subject

---

[10] § 74. College of Occupations in the Business Sector. Students gain higher commercial education for all branches of economy.

[11] § 76. College of Management and Service Industries. They serve to gain higher economical education to take up higher jobs in the fields of economy, administration, nourishment, tourism and culture.

[12] The IV. form corresponds to the 8th class of grammar school or the 12thlevel of education.

"electronic data processing" developed in the Schools and Colleges of Engineering, Arts and Crafts into the subject "electronic data processing and applied electronic data processing", then into "applied informatics".

Topics such as word processing, spreadsheets and data bases were added. Also the social effects of electronic data processing were soon part of the curricula.

New contents came into being due to electronic communication networks and the internet. To supply all schools with internet accesses with suitable bandwidth was a great challenge in the following years. With the help of fast internet accesses which are permanently at hand the assignment to induce pupils to self-study could be fulfilled. Although the standard increased the amount of lessons remained unchanged.

### 3.2  Informatics as a Special Form of Education

With "electronic data processing and organization" a new branch was established 20 years ago. Since then it predominantly trained technicians for electronic data processing on a grand scale and for commercial application of electronic data processing. From our present point of view this branch can best be compared with "business informatics".

Divisions such as "engineering with business administration – business informatics" or "electronics - technical informatics" followed. Terms like "information technology" or "informatics" were combined with further expressions such as from civil engineering.

## 4  Information Technology as Example of an Educational Branch

The final development, starting with the school year 2001/02, is the division for information technology[13]. At present this form is run as an educational experiment.

The curriculum has chosen three main areas[14]:

- network technology
- systems and information technology
- internet and media technology

In each year of education there are about 37 lessons per week. The regular education which is the same for each main area comprises the following subjects (the figures in the last column indicate the complete amount of lessons per week)

For deepening the subject matters in the three main areas another 5, 14 and 14 lessons per week are used in the 3rd, 4th and 5th year.

However, this balanced distribution was disturbed by the liability to save two lessons per week every year.[15]

Curricula are general frameworks, this means that the contents are listed only very generally. The outline of one subject which is taught over a couple of years is for in-

---

[13] The curricula can be found at: http://www.htl.rennweg.at/recht/erlaesse/it-stdt.pdf.

[14] See also http://www.zeugnisinfo.at/xml/3897/3897.pdf.

[15] "Entlastungsverordnung" June 2003 (BGBl. II Nr. 283/2003).

stance hardly more than half a page in print. Due to the fact that the technology develops very fast in informatics, the subject matters of current interest must be adapted again and again. On one hand, the lecturers themselves are responsible for that, on the other hand, the current development is coordinated in work groups among the individual locations.

| Religion | Religion | 10 |
|---|---|---|
| German language | Deutsch | 11 |
| English language | Englisch | 12 |
| History and polical education | Geschichte und politische Bildung | 4 |
| Physical exercise | Leibesübungen | 8 |
| Geography and economics | Geographie und Wirtschaftskunde | 4 |
| Economy and law | Wirtschaft und Recht | 6 |
| Applied mathematics | Angewandte Mathematik | 14 |
| Applied physics | Angewandte Physik | 4 |
| Applied chemistry and ecology | Angewandte Chemie und Ökologie | 5 |
| Applied programming | Angewandte Programmierung | 10 |
| Basics of electrical engineering and electronics | Grundlagen der Elektrotechnik und Elektronik | 6 |
| Basics of computer science | Grundlagen der Informatik | 5 |
| Media engineering | Medientechnik | 6 |
| Business economics | Betriebswirtschaft | 4 |
| Operating systems and computer architecture | Betriebssysteme und Computerarchitektur | 6 |
| Network engineering | Netzwerktechnik | 8 |
| Data base systems | Datenbanksysteme | 4 |
| Projects and project management | Projekte und Projektmanagement | 15 |
| Qualitymanagement | Qualitätsmanagement | 2 |
| Practical training on computers | Computerpraktikum | 8 |

An example for this is "voice over IP". Although it is not expressly mentioned in the curriculum, the technology is also put into practice: interested schools join the project at43[16]! VoIP offers reasonable options for communication for our economy and consequently competitive advantages. It is up to the technical schools to convey the fundamentals of implementation.

## 5 Summary

Informatics has had a long tradition in vocational schools. New curricula take current developments into account. The subject matters describe a wide spectrum from modest beginnings of a programming course to contents which need not frighten comparison with the education provided by advanced technical college (FH).

---

[16] The project at43 is carried out by The University of Vienna and the Internet Private Foundation Austria: http://www.at43.at.

# The Transition from School to University: Would Prior Study of Computing Help?

Martyn Clark and Roger Boyle

School of Computing, University of Leeds, UK
{martyn, roger}@comp.leeds.ac.uk

**Abstract.** We investigate issues in the preparation of students for undergraduate study. Specifically, we focus upon the question of whether
computer science students would be better prepared if they were required
to pass a school level qualification in the discipline. Thus we investigate
the school level curriculum in detail and make a comparison with the
demands of a typical UK university first year. We conclude that there is
no reason necessarily to see a school level qualification as assisting the
preparation of students for undergraduate study in computer science.
Rather, we hypothesise that the value of the qualification will depend
heavily on the nature of the teaching experienced.

## 1   Introduction

The preparation of students for university entry is known to be very influential
on their success [1]. Further, the preparation of students for university study of
computer science has recently been highlighted as a key issue [2, 3, 4]. Thus we
address the issue of school level computer science as preparation for studying
the discipline at university.

Specifically, we compare the English school level computer science curriculum
with the requirements of a typical university first year and ask what grounds
exist for believing that an applicant with a school level computing qualification
will perform better in a university computing course than another applicant who
has not studied the discipline before.

The paper is structured as follows. Section 2 provides background relating
to university admissions and pre-university qualifications in England together
with the methodology for the study. Section 3 details findings and these are
discussed in section 4. The paper ends with conclusions and an outline of plans
for further work.

## 2   Background

In England, compulsory education ends at age sixteen but most individuals do
not move on to university until the age of eighteen. While a variety of alternative
routes exist, most university candidates spend the intervening years at tertiary

R.T. Mittermeir (Ed.): ISSEP 2005, LNCS 3422, pp. 37–45, 2005.

institutions studying in preparation for A-level examinations. These examinations are offered in a wide range of subjects and most candidates will attempt three or, perhaps, four subjects. In the majority of cases results will play a major part in determining which universities and which degree programmes will accept the candidate.

Indeed, to be accepted at a particular English university candidates must satisfy up to three types of admission requirement.

- Matriculation requirements are designed to allow candidates to demonstrate that they have the potential to benefit from the university experience. For example, in addition to passing at least two A-levels at grade E or above, many universities require candidates to do well in at least five subjects in pre-A-level examinations taken at age 16.
- Popular and prestigious institutions and courses will normally set entrance requirements somewhat above this minimum level. For example, to study history at a member of the UK 'Russell Group' of leading research universities candidates must pass three A-levels at grades BBB [5].
- In addition, entry to many degree programmes is conditional upon passing an A-level in the student's discipline of choice. Thus applicants to physics should offer an A-level in the discipline at grade A or B.

We are aware of no degree course in computer science which requires students to have passed an A-level in the discipline. However, at our institution approximately half of each cohort present with this qualification [6, 7] and we are interested in whether these students have an advantage over their peers who are computing neophytes. An academic truism that entry qualifications are at best poor indicators of student achievement on graduation is supported by a growing body of research including our own study of computing [8, 9, 10, 11, 12]. However, these are complex issues and at least one large-scale quantitative study appears to contradict this finding [13].

Nevertheless, we are aware of no research which attempts to move back a step in the analysis and ask why A-levels, or any other tertiary exit qualification, *should* be a good predictor of university performance. Thus we ask: what grounds exist for believing that undergraduates with a school level computing qualification should get better marks than their peers?

A-level examinations are run by examination boards. *Inter alia*, examination boards publish specifications setting out the precise nature of the qualification, including the syllabus to be examined. They also set and organise examinations, including the marking and publishing results. A number of boards exist and although their respective A-level computing specifications are not identical, they are, of necessity, comparable. Indeed, the supervisory regime which assures the quality of A-level qualifications ensures that significant elements are common to each board's specification in a given subject. We examined the current A-level computing specifications offered by two of these examinations boards: the Assessment and Qualifications Alliance (AQA) and the Oxford, Cambridge and RSA Examinations Board (OCR). The selection of these boards largely reflects the accessibility of data but by studying two boards' specifications we were able to consider the relevance of their different emphases to our findings.

We compared these specifications with the first year undergraduate curriculum in order to consider the extent to which experience of an A-level course might prepare students for the university experience. The approach is subjective and relies on our judgements as teachers of computing. However, we argue that this process mirrors that undertaken in tertiary establishments when teachers receive an A-level specification and plan activities to prepare students to sit examinations based upon it. Further, the analysis could be applied to other school level qualifications and to the entry level curriculum of other universities both in England and further afield.

## 3    Findings

Our findings, which necessarily rely on our interpretations of both university and A-level curriculum documents, are designed to identify those aspects of the level one curriculum in which students who have passed A-level Computing might be thought to have an advantage over their peers who have not.

The level one undergraduate curriculum under consideration is specified as twelve modules addressing ten sub-disciplinary areas; there are two modules each of programming and mathematics. For each module we report on the extent to which we perceive the A-level as preparation. Modules are grouped into: those we judge to be new even to students who have the A-level (*new challenges*); those we consider most likely to reveal an advantage for these students (*familiar territory*); and those where we feel the A-level may represent a good foundation, although this may not be revealed in results (*firm foundations*).

### 3.1    New Challenges

Two areas of the undergraduate level one curriculum emerge as being highly distinct from the A-level experience: mathematics and artificial intelligence. There is evidence that some mathematics did feature strongly in earlier versions of the A-level curriculum [14], while artificial intelligence is a particular specialism of the department under consideration. In our judgement A-level Computing should not be a discriminator in these modules.

- English students are not alone in finding that the importance of mathematics to the practise of computing often comes as both a surprise and a disappointment [15]. However, a variety of mathematical concepts and techniques are fundamental to computing and undergraduates are expected to become familiar with areas such as algebra, discrete mathematics, logic, geometry, probability and statistics.

  In contrast, the A-level syllabus contains almost no mathematics. Each Board's specification includes a requirement to study number systems but this is the only mathematical content we identify in the specification. It should be noted, however, that an A-level in mathematics exists and that a number of computing degree programmes make a pass in this subject a prerequisite.

- The artificial intelligence module is designed to help students to develop understanding of the fundamental ideas, issues and techniques of artificial intelligence. Its key syllabus content, knowledge representation and reasoning, leads to a survey of the main sub-areas including computer vision; computing using natural language; computer learning.

  While equivalents for the remainder of the level one modules are almost certain to be found in any university level one computing curriculum, artificial intelligence is a particular specialism of the department concerned. It is, therefore, not surprising that we found no evidence that these topics are included in the A-level curriculum.

## 3.2    Familiar Territory

In contrast, there may be grounds for believing that undergraduates who have taken the A-level Computing will get better marks than their peers who did not in the database, professional development, and architecture modules. The close relationship between the curriculum requirements of these modules and the A-level specifications suggests that while the translation from the school regime to that of the university may require some effort, students should be on familiar territory.

- Introductory databases focuses upon databases as programmable systems. The curriculum is based largely around data modelling techniques and the use of the Structured Query Language (SQL) to develop, maintain and manipulate relational databases.

  Databases are a major topic in the A-level curriculum which refers specifically to the SQL, relational models and a number of other concepts which feature in the level one curriculum. However, the extent to which this is made specific differs between the Boards considered: while the AQA specification clearly addresses many of the issues included in the level one curriculum, the OCR specification addresses them, but less obviously.

  Of course, expectations at undergraduate level will not be identical with those at A-level, but our judgement is that students who have considered the concept of the relational database and used the SQL should have skills and knowledge on arrival at university that other students must learn during their level one studies. Refining understanding as concepts and techniques are encountered in new contexts should be less challenging than starting from scratch.

- The inclusion of professional development as a topic in the undergraduate curriculum reflects the close relationship between the theory and practise of computing. Students are encouraged to become aware of managerial, social and legal issues arising from the practise of computing and are given opportunities to develop and refine various generic skills such as report writing, working in groups and communication skills. Professional organisations, such as the British Computer Society [16], offer additional accreditation to degree programmes and in the UK this form of accreditation is widely sought by university departments as a form of endorsement of quality and comparability. These organisations see professional development as a particularly important aspect of the undergraduate curriculum.

These issues feature strongly in the A-level curriculum. Each of the specifications considered makes specific reference to legal, social, historical and ethical issues in computing. Therefore, we judge that students who have taken the A-level may be aware already of many of the issues of professionalism that this module seeks to highlight.

- The syllabus for the architecture module refers to computer internals, performance measures, arithmetic and logic operations and CPU internals. The A-level specification refers to many of these concepts specifically, including the expectation that students develop an historical perspective. This module, therefore, has the potential to highlight any advantage for students who have passed the A-level.

### 3.3    Firm Foundations?

The potential for undergraduates holding the A-level qualification to be advantaged in the remaining modules is less clear. Certain aspects of the undergraduate curriculum are specified for study at A-level, but there is clearly scope to address them in more or less detail depending on the Board chosen, the facilities available, and the interests of teachers and students.

In these modules the A-level may provide a useful foundation but we judge that, as activities at undergraduate level will tend to focus on the more advanced material, module results may not reveal much advantage for A-level holders.

- Introductory networking introduces ideas about operating systems and computer-to-computer communication. Key concepts from this area are required at A-level, for example, client-server models of communication, hyperlinking and the World Wide Web, and common network environments. Clearly, however, the undergraduate curriculum goes further, for example, it includes CGI scripts, data compression, and distributed applications.
- Similarly, the basics of human-computer interaction are specified as topics for A-level study including, for example, user models and interface design. The undergraduate curriculum builds upon the basics by discussing why interaction is as important as processing and analysing 'human factors', such as vision and memory, which are important in the design of interactions.
- Analysis of algorithms is a theoretical, rather than practical, module which, in addition to introducing data structures, invites students to consider particular problems and how they might be tackled using a computer. While the A-level specification does call for a familiarity with simple data structures and some description of algorithms we judge that the undergraduate curriculum requires a significantly more sophisticated understanding.
- The information systems module introduces a more 'business-oriented' or less technical ('softer') perspective on computing. It is concerned with concepts

relating to systems and information and requires students to consider different perspectives on the process of developing information systems. These concepts do not feature prominently in the A-level curriculum. However, courses based upon these specifications should consider the relationship between data and information which is an important foundation for undergraduate study. Similarly, the uses of computers in organisations, particularly management information systems, is part of the A-level specification.

### 3.4    The Special Case of Programming

Software engineering is a major component of any undergraduate programme in computing. The ability to program is one of the defining characteristics of members of the computing community [15]. Experience suggests that learning to program dominates their first year at university for a large number of computing students. Further, students who do not pass these modules are unlikely to enter level two.

The level one programming modules focus on the syntax of a programming language and techniques for ensuring that robust and reliable programs are developed which meet requirements: that is, techniques for engineering software. In contrast, the A-level specification does not require programming specifically. Rather, the emphasis is on systems development: an expression which could mean programming, but equally could refer to the development of systems using applications such as database management systems (e.g., Microsoft Access). Our judgement is that students arriving at university able to program would be at a substantial advantage but there is no guarantee that the A-level would deliver this.

Aspects of software engineering are required by the A-level specifications: particularly, aspects of design and testing. However, we consider these topics alone insufficient to confer a significant advantage because in comparison with programming they are not significant topics in the software engineering modules.

## 4    Discussion

We have identified certain university modules as being highly convergent with the school level curriculum, but this is balanced by other modules where no relationship is apparent. This finding is consistent with the results when we compared the first year grades attained by students who were admitted with A-level Computing and those attained by students with no prior experience of studying the discipline; students with the A-level were shown to do better in databases, professional development and computer architecture but not in other modules [6]. Is this sufficient to make prior study of the discipline a requirement for university entrance?

The reasons for a university to view school level experience as a prerequisite for the study of a discipline are rarely made explicit. We suggest there are two main perspectives;

- Necessary preparation: the learning of material essential to even the most elementary study at university. An example might be an understanding of calculus to study mathematics – without it, the student would find it very difficult to participate in disciplinary conversations. Thus an accepted starting point for university study is defined.
- Gate-keeping: supplementing basic entry entry requirements in a largely arbitrary way for courses where applications exceed significantly the number of places available.

Whilst recognising that if the number of places is oversubscribed some means must be found for selecting candidates for admission, we see little to commend the latter approach. Similarly, we do not see in these findings a case for adopting A-level Computing as a prerequisite for university study on the basis of necessary preparation. Not only does the A-level appear to confer a significant advantage in only three modules but we suggest that crucial differences in the way computing is experienced at the school level may have significant implications for the relevance of this qualification as preparation for joining a university department.

In the UK the origins of a discipline of computing lie in the creation of computing facilities designed to service research in mathematics and the science and engineering disciplines [7]. Thus, ideas about a *higher* education in the discipline are founded not only upon relatively easy access to equipment of a certain standard but upon the methods and techniques devised in universities for the using computers in the solution of numerical problems. In contrast, while school level computing appeared in the late 1960s, the subject did not become widespread until the general adoption of the personal computer eliminated the issue of access to equipment [14].

Prior to the commercial development of microprocessors and home computers, school computing tended to rely on a postal service to a mainframe (commonly at a university or local government facility). While slow and cumbersome, such access at least guaranteed a quality of service; pupils were operating in the same computing environment as academics and professionals (albeit remotely). We hypothesise that the introduction to schools of personal computers changed this.

Of course, personal computers are used in undergraduate computing courses and many graduates of computing degree programmes go on to support their use in business and other environments. Significantly, however, much professional and academic work in such matters as programming, database management, the Internet, etc. is undertaken using equipment that would not normally be found in the average office or home. If this hypothesis is correct, one reason that A-level Computing is of limited relevance as preparation for university study is that pupils do not operate in computing environments typical of much professional and academic work.

A second hypothesis which may have relevance to the utility of A-level Computing as preparation for university study in the discipline relates to staffing. Universities began to offer post-graduate courses in the discipline during the late 1950s with undergraduate courses being introduced in the 1960s. The number of places available has grown dramatically, particularly during the 1990s, but we hypothesise that demand from industry for the graduates of these courses, and the consequent pay differential, has meant relatively small numbers of computing graduates have entered the teaching profession.

If this hypothesis were correct it might help to explain why the A-level Computing specification does not require that candidates learn computer programming. Access to equipment is unlikely to be an issue with respect to programming which can be learnt using personal computers and commonly available software. Rather, the absence of programming from many A-level courses may reflect the fact that many A-level teachers are not computing specialists. That is, although computing academics perceive significant differences between their discipline and skills associated with the *use* of computers, the implication of this hypothesis is that this distinction is less clear at the school level; computing is taught from the perspective of using rather than building computer systems.

This is not intended to be derogatory; the ability to use information technology efficiently and effectively has become an important life skill. However, we argue that the ability to manipulate applications such as Microsoft Access or Macromedia Dreamweaver via user-oriented graphical interfaces is a relatively poor preparation for studying a discipline concerned with what happens behind the interface. Certainly, the ability to program would be significantly more beneficial than the most highly developed IT skills in the study of computing.

## 5    Conclusions

We have argued that there is some convergence between the school level curriculum in England and a typical first year university computer science curriculum. Students entering university with prior experience of the discipline are likely to have encountered already a number of ideas that computing neophytes will meet for the first time. However, unless students learnt to program as part of their A-level studies this advantage is unlikely to be significant. Thus we do not advocate making prior study of the discipline a condition of entry to university computer science degrees.

Our findings highlight the importance to university computer scientists of awareness of the treatment of the discipline in the school curriculum. In particular, support for the teaching of programming would appear a priority. Further our findings highlight the need to support students who have not studied the discipline before who may become demotivated if they struggle relative to students who have seen some of the subject matter before.

Finally, in this research we have relied upon our interpretations of A-level specification documents. Whilst we argue that our interpretations are sufficiently relevant for the findings presented here to be meaningful, it would be interesting to study students' experiences of the A-level courses based upon these documents. That is, further work will seek to compare our understanding of the requirements with the reality of studying computer science at school level.

## Acknowledgements

Some of this work was conducted with grant assistance from the Learning and Teaching Support Network for Information and Computer Sciences, University of Ulster, which we gratefully acknowledge. We are also most grateful for the significant assistance provided by the archive sections of AQA (Hilary Nicholls), AEB (Jane Bradshaw) and UCLES (Gillian Cooke) and to Miriam Zukas for comments on an earlier draft of this paper.

## References

1. Ozga, J., Sukhnandan, L.: Undergraduate non-completion: Developing an explanatory model. Higher Education Quarterly **52** (1998) 316–333
2. Clark, M.: Teaching computing in the liquid modern world. Presented at Grand Challenges in Computing, University of Newcastle, 29-31 March (2004)
3. Utting, I.: Mind the gap! Presented at Grand Challenges in Computing, University of Newcastle, 29-31 March (2004)
4. Johnson, C.: What do students want ... Presented at Grand Challenges in Computing, University of Newcastle, 29-31 March (2004)
5. University of Leeds: Coursefinder 2003 (2002) Available at: `http://tldynamic.leeds.ac.uk/ugcoursefinder/2003` [accessed 3.6.04].
6. Boyle, R., Clark, M.: A-level computing: its content and value. University of Leeds School of Computing Report No. 2002.15 (2002)
7. Clark, M.: Constructing the discipline of computing: implications for the curriculum. unpublished PhD thesis, University of Kent, UK (2004)
8. Lizzio, A., Wilson, K., Simons, R.: University students' perception of the learning environment and academic outcomes: implications for theory and practice. Studies in Higher Education **27** (2002) 27–52
9. Osborne, M., Leopold, J., Ferrie, A.: Does access work? The relative performance of access students at a Scottish university. Higher Education **33** (1997) 155–176
10. Brown, M., Macrae, S., Rodd, M.: Mathematics undergraduates' attitudes to their course (2004) In preparation.
11. Child, D.: A-levels as a predictor: the correlation between A-level grades and degree results for the 1981 entry to Leeds. The Reporter: The University of Leeds newsletter (1986) 4 Number 255.
12. Boyle, R.D., Carter, J.E., Clark, M.A.C.: What makes them succeed? Entry, progression and graduation in Computer Science. Journal of Further and Higher Education **26** (2002) 3–18
13. Bekhradnia, B.: Who does best at university? (2002) Available at: `http://www.hefce.ac.uk/learning/whodoes` [accessed 3.6.04].
14. Boyle, R.D., Clark, M.A.C.: A-level computing: its history and development. IEEE Annals of the History of Computing (2004) Forthcoming.
15. Alexander, S., Amillo, J., Boyle, R.D., Clark, M.A.C., Daniels, M., Laxer, C., Loose, K., Shinners-Kennedy, D.: Case studies in admissions to and early performance in computer science degrees. SIGCSE Bulletin **35** (2003) 137–147
16. British Computer Society: Exemption & accreditation for higher education institutions. Available at: `http://www.bcs.org/BCS/Products/HEAccreditation` [accessed 7.6.04] (2003)

# Informatics and ICT in Polish Education System

Ewa Gurbiel, Grazyna Hardt-Olejniczak, Ewa Kolczyk,
Helena Krupicka, and Maciej M. Syslo

Institute of Computer Science, University of Wroclaw,
ul. Przesmyckiego 20, 51-151 Wroclaw, Poland
tik@ii.uni.wroc.pl

**Abstract.** The reform of the Polish national education system started in the school year 1999/2000. One of the main features of it is the plan to integrate Information and Communication Technology (ICT) into almost all school subjects. The second important feature is preparing students to use computers and software in other subjects during separate ICT lessons. The separate lessons on using computers and ICT are called informatics. Informatics lessons are obligatory in primary schools and in middle schools (gimnazjum). In high schools (liceum) there is an obligatory subject called information technology (IT) and an elective subject called informatics (computer science). It is possible to take the maturity exam in informatics when someone has graduated from the high school. The authors work as a team, and have prepared subject curricula, informatics textbooks, electronic materials for students and accompanying guidelines and books for teachers for all stages of the education system. We are also engaged in teacher-education and in-service training. We want to exchange our ideas, as realized within these materials, and we would like to present our experience in making these ideas alive in our schools. The realization of informatics education in secondary schools is a continuing process. We are at the moment, in the year 2005, when the first graduates of the new education system will come to study in our universities. So it is necessary to make some reflections on the past.

## 1 Introduction

Since September of 1999, the education system in Poland is divided into: primary school (6 years), middle school (called *gimnazjum*, 3 years) and high school (called *liceum*, 3 years). Children begin the school education when they are seven.

The Ministry of National Education published a document *Guideline for teaching mandatory topics in the primary, middle and high school* [2], which can be considered as **the education standards** for subjects in all types of schools. Regarding information and communication technology (ICT), it is emphasised there that the teachers and schools are responsible for enabling all students to learn how to:

**Search, sort and make use of information coming from different**

**sources and effectively use information technology for that purpose.**

Students should learn to communicate information to others through a variety of means. One of the main objectives of the modern school is to **prepare all students to**

R.T. Mittermeir (Ed.): ISSEP 2005, LNCS 3422, pp. 46–52, 2005.

**live and work in the information society** [1]. To this end, ICT has been included in all school subjects in the standards. Students therefore should first be introduced to ICT and then they should have every opportunity to use ICT across curriculum, in studying all other subjects. It requires to:

- propose new informatics and ICT curriculum,
- integrate ICT with all other school subjects across the curriculum,
- elaborate and publish new education packages consisting of textbooks for students, software and electronic data, teacher's manual and Internet service,
- prepare teachers for introducing students to ICT and for using ICT in their teaching.

The authors, in collaboration with the publishing house Wydawnictwa Szkolne i Pedagogiczne S.A. (WSiP), started in 1997 with the project *Meetings and Learning with Computer*. The main goal of this project is to address all four areas, that is, to prepare curricula integrating ICT, elaborate learning and teaching materials for new curricula, and train teachers in using new curricula and materials.

## 2  Main Assumptions

The project is a realization of the education standards, and its main goal is to integrate ICT into all school subjects, with learning activities for students and teaching activities for teachers. It is assumed that the introductory classes on using computers and ICT, called *meetings with computer*, are oriented towards preparing students for *learning with computers*.

The project is addressed to primary, middle and high schools. For each type of school, the following items are elaborated and published:

1. **Curricula** for: Introductory ICT, ICT across curriculum, and for other subjects in the area of using ICT.
2. **Education packages** for students, e.g. textbooks[1] [9], [11], [12], software and electronic data.
3. Teacher's manuals[2] [10], [13].

---

[1] Gurbiel, E., Hardt-Olejniczak, G., Kołczyk, E., Krupicka, H., Sysło, M.M., *Informatyka, Podręcznik dla ucznia szkoły podstawowej, klasy 4-6*, WSiP, Warszawa 1999.
Gurbiel, E., Hardt-Olejniczak, G., Kołczyk, E., Krupicka, H., Sysło, M.M., Informatyka, Podręcznik   dla   ucznia   gimnazjum,   WSiP,   Warszawa   2000.
Gurbiel, E., Hardt-Olejniczak, G., Kołczyk, E., Krupicka, H., Sysło, M.M., Technologia informacyjna, Podręcznik dla liceum ogólnokształcącego, liceum profilowanego i technikum, WSiP, Warszawa 2002.
[2] Gurbiel, E., Hardt-Olejniczak, G., Kołczyk, E., Krupicka, H., Sysło, M.M., *Informatyka, Poradnik dla nauczycieli szkoły podstawowej, klasy 4-6*, WSiP, Warszawa 1999.
Gurbiel, E., Hardt-Olejniczak, G., Kołczyk, E., Krupicka, H., Sysło, M.M., *Informatyka, Poradnik   dla   nauczyciela   gimnazjum*,   WSiP,   Warszawa   2000.
Gurbiel, E., Hardt-Olejniczak, G., Kołczyk, E., Krupicka, H., Sysło, M.M., Technologia informacyjna, Poradnik dla nauczyciela i program nauczania w liceum ogólnokształcącym, liceum profilowanym i technikum, WSiP, Warszawa 2002.

4. In-service training courses for teachers who decide to work in schools using proposed materials.
5. Internet service [3].

# 3  Curricula

There are three types of curricula, prepared in the project, for each type of schools:

– ICT across the curriculum, with a realization of the school's and teachers' tasks in information technology.
– Informatics and ICT curriculum, as a separate subject, which prepares students to use ICT.
– Connections between the above curricula.

The main emphasis in the project is put on the spiral introduction of new and more advanced topics. The topics in the curriculum have been divided into five groups:

A. The use of a computer and its peripheral devices.
B. The influence of ICT on personal life, the local community, the outside world, and society.
C. The use of ICT tools, i.e. different kinds of software packages.
D. Communication, searching and using information, mainly with the help of ICT.
E. Solving problems and decision making using ICT.

Topics from group **A**, **B** and **C** are mainly assigned to separate lessons. The main objective of these lessons is making students familiar with the rules of using computers, networks and applications designing for information processing. Topics from group **D** and **E** more often require some material from other subjects, because processes of communication, searching information, solving problems are common for all domains of science and real life. The exception to this rule is the informatics curriculum for high schools, in which topics from group **E** concern computer science methods of solving problems.

## 3.1  ICT Across Curriculum

**The ICT across curriculum** is not divided into subjects since it concerns the activities of the whole school. It has been constructed by taking from the education standards of different school subjects: teaching goals, topics and skills, related to ICT [4], [5], [6] [7]. In particular, it was taken into considerations:

– formulations which *explicitly* refer to ICT and computers, contain notions and tools related to informatics education;
– formulations which refer to different aspects of information, which today, or in the near future, need the use of ICT;
– topics and goals which, when ICT is used, may increase the students' competence in using computers and ICT;
– topics and activities, which can be supported and enhanced by using ICT.

## 3.2  Informatics and ICT Curriculum

The separate lessons on using computers and ICT are called **informatics**. The Informatics curriculum is in fact a realization of the statements from the education standards.

The main goal of informatics classes **in primary schools** is to prepare students to use computers and their software, mainly to be able to use them in other subjects. It was assumed in the education standards that, at this stage of education, students should use a computer environment adjusted to their abilities (e.g. to age) and needs. To this end, a special software system has been designed and produced, which is an easy and spiral introduction to the professional MS Windows environment [14], [15].

**In middle schools** (*gimnazjum*), during the informatics classes, students are prepared to use computers, computer networks, and multimedia on a more advanced level. It should give students a more solid background for using ICT in other subjects. Moreover, students are introduced also to problem solving with algorithms. The language of implementing algorithms is Logo. The MS Windows environment is used at this stage of education.

**In high schools** (*liceum*) there are two subjects. One of them, called information technology (IT), is the continuation of earlier students' preparation in using computers, networks and multimedia tools for managing information. The stress is put on working with information in a good style, using possibilities of some tasks' automation. There is nothing about algorithms and programming. Informatics (computer science) is an elective subject addressed for young people who are interested in computer science as an element of their future education. The informatics lessons are expecting to show computer science as a discipline connected with designing and implementing new systems of information processing. It should include ways of solving problems in the following stages: analysis of a problem situation, making specification, designing the solution, realization and testing the solution. Students are introduced to classic algorithms, programming languages, theory of data bases, programming interactive websites.

# 4  Informatics Maturity Exam

Students who take the informatics subject in high school, could also take the maturity exam in it. The examination standards [16] are formulated in three areas:

– knowledge and understanding of basic concepts, methods and processes connected with informatics,
– using knowledge and information in solving theoretical and practical tasks,
– using informatics methods in creating new information and problem solving.

There are two parts of the exam: theoretical (without the use of computers) and practical. In both cases, the student should prepare appropriate documentation in which his or her solution is described. The student's work is externally moderated.

# 5    Reflections

## 5.1    ICT in Other Subjects

The placement, and the ways of developing computer learning support, should be precise in the curriculum of particular subjects. It should concern curriculum content, as well as appropriate new content and skills, which are possible only by using ICT methods and skills. Changes in the curriculum should take into account the possibility of computer deployment, which really will enrich known and established methods of working.

Computer use and ICT should appear (in subjects other than computer science) in two roles: as a didactical support, which enriches learning and teaching processes; and as an element integrated into particular school subjects, as elements which are inseparably connected with particular subjects.

Success in using computers in teaching depends on the level of their integration within established methods of learning and teaching – on their integration in curricular and in didactical support for students and teachers.

Research results concerning the efficiency of computer didactic aids indicated that lack of effects in this field (computer use in education) is caused by their insufficient integration with the school subjects. It is not enough to stand these machines "next to" the teacher, to have some positive results. Their conceptual "placement" in each region of teaching and the learning process is vital, as well as their mutual integration [8].

In the project *Meeting and learning with computer* a proposal for integrating computers with the teaching process is realized on two levels. First of all, the ICT curriculum (addressed to the whole school) is accompanied by content from curricular guidelines of all subjects and their connections with these curricula. Next, we propose integration activities with ICT used in other school subjects. For this purpose we prepared for use in other school subjects a textbook for students at the middle school [9] and accompanying teachers' manual [10]. In the students' textbook we demonstrate how to use computers in other school subjects using their curricula and textbooks and taking into account how students have been prepared within their informatics classes.

In the book *Learning with computer in the middle school* [9] we present typical exercises from the textbook for different subjects (on the middle school level). We demonstrate how the student can use in doing exercises: a computer, software, multimedia, and the Internet. In all exercises skills from computer science classes are used. The computer doesn't replace the teacher but it could be a means of doing some operations easier and faster than without it as well as broadening knowledge and skills. In the examples and exercises we don't use educational software. The three main goals of our class scenarios are: the application of skills from the informatics classes; using them to create active ways of performing in other school subjects, and to enrich students' skills such as using software applications, using Internet sources and services, or multimedia files on CD-ROM disc.

Our solution that there is a separate textbook with exercises from different subjects is not the best way of integrating ICT with the whole school curriculum. These exercises should be placed in textbooks for these subjects. But there is a long way to go in changing the teachers' and authors' of educational materials approach to using computers and networks in the learning process. We are satisfied that our textbook plays some role in teachers-education in different departments. They could consider it as an example of good practice.

### 5.2 Algorithms and Programming at Middle School Level

The informatics curriculum for middle schools includes topics concerned with problem solving, algorithms and basic programming skills. It is the only subject in a new education system which has a disadvantage well-known from previous solutions. The disadvantage is a result of linking together topics typical for computer science with topics connected with the effective use of the computer and its software. One of the reasons that this kind of connection does not succeed, is the level of the teachers' preparation. It's obvious that teaching difficult and abstract concepts at a basic level requires some extra competencies from a teacher. Our experience shows that it is a great difficulty to realize these topics in schools. Many teachers do not even try to do it.

Another question: is problem solving, algorithms and development of programming skills really essential for middle stage education? One answer is yes, because young people at this stage of their education should understand what the areas of interest in different knowledge disciplines actually are.

### 5.3 IT and Informatics Subjects at the High School Level

The problem we describe in the previous section is closely connected with informatics education at the high school level. Young people who like playing computers and surfing the Internet declare their interest in opting for an elective subject. They do not know what it is really about, because there was no signal at the middle level that problem solving, algorithms and programming need some skills of thinking, reasoning, and understanding mathematical concepts.

Another problem is, once again, teachers' preparation. Informatics subject in the form described in the document *Guideline for teaching mandatory topics in the primary, middle and high school* and defined by maturity examination standards is a great challenge for the teacher. In our opinion, teachers of informatics subject in high schools should be graduates of a computer science department. At our university, we prepare computer science students to become teachers. And we can point to good practice examples, when after graduating from university they work effectively and successfully in high schools.

## 6  Conclusions

We have finished the work connected with education standards, curricula and learning materials for all stages of the education system. In the year 2005, the first graduates of the new education system will come to study in our universities. According to the assumptions of the education system reform, they should be better prepared for using ICT in their work.

The problem that concerns us is the shape of an informatics education more connected with the introduction to computer science in secondary schools. The question of the content and the methodology employed in introducing the basic concepts of computer science at the secondary level is extremely important.

The second important question is, how could we facilitate and speed up integrating ICT with other subjects? What kind of activities are the most effective?

Now, as university workers, we are engaged in changing the shape of teacher-education. The Ministry of National Education has recently published standards of teachers education, so it will cause further changes in the study programmes.

# References

1. Apple Computer Education Team, Education Notes 2, 1996.
2. *Guideline for teaching mandatory topics in the primary and high school* (in Polish), http://www.men.waw.pl/prawo/rozp_14.html
3. Gurbiel, E., Hardt-Olejniczak, G., Kołczyk, E., Krupicka, H., Sysło, M.M., Project *Meetings and Learning with Computer* (in Polish), http://www.wsipnet.pl/kluby/informatyka.html
4. R. Heinich and others, *Instructional Media and Technologies for Learning*, Prentice Hall, 1996.
5. *Informatics for Secondary Education — A Curriculum for Schools*, UNESCO, Paris, 1994.
6. *Information Technology in the National Curriculum*, England and Wales, January 1995.
7. Ch. Moersch, Levels of Technology Implementation, The ISTE Journal of Educational Technology Practice and Policy, v.23, 3 Nov. 1995.
8. de Corte, E., *Spojrzenie wstecz i przed siebie na uczenie się wspomagane technologią z perspektywy badań nad uczeniem się i nauczaniem*, Conference "Informatics in Schools" proceedings (in Polish), Lublin 1997.
9. Gurbiel, E., Hardt-Olejniczak, G., Kołczyk, E., Krupicka, H., Sysło, M.M., *Learning with computer in the middle school*, (in Polish) WSiP, Warszawa 2001.
10. Gurbiel, E., Hardt-Olejniczak, G., Kołczyk, E., Krupicka, H., Sysło, M.M., *Learning with computer in the middle school*. Teachers' manual, (in Polish) WSiP, Warszawa 2001.
11. Gurbiel E., Hardt-Olejniczak G., Kołczyk E., Krupicka H., Sysło M.M., *Informatyka. Część 1. Kształcenie w zakresie rozszerzonym. Podręcznik dla liceum ogólnokształcacego*, WSiP S.A., Warszawa 2002.
12. Gurbiel E., Hardt-Olejniczak G., Kołczyk E., Krupicka H., Sysło M.M., *Informatyka. Część 2. Kształcenie w zakresie rozszerzonym. Podręcznik dla liceum ogólnokształcacego*, WSiP S.A., Warszawa 2003.
13. Gurbiel E., Hardt-Olejniczak G., Kołczyk E., Krupicka H., Sysło M.M., *Informatyka. Poradnik dla nauczycieli*, WSiP S.A., Warszawa 2004.
14. Gurbiel, E., Hardt-Olejniczak, G., Kołczyk, E., Krupicka, H., Sysło, M.M., Junior Windows und Junior Office. Einfürung in die ICT, Paderborn (Germany), Infos 2001, 17-20.09.2001.
15. Gurbiel, E., Hardt-Olejniczak, G., Kołczyk, E., Krupicka, H., Sysło, M.M., Junior Windows and Office-Environment for Introducing ICT w Networking the Learner, 7th IFIP World Conference on Computers in Education WCCE 2001, 29.07.-3.08.2001, Dania.
16. Informator maturalny od 2005 roku z informatyki (in Polish) http://www.cke.edu.pl/podstrony/inform_matur/inform_matur.html

# Teaching Information Technology in General Education: Challenges and Perspectives

Valentina Dagienė

Institute of Mathematics and Informatics,
Akademijos str. 4, LT-08663 Vilnius, Lithuania
dagiene@ktl.mii.lt

**Abstract.** During the last years a need of a new policy for implementing information and communication technology (ICT) in education has emerged. The Strategy for ICT implementation in Lithuanian education for 2005-2007 has been developed. Standards for school students' as well as teachers' computer literacy have been prepared and implemented. Teaching and learning information technology (IT) course in schools is one of the most relevant issues in information society. The paper deals with the goals and nature of the IT introducing into curriculum. It discuses the links with other school subjects and estimates the relationship between the compulsory IT course and the integrated parts as well as elective modules. The issues of general competencies essential for a contemporary citizen and the role of ICT in their development are also being discussed. Some suggestions in respect of developing IT curricula and general content are presented.

## 1 Introduction

The Lithuanian school education mainly consists of three stages: elementary ($1^{st}$-$4^{th}$ grades), basic ($5^{th}$-$10^{th}$ grades), and secondary ($11^{th}$-$12^{th}$ grades). Full-time education is compulsory for all children from the age 6 or 7 to 16. Almost all the secondary level schools are state schools. There are approximately 1100 comprehensive schools (basic and secondary) with about half a million students in the country (there are 3.5 million inhabitants in Lithuania).

ICT has rather firm position in education; its availability for teaching and learning becomes increasingly obvious. The main discussions go on different aspects of methodology: what are the most reasonable ways of its implementation, how the teaching should be improved, etc.

Following the results of International Association for the Evaluation of Educational Achievement we can get rather value-free prospect of the implementation of computers into comprehensive schools of different countries [10, 11, 12].

We clearly may trace four main trends: 1) informatics as a separate educational subject; 2) development of applied computer skills; 3) training of information skills; 4) integration of informatics or information technologies in the other educational subjects.

R.T. Mittermeir (Ed.): ISSEP 2005, LNCS 3422, pp. 53–64, 2005.

The model of informatics as a separate course in a comprehensive school dominates in majority of East European countries, in which the fundamental and academic trends of teaching are rather more dominating until nowadays. Lithuania also falls under that category. Informatics as a separate subject was established in late 1970s and early 1980s. As a compulsory or partly compulsory subject it has been delivered in Belarus, Bulgaria, Czech Republic, Latvia, Poland, Romania, Russia, Slovak Republic, Hungary, Germany, and other countries [13, 5]. The course is being changed permanently: teaching about computer and training of the programming skills used to get more attention ten years ago, while nowadays much more consideration is devoted to developing the skills of practical ICT use in teaching and learning.

In today's world all countries give rising attention to ICT implementation in education [9]. Those countries which have informatics as a separate subject usually treat ICT as a part of it; however, most of the time and place in the teaching process is assigned to the technology itself, but not to its applying to the process of teaching and learning. In order to emphasize novelty of the course in informatics and the aspect of its applicability most of the countries, including Lithuania, have renamed it into Information Technology.

The second trend – development of applied computer skills – actually is the part of the course of informatics, and especially of IT. The trend is emphasized by those countries which previously didn't have academic course in informatics and which don't use the centralized way of providing computers for education but follow the will and the possibilities of the schools themselves.

Developing of information skills in fact embraces IT trend, but is slightly more of humanitarian studies and is coherent with libraries. J. Herring has introduced the model for developing information skills called PLUS [6]. The further works of this scholar is devoted to the issue of implementation of internet in educational process [7]. There is opinion that internet and CD will become main information sources and school will seriously have to consider this.

Implementation of computer-based technology during the lessons of each subject is one of the main goals of informatics or IT. Such process develops in all countries, although in a different way: it's closely related to economical level, infrastructure and state's priorities over the information society, etc. Some countries and especially those who have deep traditions of integrated teaching (for example, Denmark) implement integrated course of IT more successfully [8]. The parallel processes are preceded in many West European countries: on one hand, the IT trends are taken into account, on the other hand, IT is implemented in different school subjects.

East European countries have much more problems with such integration. The main reasons for it are the following: 1) lack of the technical means in schools; 2) inadequate or partly inadequate curricula or even lack of it; 3) low preparation level of teachers of different subjects to implement ICT in their teaching; 4) domination of academic way of teaching, *i.e.* subjects are being taught separately and have very little connection one to each other. Unsatisfactory attention to new teaching methodologies which require computer-based implementation in subject's teaching and the lack of qualitatively new teaching means have also to be mentioned here.

## 2  ICT Implementation and Education Goals

ICT implementation is a complex task which includes all elements and areas of education and influences the concept and the system of education. Different motives have revealed the variety of educational goals that may be reached with the help of ICT. The Strategy for ICT implementation in the Lithuanian education (for the years 2000-2004 and the new one for the years 2005-2007) provides that implementation of ICT in education should help to realize the Lithuanian education reform, should fit into general school objects and should satisfy public process and trends of economy in country [15]. Therefore the declared aims are based on the upbringing goals provided in general curricula of Lithuanian comprehensive schools and in conception for Lithuanian education as well as on the general values and principles of school work.

Analysis of Lithuanian comprehensive schools and evaluation of goals that are declared by educational reform has revealed that ICT implementation in comprehensive schools would be useful for different educational purposes, such as: 1) obtaining of a comprehensive education (on one hand, computer literacy is a concurrent part of the comprehensive education, and on the other hand, computers are tool allowing to get latter-day education); 2) upbringing the skills of continual and autonomic learning as well as ability to get handle on the different information sources; 3) stimulation of the communication and the cooperation as well as contribution in understanding of the main principles and values of democratic society; 4) as a result of its cultural, cognitive, and cooperational nature it may benefit an influence on each citizen's cultural self-consciousness and humanistic values.

All of this shows that the role of ICT in Lithuanian education should be regarded as multidimensional. Regarding the synthesis of general motivation for ICT implementation and analysis of Lithuanian education goals, the strategy for the years 2000–2004 has provided three main goals of IT implementation: 1) to provide the prospects and trends of integrating ICT into the Lithuanian general education, 2) to harmonize activities of various institutions, 3) to effectively use the funds allocated for the computerization of education. Strategy for the years 2005–2007 is concentrated on the following goals: 1) breakthrough of ICT implementation in school teaching and learning; 2) creation of educational computer network – well-stocked electronic space designed for teaching and learning as well as nurturing the conditions for modernization of education management and communication between school societies; 3) improvement of all inhabitants' computer competence helpful for solving the problems of social imparity. The goals of both previous and recent strategies embrace economical, social, pedagogical and other objectives.

## 3  From Informatics to Information Technology

The course in informatics started to be taught in Lithuanian comprehensive schools 20 years ago. The contents of the course, evaluation, and even the name were changed several times; nevertheless IT has remained as a separate subject. Besides, one of the most important components of IT is to make students of comprehensive schools ICT literate [2]. Today so called IT course is compulsory for the 9th and the 10th grades of basic school (68 hours in total) as well as for upper secondary school (11th and 12th grades, also 68 hours). Students in the 11th and the 12th grade may also choose the optional (advanced) course of the subject. Students have to learn content defined in the course curriculum and obtain the capability defined in the educational standards. IT course usually is taught during the individual lessons of the subject. During the lessons, however, an integrative nature of the course is being stressed; students are prompt to see parallels with other subjects, to employ modern methods, to differentiate contents, etc.

The major developments of educational reforms in Lithuania occurred in the field of curriculum development. The new curricula and standards seek to strike a balance between the quantity of necessary knowledge on one hand, and the acquisition of intellectual, social and civic fluency on the other hand. Recently, IT general curricula and general education standards for basic and upper secondary levels were developed [3, 4]. At the moment the IT curriculum for basic education ($5^{th}$-$10^{th}$ grades) is being revised. An integration draft should be prepared before long.

The main aim of teaching IT in general education is to develop students' information culture (literacy) in a broad sense. This goal is timely, urgent and of constant value. With the course of time the conception of information culture may change. Both basic and secondary school are striving for this goal. However, in the latter the conception is deeper and more comprehensive.

In our opinion, the information culture is a wide concept, considerably wider than information skills or abilities to work by computer. We consider that at present the conception of information culture covers various abilities and skills [3, p. 367]:

- to systematize the knowledge of ICT that the students have gained before the school or outside of it;
- to develop logical and operational thinking, operation planning skills, creativeness, ability to improvise, self-confidence;
- to refresh their IT knowledge and improve their skills to think and act;
- to give an opportunity for students to choose the direction of their further studies in the field of informatics;
- to develop a general literacy of students' information activities together with other school subjects;
- to get familiar with the elementary ICT and the related concepts and to be able to apply that creatively in daily life and cognition;
- to learn the basic concepts of ICT and understand their meaning, and put it into practice;
- to get familiar with the history and development of IT and their impact on the evolution of society and its culture;
- to improve their skills on ethical issues: to operate with ICT legitimately and reasonably, to link ICT with general issues of the culture of the society;
- to foster a resolve to continuously develop the content and style of one's information activities.

The goal of information culture is understood as an ideal towards which all the information education at schools should be directed, including compulsory and optional courses devoted to informatics.

The content of information culture's notion is constantly changing and is reliant on technological transformations. General tasks and goals of IT teaching and learning are defined also after the notion of information culture. It embraces a broad range of students' cognitive and other abilities and attitudes: starting with acquisition of the main IT terms and ending with creative abilities of improvisation, curiosity for innovations, and perception of cultural and ethical issues related to ICT.

Principle competencies of educated person (reading, writing, and arithmetic) which were dominating for several centuries nowadays are replaced by other ones, such as: information search (Web), text layout (word processing), and handling of numeric data (spreadsheet) (Fig. 1).

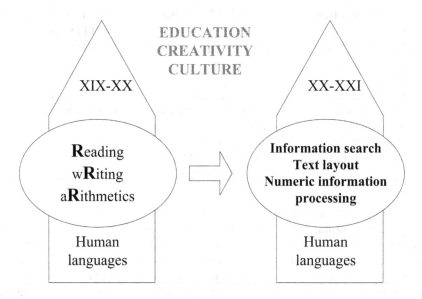

**Fig. 1.** Changing of basic competencies in society

IT curriculum emphasizes the value-based attitudes and general skills. However, these abilities are the objective of all informational training. The aims of separate IT course are much more narrow and pragmatic. In the last two grades of basic school (9th and 10th) students are taught to summarize ICT knowledge that was obtained in school and out of it, improve their ICT skills, and are prompted to get deeper awareness of informatics as a science which might encourage them for further studies of the subject. The aims of general course of IT for the 11th and 12th grades are cognitive as well, while the advanced course is intended for the training of specific application skills in one of the three chosen areas of ICT (data base, programming or multimedia) [4].

IT standards and contents of its courses are divided into the main ICT topics as it is shown in Table 1. The intended aims for the 9th-10th and the 11th-12th grades are essentially different. The IT standards for the 9th and 10th grades very precisely define the ICT knowledge and skills the students should obtain. The IT standards for the

11th and 12$^{th}$ grades are combined from two components. The first one describes general ability, while the second one is provided to define the particular achievements related to particular topics and chapters. General ability is rather broad and matches the common goals of the course. The content of curriculum is close to that of European Computer Driving License (ECDL), thus the main stress is placed on the substantial intelligence of ICT and on the formation of practical skills.

**Table 1.** Contents of IT subject curricula

| Compulsory course, 9-10 grades | Compulsory course, 11-12 grades | Advanced (optional) course, 11-12 grades |
|---|---|---|
| 1. Computer (principles of the work with computer) | 1. Advanced elements of text editing | 1. Data base |
| 2. Text processing | 2. Presentation | 2. Multimedia |
| 3. Information (basics of information handling) | 3. WWW and electronic mail | 3. Programming |
| 4. Algorithms (main concepts and commands) | 4. Social and ethical issues of using IT | |
| | 5. Using spreadsheet | |

Before graduating from the 12$^{th}$ grade students can chose IT school-leaving examination (starting with 2006 it'll be possible to choose State school-leaving examination in programming). The topics of school examination fully matches the curriculum and standard of IT compulsory course, while State examination additionally embrace the programming module of advanced course. Both examinations include test questions on theoretical part (mainly) and practical tasks which rather reveal practical skills of problem solving.

## 4  Students' General Computer Literacy Standard

Training of ICT literacy is closely related not only to IT course, but also to the Students' General Computer Literacy Standard [14], which is the key to the evaluation in a way as well.

The term *computer literacy* used in the Students' General Computer Literacy Standard covers a wider aspect - not only skills to work with the computer but also skills to implement IT in teaching and learning meanwhile acquiring the most general information skills. Name of the document quite nicely reveals a generality - value on which computer literacy's conception is based.

Computer literacy training is based on the attitude of integrity. The Standard clearly reveals the importance of computer literacy in training process and its connection with IT course: "The Standard defines such computer literacy which can be achieved only by integrating ICT into the process of education: lessons of various subjects and activities after school, use of ICT in the school libraries. All-rounded computer literacy cannot be achieved just by using IT during the lessons of IT subject" [14, p. 2-3].

Standard emphasizes the necessity of value attitudes in order to apply ITC properly and effectively in training. Student's experience obtained in lessons of different subjects which implement computer technology has a main role in formation of those values.

The Standard specifies the guidelines of the most general value attitudes of students: 1) to perceive the importance of learning in the life of society and the importance of ICT in learning during lifetime, 2) to grasp the importance of ICT in professional activities as well as in everyday life and to become citizens enjoying full rights and taking an active part in society, 3) to penetrate not only the advantages provided by ICT, but also its dangers to equal opportunities of learning and democracy, 4) to understand that ICT shall be based on respect for traditional values of the state and people and shall assist to use the Lithuanian language correctly, 5) to be able to use the opportunities provided by ICT with great responsibility and perceive the importance of observing ethical norms in this area, 6) to be interested in the progress of ICT, improve and update skills of technology application, and enabling to feel safe and confident working with hardware and software with great responsibility.

Standard provides guidelines which are kind of more comprehensive notion of computer literacy. These are the following: 1) value attitudes; 2) general ability (for learning, work, communication, problem solving and research, critical thinking, and evaluation); 3) thematic fields of computer literacy (main principles and notion of the work by computer, basics of information handling, text processing and providing of information, acquaintance with a spreadsheet and data base, social, legal, and ethical issues).

## 5 Future Directions of IT Implementation into Education

The strategy of ICT implementation in Lithuanian education (for the year 2005-2007) schedules the systematic ICT teaching from the first grades of basic school. A team of experts has approved the IT course for the $5^{th}$ and the $6^{th}$ grades (68 hours in total). If some schools do not manage to prepare for these changes starting from the year 2005, they will be allowed to start such course one year later having more intensive course in the $6^{th}$ grade. IT involvement into comprehensive schools' curricula of younger grades and its integration with other subjects is based on the following:

- wide spread of these technologies and its wide range of facilities;
- natural demand of students, their parents, teachers, and a whole education society;
- necessity of IT implementing in everyday and school life;
- inclination of young people to technological innovations.

It's considered that IT course in the younger grades will determinate the retraction of compulsory IT course in upper grades (especially in $11^{th}$ and $12^{th}$ grades) and will encourage students to implement their ICT skills in other subjects and out-of-class activities. However, during the transition period (2005-2010) IT course will be held in both younger and upper grades. At the same time the IT integration to other subjects should increase (Fig. 2).

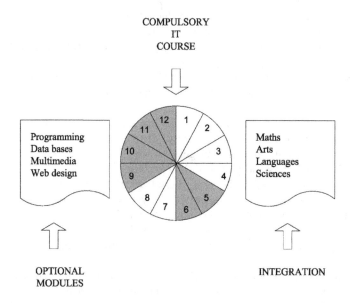

**Fig. 2.** Compulsory, optional and integrated courses in Lithuanian education

The main purpose of IT course in basic school is to use the IT knowledge and skills for better understanding of all subjects, to acquire the ability and desire for civilized communication not only within the school community but also within the contemporaries of the word. ICT provides a wide range of abilities especially in students' everyday life and encourages continuous perfection of person: it provides more skillful use of writing, speaking, and image as tools for communication and collaboration, cultivates self-support, continuous search of information and its processing, skills of activity planning, and helps to form logical and systematic thinking.

IT course should help to create conditions for students to obtain skills, knowledge, and experience in contemporary IT; however it also should be related to perfection of the learning process and involvement into life of information society.

Information training and encouragement of effective and proper implementation of ICT form not only computer literacy and skills for modern work, but also evolve moral values, if only content and training methods properly match one with each other. Systematic IT training from the younger grades and its reasoned integration with different subjects and themes would qualitatively improve students' modern competencies which are necessary for superior learning.

In the 5$^{th}$ and 6$^{th}$ grades IT course of 68 hours is suggested. Besides this, 34 hours of IT training should be integrated into different subjects (Table 2). Such integration could be shifted into the art lessons (e. g. theme "Computer drawing") and Lithuanian and foreign languages' courses (e. g. theme "Acquaintance with internet"). The approached themes are directly connected with already mentioned subjects. Nevertheless, other subjects are also encouraged as well as designed activity in several subjects.

Table 2. IT curriculum design: distribution time and themes for 5-6 grades

| Themes, subthemes | IT hours | Subjects, integration is addressed to | Integrated hours |
|---|---|---|---|
| **1. Introduction to computer programs**<br>– Calculator, clock, calendar<br>– Simple educational programs<br>– Educational computer games | 10 | | |
| **2. Principles of computer use**<br>– Storage of information<br>– Files, directories<br>– Saving information<br>– Archiving<br>– Search information in computer<br>– Computer and health | 6 | | |
| **3. Drawing with computer**<br>– Introduction to graphic editor<br>– Drawing tools<br>– Operations with graphic objects: rotation, flip, inversion<br>– Gallery<br>– Elements of animation | 4 | Art | 10 |
| **4. Text and keyboard**<br>– Keyboard, levels<br>– Keyboard typing tutor<br>– Writing with computer<br>– Lithuanian characters<br>– Fonts<br>– Styles<br>– Formatting of paragraphs<br>– Spell check<br>– Inserting graphics into texts<br>– Introduction to text layout<br>– Printing | 14 | Lithuanian language | 10 |

**Table 2.**(*Continued*)...

| | | | |
|---|---|---|---|
| **5. Internet and electronic mail** <br> – Information search in Web <br> – Internet and its dangers <br> – Downloading documents, files <br> – Web mail <br> – Reading, writing, sending emails <br> – Attachments, viruses in attachments <br> – Chats | **10** | Lithuanian language <br><br><br> Foreign language | 4 <br><br><br><br> 10 |
| **6. Projects with Logo** <br> – Computer control understanding through Logo program <br> – Control the dynamic object (turtle): by commands, keyboard, mouse <br> – Repeating <br> – Drawing, scanning, composition <br> – Using several objects (turtles) <br> – Turtles and their shapes <br> – Basics of animation | **24** | | |

In the 7th and 8th grades IT course should last 34 hours and integration part in other subjects should include 68 hours. The integration could be addressed to Lithuanian language (themes "Text processing" and "Document creation and publication"), art (theme "Presentation and its arrangement", subtheme "Design elements in websites"), and math (theme "Principles of table processing") courses.

In the 9th and 10th grades IT course should summarize students' knowledge, prompt them to use their skills purposefully and pay attention to right technology implementation and its validity. For those who would like to learn more about computer working principles, a special course on algorithms should be provided. In the 9th and 10th grades IT course should last 34 hours and embrace 17 integrated hours. IT course for these grades should be more specific, intense, and claiming for the ordered and systematic generalization of knowledge.

The suggested course integration is conditional. If some teachers of different subjects have ability and conditions for effective IT implementation in their lessons or other cultivation, ICT integration into these subjects should be promoted. Integrated course should be held by teachers of both subjects, at least at the beginning. It's necessary to properly consider the content of the lesson or lessons, synchronize actions, provide particular tasks, etc. That is the only way to reach a proper level of appropriate abilities. IT teacher with the help of teachers of other subjects will be able to plan the helpful skills for other courses.

# 6  Conclusions

Learning with ICT is one of the main concepts in education. At the beginning, Informatics has been taught as an academic, knowledge-based course. Progressively the course of Informatics has been changing to practical-based activity, which pays main attention to information technology. IT course, as it is now called in many countries (and Lithuania too), has become ternary one. Firstly, it's a separate part of the course intended to form the most general information skills and knowledge, separate and compulsory course for all. Secondly, the course can be regarded as a component of all subjects. It may be compared with the reading skills that are necessary in all fields. Thirdly, it's more specific and deep knowledge of professional informatics and ICT. We may constantly feel the increasing need of these skills from industry and society in general. Therefore, school should provide optional courses and modules on different computer science issues for those who have abilities and desire to learn it. All three mentioned parts of IT course is represented in Fig. 2.

Content of the course has an extremely important role [1]. If the main competencies of the last century were regarded as a combination of "three R" – Reading, wRiting, aRithmetics – our time invites us to search for something fundamental and necessary. IT course emphasizes three main parts: information search (Web), text layout (text processing), and work with numerical data (spreadsheets). These three are relevant everywhere and for everybody. The fact may be testified by the use of software designed exactly for the mentioned tasks. Consequently, these are the things that should draw the main part of IT school course compulsory for all.

# References

1. Anderson, J., Weert, T.: Information and Communication Technology in Education. A Curriculum for Schools and Programme of Teacher Development. Unesco (2002)
2. Dagiene, V.: The Model of Teaching Informatics in Lithuanian Comprehensive Schools. Journal of Research on Computing in Education, Vol. 35, N. 2 (2002-2003) 176-185
3. General Curriculum and Education Standards: Pre-school, Primary, and Basic Education. Vilnius, Ministry of Education and Science (2003) [in Lithuanian]
4. General Curriculum for General Education School in Lithuania and General Education Standards for Grades XI-XII. Vilnius, Ministry of Education and Science (2002) [in Lithuanian]
5. Hawkridge, D.G.: Educational Technology in Developing Nations. Plomp, T., Ely, A.D. (eds.) International Encyclopedia of Educational Technology, 2nd ed. Great Britain, Pergamon, (1996) 107-111
6. Herring, J.E.: Teaching Information Skills in Schools. London, Library Ass. Pub. (1996)
7. Herring, J.E.: Exploiting the Internet as an Information Resource in Schools. London, Library Ass. Pub. (1999)
8. Ipsen, A., Thorslund, J.: Curricular Reform and Life-skills in Denmark. Curriculum Change and Social Inclusion: Perspectives from the Baltic and Scandinavian Countries. Final Report of the Regional Seminar, Unesco (2002) 64–69

9. OECD Schooling for Tomorrow. Learning to Change: ICT in Schools. Education and Skills. OECD publications. Paris, OECD Center for Educational Research and Innovation (2001)

10. Pelgrum, W.J., Anderson, R.E. (eds.).: ICT and the Emerging Paradigm for Life Long Learning: a Worldwide Educational Assessment of Infrastructure, Goals, and Practices. Amsterdam, IEA (1999)

11. Pelgrum, W.J., Plomp, T.: The Worldwide Use of Computers: a Description of Main Trends. Computers in Education, Vol. 20, N. 4, (1993) 323-332

12. Plomp, T., Anderson, R.E., Kontogiannopoulou-Polydorides, G. (eds.): Cross National Polices and Practices on Computers in Education. Dordrecht, Kluver Academic Pub. (1996)

13. Sendova, E., Azalov, P., Muirhead, J. (eds.): Informatics in the Secondary School – Today and Tomorrow. Sofia (1995)

14. Students' General Computer Literacy Standard. Information Technologies at School. Vilnius (2002) 118-127

15. Summary of the Strategy for ICT Implementation in the Lithuanian Education. Information Technologies at School, Vilnius, (2002) 85-103. Available: http://www.emokykla.lt/

# Educational Standards in School Informatics in Austria

Christian Dorninger

Ministry of Education, Science and Culture,
Minoritenplatz 5, 1014 Wien, Austria
`christian.dorninger@bmbwk.gv.at`

**Abstract.** In the last two years educational standards have been an important issue when discussing the different student achievements in upper secondary education of the EU member countries. Standards are an indicator of quality at school and should be applied to different subject areas in general and to vocational education (and training). Computer science or information technology is one of the most interesting subjects in this context: It is pretty new in all curricula and is strongly linked to practice. The definition of different achievement levels to understand important models and patterns of school informatics is rather easy. There are also good links to certification standards in industry and expert circles. Therefore, the paper outlines a model of four levels for standards of certification in information technology skills. It fits well for 13 year (7th grade) to 18 – 20 year (12-14th grade) old students. Critical success factors are discussed. First experiences with the model have been analysed.

## 1 Introduction

A government initiative in Austria from 2001 to 2004 has created and initiated a number of projects and perspectives for schools, colleges and universities. Branding "eFit-Austria" (www.efit.at), a support programme with about 30 Million Euro was established, where pupils, students, teachers and educational institutions as a whole can participate. The main activities of this initiative are as follows:

- The campaign to promote "New media in teaching at schools and universities" with platforms and e-learning and internet skills programmes for teachers and a project application procedure for university teachers and institutes;
- A support structure (funding, organisation, evaluation) for e-learning projects of educational institutions (also adult education) and student groups;
- An electronic learning portal www.bildung.at, where community building and content provision is being managed;
- A new approach to reshape the computer science studies at Austrian universities has been established (computer science bachelor, master, and teacher-training programmes at some universities);
- With regard to private-public-partnerships there is intensive cooperation with industry to provide internationally acknowledged IT-certificates like Network Academies, Networking operation systems, ERP-Software and Internet –script languages (JAVA, PHP, ASP,…) for students (from the age of 16);

R.T. Mittermeir (Ed.): ISSEP 2005, LNCS 3422, pp. 65–69, 2005.

- An open source software initiative was launched in December 2002 to promote working with software like LINUX, Staroffice or shareware learning platforms. A certificate for students and teachers will raise acceptance of "free software" and support training structures.
- Some first ideas of developing educational standards of IT subject areas in secondary education (general education and vocational education and training) will be launched.

Recent developments in pedagogy have focused on shifting from instruction to problem solving. The higher independence of the learner from teacher instruction or fixed learning programmes based on behaviouristic ideas has changed to elements of cognitivistic or constructivistic learning models. Not only teacher-student interaction but also working in learning environments or professional support structures (simulation of real working places) increasingly influence the learning culture.

One important issue is to implement quality assurance at schools. This is to ensure that the objectives of subject areas in different years can be fulfilled. One of the most important vehicles to maintain quality is to define educational standards for important subject areas. In Austria educational standards will be introduced for subjects like Maths, English and German in grade 8. As for vocational education and training, in subject areas like information technology it is easy to define valuable and reliable educational standards.

## 2  What Are Educational Standards?

Educational standards define the demands on teaching and learning. They describe objectives and aims are named for the educational work, expressed as learning outcomes of students. Specific tasks and group of tasks must be fulfilled to master these targets.

Educational standards describe the competences of students necessary to meet the objectives. The competence based models depend on a specific grade and will be written in a way to derive concrete tasks and formulate levels of testing.

Educational standards should be developed in different subjects, also in computer science or information and communication technology. In the field of IT-skills, important work has been done: There are lots of certificates available in the IT-sector to get expertise in different IT-skills and in information technology some basic skills were defined already in 1997 in Finland, Sweden or Ireland.

## 3  Education and Training in Information Technology

School informatics as a subject area in secondary school syllabi is fairly young and does not have traditional approaches. School books are not really important, a lot of spontaneous work is done and the laboratory character of the students` work is impressive. Syllabi and curricula are very general and aim at implementing concrete skills. The content is "open" to be designed.

All European countries have recently introduced learning standards, national ones or international ones like the ECDL (European computer driving license). So the basic

IT-skill segment is well defined and was approved a number of years ago. The pedagogic component of IT basic skills is not fairly outlined in the ECDL syllabus – like group work, project work or problem solving technics. Combined with a suitable pedagogical approach, the ECDL plus pedagogical items would be a good example of such a quasi standard.

In Austria, further steps have been taken to deal with higher level skills: IT industry certificates were introduced and sometimes even new ones developed. Examples are the CISCO-networking academy, the Microsoft IT-academy, skills to use ERP-software like MySAP (specific customising for county typical accounting) or database qualification in the world of ORACLE. Also a certificate for open source software (LINUX et al) has been developed.

Even if one can see some disadvantage like product near working – and loss of general IT approaches - or the short life cycles of software versions, there is evidence of positive development: near to expert practice, world wide accepted and sometimes linked to e-learning courses with really good material like the CISCO-network academy.

As the well known certificates require high level expertise (like Linux Professional Institute modules 101 or 102), for open source software and LINUX a student skills package to enter this new world was created. The EOSC (European open source certificate) is now offered to young people to prove their often acquired informally qualifications in this field.

## 4  A Model of IT Standard – Four Levels of Competence

Standards for IT at school informatics are related to similar constructs in language learning (the TOEFL –test in English for example), in training of special technology skills like in welding, manufacturing, or in quality assurance. Providing access to these "external" certifications and integrating the required knowledge and skills into vocational education and training school curricula has a longer tradition in Austria.

The experience in these areas forms an important basis for the discussion on standards. Because of "open" syllabi the main responsibility is delegated to the teachers. Quite different profiles in different schools developed – from low level ranking in student test achievements like PISA (programme of international students assessment) to high level ranking of good or best schools. The gap between the good and the worse performers is to large, decided an expert group of the Austrian minister (Bericht der "Zukunftskommission" des bm:bwk; Vienna, 2003).

Therefore, an "evaluation culture" in the Austrian education system must be established. School programmes and system monitoring form one part this evaluation culture, educational standards in groups of subjects another.

In information (and communication) technology four levels can be defined to standardise skills and knowledge:

- The first level is ECDL (seven modules from general IT-knowledge, operating system, office products to internet access) combined with a pedagogical approach of knowledge in school informatics.
- The second level is a problem solving approach including programming language skills and dealing with moderate algorithm in computer science. There should be a

link to change standard software like office products by using different data models (e.g. to extend the knowledge of office products with macro programming via Visual Basic for Application).

- The third level is a first expert level. External certificates are awarded. It can be done in different subject areas like networks, database-programming, network operation systems or web technologies. A clear occupational sub-area must be linked to this level.
- The fourth level has to do with excellent programming knowledge and software design concepts of computer science disciplines and basic research work together with a grade in higher education.

With this level concept the range from grade 7 or 8 (ECDL) to higher education can be covered. Level two can be met with upper secondary graduation, level three with specific vocational training, practice and certification (career in an ICT- profession field or bachelor degree in applied computer science), level four relates to a university diploma in ICT disciplines.

## 5   First Experiences with IT Standards Since About 2000

After three years of practice, we have come to the following conclusions:

1. For rather a simple learning process and exam content in terms of basic skills, it may be easier to define standards and norms. Complex know-how in IT and knowledge in upper secondary and higher education are not easy to standardise. We have high numbers who achieve level 1 (100.000 ECDL graduates in 3 years in Austria!). Those, who acquire IT industry certificates, are fewer in numbers. Educational content and skills required in the exams must be part of the school syllabi or it must be easy to integrate it. Exams outside school programmes form a high barrier and are not widely accepted (the CISCO academy syllabus comprises 4 semesters and the semester exams are taken by a broad group of students and teachers. But only 30% of them take the last exam "outside the course" – a summary of the 4 semesters. So the implementation of standards is important and possible, but they must be implemented within the regular programme.
2. For standards there should be a kind of guarantee of acceptance in the professional fields. If they are linked to career pathways, it is easy to argue their importance. The more global (world wide) standards one can introduce, the bigger the link to labour market needs, the easier IT standards will be accepted by a larger amount of students. In vocational education and training it may be easier to get a feeling for these developments. Standards in IT subjects are mostly world wide, connected to specific software or products and have a short lifetime. Not really easy to integrate them in the slow moving education sector!

Educational standards will continue to dominate parts of the discussion of school efficiency and the way to demonstrate the beginning of lifelong learning. IT has experience with certification and could feed its expertise into this discussion.

# References

1. bm:bwk, eFit-Austria, Jahresberichte 2001, 2002 und 2001 bis 2003, Vienna, 2004.
2. Günter Haider et al., Zukunft:Schule–Strategien und Maßnahmen zur Qualitätsentwicklung, Vienna, 2003.
3. Peter Micheuz (publisher), Standards in der Schulinformatik, Völkermarkt, 2004.
4. Eckhard Klieme et al., Zur Entwicklung nationaler Bildungsstandards, Expertise des DIPF (Deutsches Institut für Internationale Pädagogische Forschung, 2003; www.kmk.org/aktuell/Bildungsstandards
5. Werner Specht, Zum Stand der Entwicklung nationaler Bildungsstandards, Grundsatzpapier des österreichischen Bildungsministeriums, ZSE (Zentrum für Schulentwicklung) in Graz, 2003.
6. Helmut Heugl, Marlies Liebscher, Bildungsstandards aus Mathematik für die Sekundarstufe II, Jul 2004.

# Russian Educational Standards of Informatics and Informatics Technologies (ICT): Aims, Content, Perspectives

Aleksandr A. Kuznetsov and Sergey A. Beshenkov

Russian Academy of Education, Pogodinskaja 8, Moskow, 119121, Russia

**Abstract.** Educational standards fixes three main parameters in informatics and informatics' technology: the goals for every step of education (primary step, intermediate step and pre-professional step), the obligatory component of the content, and the level of it's acquaintance. The basic course is the course of 8-9 classes. Informatics' technology of solving tasks is in the focus of the basic course. There are three aspects of the technology: "Informatics' processes and their automatisation", "Informatics models" and "Informatics' point in managing". The three aspects are fixed in the standard and are common for the permanent course of informatics (taught from the second to the eleventh class).

Educational standards set three main parameters for studies in informatics and informatics technologies: the purpose for every step of learning (introductory, intermediary and pre-professional), the obligatory component of the content, and the level of its acquaintance.

The issue of the content of education is one of the main issues of the course in informatics. In Russian schools this course is provided as a part of general education in schools as well as universities and teachers training colleges.

As with any course which constitues a part of general education in Russia, the contents of a course in informatics is based on two main principles:

- the requirement to cover the main issues of informatics; and
- the emphasis on the main types of information activities.

This approach leads to segregation of two concenters of the content of the course in informatics, namely "informational processes" and 'informational technologies". "Informational technology" is a process resulting in the creation of information products with specified qualities, in particular with the aid of computer and its software.

According to the modern standards and basic curriculum of Russian schools, a course in informatics is given continually from the $2^{nd}$ to $11^{th}$ (last) year of school and, as a rule, at universities. There are three main learning steps: introductory ($2^{nd}$ to $5^{th}$ years of school), intermediary ($7^{th}$ to $9^{th}$ years) and pre-professional ($10^{th}$ and $11^{th}$ years). To maintain the uniformity of all steps, the course in informatics is based on three main topics which are covered throughout the course and are the sort of "axiomatic statements" of the modern course in informatics: "Information and informational processes", "Informational modelling" and "Informational basics of management".

R.T. Mittermeir (Ed.): ISSEP 2005, LNCS 3422, pp. 70–74, 2005.

These three continuous course topics in informatics are covered at every step of learning but of course in various depths. We will consider below those topics in more details.

The scope of issues traditionally covered by the topic "Information and informational processes" is significant for the course in informatics. At the introductory step, the choice of tasks and learning materials is aimed at providing full description of the concept of usage of multimedia in all fields of human activities and problems of subjective interpretation of information. It lays the grounds for further studying of informational modelling, algorithms etc.

In the pre-professional step, the procedure of interpretation of information is again in the foreground, but in a different light. Here, the perspectives are the as various ways of interaction with technical and social systems. Generally, the steps of learning of informational process are described in Table 1.

**Table 1.** Main learning steps of the topic "Information and informational processes"

| Learning step | Aspects of the course in informatics | Main studied processes |
|---|---|---|
| Introductory | Information as a message in the form of sequence of symbols | Encryption, interpretation |
| Intermediary | Information as a message in the form of sequence of symbols that are stored, transferred and processed through technical equipment | Storing, transferring, processing |
| Intermediary and pre-professional | Information as a message transferable via channels which can be kept and processed according to certain rules | Modelling, characterisation, algorithmisation |
| Pre-professional | Information as data and methods of its processing | Information technologies, automatisation |
| Pre-professional and higher education | Information as semantical feature of matter | Interpretation, methods of learning and communication |
| Higher education | Information as a resourse, product, tool and instrument of professional activities | Methods of practical activities, decision generation and decision making |

The modern stage of the development of education is characterised by increased attention to the notion of model and the methodology of modelling.

**Table 2.** Main learning steps of the topic "Informational modelling"

| Learning step | Aspects of the course in informatics | Main studied processes |
|---|---|---|
| Introductory | Modelling as substitute for a subject in the process of learning, interaction and practical activities | Comparison, collating, examination of models |
| Intermediary | Modelling as a simplified version of a real subject. Informational modelling as a scheme, image or description of a studied subject. | Formalised representation of text, graphic, numerical, and audio information |
| Intermediary and pre-professional | Modelling as a new subject which reflects certain qualities of an original subject which are material for the purposes of modelling | Characterisation, creation and interpretation of tables, diagrams, flow charts, schemes, formulas and algorithms |
| Pre-professional | Modelling as a way of knowledge, means of communication, tool of practical activities | Structuring of data and knowledge |
| Pre-professional and higher education | Modelling as physical or informational equivalent of a subject which operates in certain characteristics in a way similar to that of an original subject | Creation of valuation criteria, valuation check of modellings |
| Higher education | Modelling as a new subject (real, informational or imaginary) different from an original subject, having and reflecting qualities material for the modelling purposes of which allow it to fully replace the original subject for the given purpose | Systematic analysis, design, impact analysis |

The course in informatics helps, to the largest extent possible, to classify the knowledge that learners have about models and conscious application of informational modelling in their learning and then in their professional activities. The creation of models in the courses of mathematics, physics, chemistry and biology is fortified by learning, in the course in informatics, about issues related to the stages of creation of models, analysis of their qualities, validity checks in respect of the model and the object and the aim of modelling, examining the influence of the choice of modelling language on the quality of obtained information etc.

The process of learning modelling should be organised in such a way as to enable a learner to try the roles of creator, observer and user of models because trying different roles is especially important in modelling.

The main learning stages for modelling in different learning steps are described in Table 2.

Informational technologies of task solutions are directly related to management techniques. The main learning steps of this topic are described in Table 3.

**Table 3.** Main learning steps of the topic "Informational basics for management"

| Learning step | Aspects of the course in informatics | Main studied processes |
|---|---|---|
| Introductory | Management as handling activities of somebody or something | Work with operators |
| Intermediary | Management as a governing act transferred by way of instructions | Algorithmisation, operating of work of computer, operators by way of instructions |
| Pre-professional | Management as directed informational interaction between a managed object and the system of management | Purpose, mechanisms, methods, results, valuation of quality of management |
| Pre-professional and professional | Management as a mechanism of self-organisation of complex systems | Systematic and functional analysis |
| Professional | Management as a sum of principles, methods, forms and ways of influence to an object of management with the purpose of reaching specified characteristics of its functioning and/or expected results of its activities | Preparation, making, realisation of management decisions |

The issues described above served as a ground for the Federal component of a Russian standard for general studies (2004). They are also employed in key textbooks that are used for the course in informatics in Russian schools, among them [1, 2, 3]:

# References

1. S.Az.Beshenkov, E.A.Rakitina. Informatics 10 -11 Sistematic course. Moskow (2000)
2. I.G.Semakin et al. Informatics. Basic course. Moskow ( 2001)
3. N.V.Matveeva, E.V.Chelak, T.A.Konotopova. Informatics - 2. Moskow (2003)

# The Present-Day Tendencies
# of Teaching Informatics in Ukraine

Oleg Spirin

Department of Information Technology, Zhytomyr Ivan Franko University,
40 vul. V.Berdychivska, 10008 Zhytomyr, Ukraine
som@zu.edu.ua

**Abstract.** The article describes the present-day situation and general approach to teaching informatics in secondary schools in Ukraine. The syllabus of teaching informatics in Ukrainian schools is described, including major topics and the number of academic hours.

## 1 Major Features of the Course in Informatics at Secondary Schools

The main objective of informatics teaching is to provide students with theoretical knowledge in the basics of informatics and the development of practical skills in using present-day information technology in students' every-day practical learning.

The theoretical basis comprises the following components: the concept of information, its properties, informational processes and systems; general principles of computer-aided problem solution based on common and application programs; problem definition; construction of corresponding informational (mathematical in particular) models; fundamentals of algorithmization and programming; principles of computer hardware; and opportunities for using the Internet).

Practical skills comprise work with information input and output devices, application software of both general and specific types: text processors, graphics editors, electronic worksheets, database management systems, search systems, teaching software tools, browsers for viewing hypertext pages, e-mail and teleconference software, searching for information on the Internet etc; also skills of development, description and implementation of some algorithms and programs based on algorithmical language tools and real programming languages.

Depending on the type of computers, teachware and software available, teachers can themselves choose the appropriate methods and techniques to achieve the aims of the course. According to the methods and techniques that are chosen, teachers select corresponding textbooks, manuals and teaching materials out of the list of resources recommended by the Ministry of Education and Science of Ukraine, combining various resources or giving emphasis to some of them.

Here is the list of the main topics and their sequence for the senior forms of general secondary schools in Ukraine [1]:

1. Information and informational processes.
2. Information system.

R.T. Mittermeir (Ed.): ISSEP 2005, LNCS 3422, pp. 75–83, 2005.

3. Operational system.
4. Fundamentals of disc handling.
5. Application teaching software.
6. General-purpose application software:
   - graphic engine;
   - text processor;
   - computer presentations;
   - electronic worksheet;
   - databases.
7. The Internet.
8. Basics of algorithmization and programming:
   - information model;
   - algorithms;
   - program. Programming language;
   - reference to algorithms and functions;
   - reference to repetitions and branching;
   - table values;
   - literal values;
   - graphic operations.

In 2003 the Ministry of Education and Science determined the procedure of final public testing in informatics [2]. Two options are available: an oral examination or defence of students' papers describing the development of application software. The students themselves choose either of these two options. The second option can be chosen only by the best students who have the highest academic performance in informatics.

Teachers of informatics offer their students a list of recommended subjects for their research papers, taking into consideration inter-disciplinary connections and needs of teaching informatics. Students are free to take any topic which is of interest for them, has practical significance and relevance. A student's paper can be of educational, demonstrational, testing or gaming nature or can combine several features. The curriculum does not allocate any specific time for development of software by students – they do it as part of their homework and out-of-class activities.

A specific activity in informatics is the annual competitions held at several levels: I – school level, II – district or city level, III – regional level, IV – national level.

## 2  Peculiarities of Teaching Informatics at School

### 2.1  Existing Syllabi

Teaching informatics to senior students of Ukrainian secondary schools follows a syllabus with three variations, depending on the facilities available at schools. The first variant is for teaching informatics without actual use of computers, the second variant is for DOS-based teaching of informatics and the third variant is for WINDOWS-based teaching informatics. This three-variant syllabus has been in use since the late 1990s. This syllabus can be regarded as a transition period syllabus. One can expect that it will remain in effect for a rather long period of time, for more than five years to come.

This is connected with insufficient and unbalanced investments in the computer facilities of secondary schools. There is still a considerable number of schools which have out-of-date computers or no computers at all. In the latter case, informatics is taught basically in terms of fundamentals of algorithmization. Computer hard- and software are studied only theoretically. Practical skills are limited to skills in mathematical simulation, development of algorithms for problem solution, their graphic description in the form of flow charts. Algorithms can be described in terms of the Teaching Algorithmic Language (TAL), specifically developed in the early 1980s. The main references in this language are similar to PASCAL operators. TAL is intended for use in paper study of algorithmization, though a translator of this language exists which is used on old teaching hardware (mid-1980s – early 1990s).

The three-variant syllabus provides that if a school has sufficient computer facilities, the course of informatics covers two years, the total amount of academic hours being 102 hours (table 1.). Informatics lessons are often distributed as follows. In the first half-year students may have one lesson a week, and in the second half-year they have two lessons a week. Then in the second year they may have two lessons a week in the first half and one lesson in the second half of the year. Depending on the school curriculum, informatics can be studied in 8-9 or 10-11 forms.

**Table 1.** Here are the main components of the course of informatics

| Topic | Amount of hours |
|---|---|
| Introduction. Information and informational processes | 3 hours |
| Information system | 5 hours |
| Operating systems | 9 hours |
| Basic skills of disk handling | 5 hours |
| Application software | 46 hours |
| INTERNET and its basic possibilities | 6 hours |
| Fundamentals of algorithmization and programming | 28 hours |

## 2.2  Further Changes in the Existing Syllabi

Since 2003 Ukrainian schools have started the transition to profile (specialized) teaching in senior forms. Its aim is to provide the students with basic knowledge and skills for the job market. This education profile makes use of new syllabi in informatics developed specifically for the changed purposes of student's training. The minimal compulsory amount of hours for informatics during two years of study is 70 hours. The syllabi under consideration present an updated version of the WINDOWS-based syllabus within the earlier three-variant syllabus.

*The first line* is aimed at solving information problems involving information search, use and processing. From the practical point of view it aims at training a PC user at a corresponding level. These syllabi are used in universal-profile forms and those specializing in Philology, the Humanities, Fine Arts and sports. In these types of forms informatics is studied during two years, with one class per week (the total of 70 hours). The syllabi of this line have insignificant differences in their contents and amount of hours.

Table 2 shows the components of the course in informatics for the universal-profile schools.

Table 2. Distribution of topics for universal-profile schools

| # | Topic | Hours | | |
|---|---|---|---|---|
| | | Total | 10 form | 11 form |
| 1. | Introduction. Information and informational processes. | 2 | 2 | |
| 2. | Information systems and their components. | 6 | 6 | |
| 3. | Application teaching software | 4 | 4 | |
| 4. | General-purpose application software (graphic and text processors, computer presentations, electronic worksheet, databases) | 34 | 14 | 20 |
| 5. | Internet | 6 | 6 | |
| 6. | Computer simulation. Basics of algorithmization and programming. | 12 | | 12 |
| | Float time | 6 | 3 | 3 |
| | Total | 70 | 35 | 35 |

Among the application software used in Ukraine is specialized computer teachware, certified by the Ministry of Education and Science, for example, „Videointerpreter of search and sorting algorithms", „Geography of continents and oceans with maps", „Ancient Rome", „Electronic course in modern history", „Dynamic geometry package DG", program packages GRAN-1, GRAN-2D, GRAN-3D, GRANWIN, „Geography. Location map", „Native language", „Your health is in your hands", „Ukraine and its regions", „Physics for a future engineer. Learning to solve problems", „Regional transport systems", interactive testing systems, etc.

*The second line* is aimed at the practical mastery of skills essential for work with the basic components of up-to-date computer software, familiarization with functions of major computer devices and the basic technologies of computer-aided problem solving, starting from the formulation and construction of information models up to the interpretation of results. These syllabi are designed for schools (or forms) specializing in physics, mathematics, biology, chemistry and technology. In such schools (or forms) informatics is studied during two years, with two classes per week (total 140 hours). The aim of the course is somewhat broader than the syllabus of the *first line*. It involves understanding the theoretical basis for processes of transformation, transmission and application of information, understanding the meaning and role of information processes in contemporary society, and the development of practical skills in the conscious and rational use of computers.

More hours (46-48) are allotted to the fundamentals of algorithmization and programming. Teaching programming involves the use of the translator of one of the programming languages (BASIC, PASCAL, C++, Visual Basic, Delphi, etc.).

It should be mentioned at this point that the syllabi of the first and second lines are not satisfactory in the opinion of certain specialists in the methodologies of informatics.

These specialists point out considerable discrepancy between the existing concept of informatics teaching, international teaching standards, effective syllabi, the concept of profile teaching and the real situation in Ukrainian schools. One of the reasons for such discrepancy is absence of options at the level of teachware. At the same time there are active disputes as regards the "Algorithmization and programming" section, its place in the syllabus, components and order of studying topics. Most university specialists insist that this topic should take the central place in the school course in informatics. It should involve visual programming as its essential component.

*The third line* of syllabi provides for the study of informatics from the 7th or 8th form. Such syllabi were developed for forms specializing in deep study of mathematics, informatics and ICT. According to these syllabi, students have 2-4 hours of informatics in the 8th-9th forms (total 140-280 hours) and 4 hours per week in the 10th form (total 280 hours).

Most syllabi provide an integrated course – "Informatics and information technology". 7-9-formers can have a basic course at the expense of the optional (selective) hours provided in the curriculum. At the same time they can have the course in technology at the expense of hours allotted to labour training.

The course in technology for 7th-9th-formers involves teaching skills of vector and bitmapped graphics for polygraphy, multi-media programming and web-design.

In the 10th and 11th forms this integrated course is studied along one of the profiles: computer-aided design technologies, object-oriented programming languages, use of electronic worksheets in economics and business, web-design, architecture and landscape design.

Besides the above-mentioned compulsory syllabi students may have access to optional (selective) courses, such as:

– fundamentals of information technology (140 hours);
– Internet-oriented graphics programming (70 hours);
– markup language (40 hours);
– object-oriented visual programming (140 hours); etc.

## 2.3  Who Defines How Informatics Should be Taught?

All of the syllabi described above are approved by the Ministry of Education and Science of Ukraine. Depending on the available computer facilities and school profile, school administrations choose a certain syllabus. The syllabus chosen is approved by the local educational authorities which fund schools.

Where students are aiming at higher education in universities majoring in computer sciences, school authorities can allot more hours for deeper teaching of informatics, negotiating the changes in the syllabus with the corresponding university.

It is up to a teacher to choose specific methods of teaching. The main thing is that the teacher should guarantee meeting the ultimate standards of knowledge and skills specified in the syllabus. Consequently, the syllabus defines only the type of obligatory software, and it is up to the teacher to select the particular version. Teachers also define the textbooks to be used in the course of study.

## 2.4  Training of Teachers of Informatics

The public system of training of teachers of informatics (Fig. 1) consists of two routes:

- 5-year university training majoring in informatics, mathematics and basic informatics, teaching of informatics at secondary schools; or 1-2-year post-diploma (further) course in informatics for university graduates;
- one-month free courses in informatics at regional institutions for further pedagogical education for teachers of mathematics and physics and for computer engineers who started their work at schools.

Working teachers of informatics take refresher courses once every five years. These one-month courses are provided by regional institutions for further pedagogical education. If school administrations have the opportunity to adopt a broader course of informatics due to improved computer facilities, teachers of these schools can take a refresher course before the scheduled time.

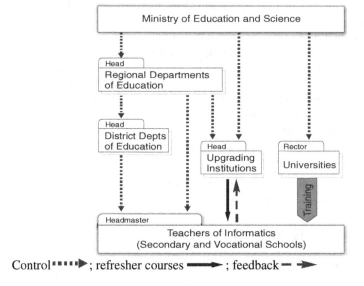

Control ▪▪▪▪▶ ; refresher courses ➡ ; feedback ⇢

**Fig. 1.** Public system of training and retraining of teachers of informatics

Teachers of informatics are motivated to upgrade their professional competence by annual competitions for the best teachers of informatics. These competitions are organized by the regional institutions for further pedagogical education. Their winners take part in the national competition. The winners of these competitions are awarded diplomas and bonuses and put forward for higher professional categories, which means higher salaries.

Teachers of informatics can upgrade their competence on their own, making use of the national monthly journal "Computer at school and family" and the national newspaper for teachers which highlights issues relating to the informatization of secondary education, theoretical and practical issues of informatics teaching, methodological recommendations concerning teaching new software, feature discussion of the present-day situation in informatics teaching and its prospects, publishes samples of final tests and assignments for the national students' competition in informatics, review textbooks and manuals, etc.

Alongside traditional schemes of teachers' upgrading and retraining, an increasing role today is played by the initiatives of individual teachers. An example of one such initiative is the "Hot Summer" project, in which teachers of informatics submit electronically their best lesson plans for consideration by experts, share their successful methods and techniques. The organizers of this project collect the database and disseminate it among the participants for further discussion and use.

Teachers of informatics have also set up regional Internet Olimpiadas, involving the solution of advanced-level programming problems.

At the same time, the availability of qualified teachers of informatics remains a problem for Ukrainian schools. The main reason for this is the low salaries of school teachers in general. As a result, young promising teachers leave schools and seek better employment in other spheres. The beginning of 2003-2004 school year witnessed about 6,000 teachers' vacancies in 21,000 schools, mainly of teachers of informatics and foreign languages.

## 2.4 Teachware

One of the major problems today is the provision of adequate teachware (textbooks, manuals, software and test programs, teaching materials) for teaching informatics. Most of the existing textbooks which were financed by the Ministry rapidly become out-of-date and can not follow the changing syllabi. The quality of the textbooks and manuals is affected by the existing imperfect expertise procedure provided by the Ministry. Often such expertise is carried out formally. Some teachers of informatics try to fill this gap with their own teachware often developed in a hurry, lacking the necessary experience and competence for this. The resulting teachware is not always of appropriate quality.

This situation brought about some drastic demands for the Ministry to stop public financing of textbooks and manuals in informatics, in order to prevent large-scale invasion of low-quality teachware. Instead, it has been proposed that publishing houses should publish textbooks in informatics on the basis of commercial risk. In this way they would be able to react to rapid changes in informatics as a science and school discipline, and teachers would be able to choose a textbook out of several proposed titles.

## 3  Some Prospects of School Informatics in Ukraine

All of the description above shows that at present informatics in Ukrainian schools is studied following a number of syllabi oriented at various specialization profiles and levels. We expect that this trend will become even more prominent in the decade to come. At the same time the teachers' main efforts will be directed at searching for ways to eliminate discrepancies between the knowledge and skill standards declared in the syllabi and the actual knowledge and skills displayed by the students.

Some definite trends relating to teaching informatics in schools are listed below:

1. The structure of the school course in informatics is likely to change. In future it is likely to comprise three levels and follow the development of students' intellectual activity: 7th-8th forms – a basic course, 9th-10th forms - the main course, 11th form – the specialized course.

2. Alongside the expected change in the course structure, the future is likely to witness separation of the fundamental (mainly algorithmization and programming) and applied (IT) aspects of teaching informatics at schools. This trend may lead to differentiation of two subjects: the fundamentals course which will be taught by teachers of informatics and the applied aspects which may be taught not only by teachers of informatics, mathematics and physics but also by teachers of the humanities. Such a change will bring about the necessity of reforms both in the school teaching of informatics and in the system of university training of teachers, their further upgrading and retraining.

3. The introduction of informatics as a subject in primary school seems quite feasible. Some schools are carrying out the experimental teaching [3] of some introductory courses, like "Computer ABC" (for the first-formers), "Steps to informatics" (for the second-fourth-formers), "Introduction to informatics" (for the fifth-sixth-formers). At the same time there is a strong belief that in primary school computers have to be used only as a means of teaching other subjects and that this should not be considered as teaching informatics proper.

4. Computers will be found not only in schools but also in students' homes. We expect that in future the students in the 5th-6th forms will show significant computer competence and in the 7th-8th forms they will have higher knowledge and better skills in using computers than ordinary teachers have today. This will have to bring about adequate changes in the syllabi and teachware, and the present-day concept of training PC users will have to be critically reassessed with the shift to algorithmization and solving typical problems.

5. A broader range of optional (selective) courses is expected. The training of PC users is expected to incorporate the comprehensive study of artificial intelligence software and general expert systems. In teaching programming there is a tendency of wider additional use of Internet-programming systems (ASP, PHP, Perl, Java, etc.) and systems of Internet publications (HTML, XML, XHTML). Some specialists [4] consider the possibility of incorporating LINUX systems into school courses in informatics. Yet we do not consider the prospect of using such operating systems and corresponding application software realistic.

6. An increase in investments in school computer facilities is quite feasible. Intensive improvement of school computer facilities is backed by the government program aimed at provision of every rural school with modern computers. Since 2001 2257 computer classrooms have been supplied to rural schools (about 1500 in 2004).

7. We can also expect a considerable inflow of well-trained teachers of informatics to schools in the immediate future. This trend is reinforced by the government's plans to conclude social agreements with university graduates, according to which those graduates whose tuition was covered from public funds will have to work at schools a specified number of years.

8. One can expect formation of a professional association of teachers of informatics.

9. One can also expect that formerly isolated system of informatics teaching in Ukraine will enter the wider international environment (EU in particular). This tendency can find its realization in experience sharing, participation in international educational projects in the field of informatics and conferences.

# References

1. Informatics. Syllabi for general secondary educational institutions. – Zaporizhzhya: Premier, 2003. – 304 pp. (in Ukrainian)
2. Methodological recommendations for the final public testing in informatics in 2002/2003 (in Ukrainian) http://www.mon.gov.ua/laws/list_1_9_39_.doc
3. V.M.Shevchenko. The structure of the course in informatics at school # 52 // Computers at schools and in the family. – 2003. - # 2 – P.27-28 (in Ukrainian)
4. Ya.M.Glynskyy, V.A.Ryazhska. Linux-practicum in informatics. Manual. – Lviv, Deol, 2004. – 248 pp. (in Ukrainian)

# Study of Information Search Systems of the Internet

Yuri Ramsky and Olga Rezina

Computer Science Department,
M.Drahomanov National Pedagogical University,
9 Pirogov Str., Kyiv, 01030 Ukraine
`rama@ukr.net, rezina_olga@mail.ru`

**Abstract.** Qualified search for information in the internet is considered to be a fundamental capability of pupils to be educated for the information society. The theory of planned formation of intellectual actions is assumed as a basis of learning of internet search systems. The paper reports on the computer teaching program "Poshuk-META" (Retrieval Aim), a system to get acquainted with searching the internet even without an internet-access.

## 1 Introduction

Information and knowledge are determinant factors of the development of modern society and a more important national resource. Information retrieval is the issue of the day in the information society. The retrieval activity is a basis in the educational process of a secondary school, an academy and a professional activity for most of people today.

The problem of information retrieval comes up before pupils at the time of self-dependent and research work, preparation for reports and papers, selection of additional materials for different subjects. This problem can be solved in the process of learning of Informatics. It's necessary to form:

- Skills to define possible sources of information and the strategy of its retrieval;
- Skills to do the semantic processing of data;
- Skills to analyse and interpret findings;
- Skills to appreciate information from the point of view of its authenticity, accuracy, adequacy for the solution of the concrete information task.

The impetuous development and active use of modern information and communication technologies have made it possible to begin the wide-ranging transformation of information to the electronic form and creating of a huge quantity of information resources. The electronic form of the representation of information makes it possible to organize the processes of preservation, processing, spreading, and retrieval of data in a qualitatively new level.

The intensive disposal of data in the internet is the fundamental direction of the technological development of information resources. The quantity of scientific, educational, cultural, social internet-resources increases all the time. They are electronic libraries and encyclopedias, electronic journals and newspapers, materials

R.T. Mittermeir (Ed.): ISSEP 2005, LNCS 3422, pp. 84–91, 2005.

about educational institutions, school and students' unions and so on. The educational potential of the internet can be effectively used in studies as well as during the solution of didactical and pedagogical problems. A teacher of Informatics should help pupils organize their work in the internet, make information retrieval easier for them, shorten unproductive expenditures of time. Pupils must know that search systems of the internet are effective means of information retrieval and exploration.

## 2 Psychological Grounds of Studying the Theme "Search Systems of the Internet"

L.Vygotsky's cultural-historic theory of development of higher psychic functions is one of the leading in psycho-pedagogical science in Ukraine. It is widely used during the discussion of problems such as person and culture, studies and development, influence of information technologies on the development of children's psychics. According to the basic provisions of cultural-historic theory, signs and sign systems, which regularly get more complicated, contribute to the development and transformation of higher psychic functions [1].

The internet can be viewed as socio-technical system, which, together with modern digital technologies, is based on traditional sign systems and contributes to their quantitative complication and qualitative transformation. According to L.Vygotsky's views, such a socio-technical system, which regularly gets more complicated, promotes the development and transformation of higher psychic functions. That's why viewing the internet as modern means of activity which stimulates psychic development of a person, is quite grounded.

In spite of the variety of internet users' activity, researchers single out three main types of activity mediated by the Web: cognitive, communicative and playing [2]. We consider the information-retrieval activity as a constituent of a cognitive activity. Considering the internet as a sign system, working with it, and notably retrieving information from it contributes to the psychic and intellectual development of a child. Hence, we suppose it necessary to study internet search systems in the school course of Informatics.

Studying of internet search systems may take place on the basis of the theory of planned formation of intellectual actions, which is grounded by scientific works of P.Galperin and N.Talyzina. The theory of planned formation of intellectual actions supposes some successive stages.

At the first stage the basic motivation of the action is formed. Researchers have come to the conclusion that internet users' activity is poly-motivistic. Among the main motives are: cognitive, businesslike, communicative, recreational and playing, affiliative (the need to feel oneself as a member of some group), as well as motives of cooperation, self-fulfillment and self-assertion [3].

We think that the task of a Informatics teacher is to form pupils' cognitive motives of activity in the internet and to compare them with social ones. To form positive cognitive motivation of studying search systems of the internet, the teacher should inform pupils about the following facts:

- A qualified internet user may get access to scientific and literary sources of the leading libraries of the world;
- The majority of scientific, popular scientific and literary journals have electronic versions available via the internet, and some journals have only electronic version.;
- The number of different electronic encyclopedias, reference-books, dictionaries, thematic sites, present in the internet, regularly increases;
- Work with such types of resources is characterized by the availability of convenient and effective retrieval means.

Social motivation of the retrieval activity in the internet may be raised or formed by adducing the following facts:

- The retrieval activity is one of the leading while studying in the academy or institute of higher education, and for many in professional activity as well;
- The majority of institutes of higher educations in Ukraine and in other country have their own internet-sites, which offer data about faculties, specializations, terms of admission and so on;
- Some sites inform of possibilities and terms of studying the finding work abroad, studying the foreign language in its native country;
- Due to the information offered by the internet-sites, one may solve the problems of rest organizing, getting goods and so on.

At the next stage of planned formation of intellectual actions there the formation of the reference scheme of the action happens, i.e. the system of reference points and instructions. Considering of which is necessary to perform the action mastered with required qualities. The reference scheme of the action of information retrieval in the internet may be like the one in Figure 1.

The reference scheme of the action presented to pupils is polished up on the basis of training tasks.

Task 1. What is the height of Eiffel Tower? (The answer should be accompanied by a reference to the internet page).

To the query *Eiffel Tower* the search engine in the first results gives out documents that contain the answer. Three first operations of the reference scheme of the action are carried out.

Task 2. Which space project aims at studying the processes of the active Sun?

Solving of this task suggests introducing a sequence of query-specifications (for example, *space project* + *active Sun*) with the analysis of the results obtained. Four operations of the reference scheme of the action are carried out.

Task 3. To find documents which inform of the results of the regional phases of the all-Ukrainian contest "Young economy". Take into account that the regional phase may be called the district one.

Solving of this task demands introducing the query *all-Ukrainian contest*, query-specification *Young economy* with the usage of the boolean operators *(regional | district) phase*. It's necessary to show pupils that simple subsequent introducing of queries *regional phase* and *district phase* will lead to the exception from the area of retrieval of documents, which contain the words *district phase*, but don't contain the words *regional phase*, which contradicts the condition of the task. All the operations of the reference scheme of the action are carried out.

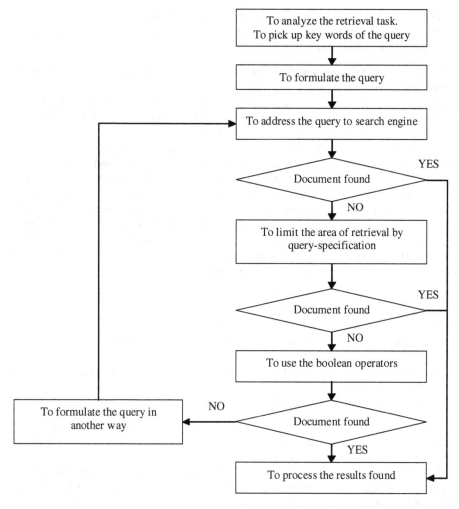

**Fig. 1.** The reference scheme of the action of retrieval in the internet

The criteria of formation of the action of retrieval in the internet is pupil's ability to find the information needed or to make sure that there is no such information in the Web.

## 3   Defining the Contents of "Search Systems of the Internet". Computer Teaching Program "Poshuk-META" (Retrieval Aim)

We suggest examining questions such as:

- Types of internet search systems (Subject Directories and Search Engines), their peculiar properties;
- The principles of functioning of search engines (the processes of scanning, indexing and ranging);

- The notions of information retrieval, relevance and boolean operators;
- The search engine on the example of which practical realization of the issues considered is carried out.

It's advisable to focus on mastering of possibilities of some search system: to define what information space it covers, to learn to formalize information needs by picking up key words and determining semantic links between them, to master boolean queries of the search system to analyze the results obtained. For Ukrainian pupils the system <META> may become such an object of studying.

Search system <META> (http://meta.ua) covers the whole Ukrainian segment of the internet, realizes retrieval according to the list of Ukrainian sites, gives a possibility of access to European information resources. <META> combines in itself the functions of subject directory and search engine, is characterized by high accuracy and speed of retrieval, processing documents by any European language with taking into account of morphology of Ukrainian and Russian. Studying of internet search systems is complicated by the fact that not all Ukrainian schools have an access to the internet. The authors have set a task to create a computer program of studying search systems without an internet-access. This was necessary :

- To present the theoretical material of the course studied in the hypertext-structure;
- To prepare examples for solving;
- To form the base of retrieval in accordance with pedagogical and educational objectives, to pick up documents, the theme of which would be interesting and urgent for pupils;
- To organize in this base a full-text retrieval of documents with the support of the boolean operators;
- To work out a system of retrieval task.

Such a program was created and it got the name "Poshuk-META" (Retrieval-Aim). Its interconnected constituents are: an electronic schoolbook, a system of examples for demonstration, a program-trainer.

The electronic school-book contains the theoretical material presented in the hypertext-structure. The systems Yahoo!, Google, Yandex (Russia) and <META> (Ukraine) are the objects of demonstration.

For creating the program-trainer from the internet there have been picked up web-documents (500 Mb), which have scientific, educational, cognitive direction. These documents were indexed by the employees of <META>, on their basis was organized a full-text retrieval with the support of the boolean operators of <META>. The program processes queries in Ukrainian, Russian, English. All the program is contained on CD.

For use of the program "Poshuk-META" there was worked out a system of laboratory works. Here are their themes and some tasks suggested for them.

### Laboratory Work №1. Simple Retrieval.
Examples of retrieval tasks:

1. What is the aim of the project Space Interferometry mission?
2. What is the firm Bolt Beranek and Newman famous for?
3. What are the peculiarities of the car Honda Civic Hybrid?

The results of the retrieval must be entered into the following table:

| Number of question | Formulation of the query | URL-address of the site where the answer is found | The answer to the question |
|---|---|---|---|
| | | | |

Drawing up of the main results of laboratory works is done in the form of tables, which enable to summarize the things studied.

### Laboratory Work №2. Boolean Operators of <META>.

Examples of retrieval tasks – to find documents, which contain certain key words, using boolean operators:

1. To find documents containing the word *school*.
2. To find documents containing the words *school* and *lyceum* at the same time.
3. To find documents containing at least one of the words *school* or *lyceum*.
4. To find documents which contain the word *lyceum* but don't contain the word *school*.

The results of the retrieval must be entered into the following table:

| Number of question | Formulation of the query | Number of documents found |
|---|---|---|
| | | |

The analysis of the results obtained enables to follow the change in the number of the documents found with the usage of boolean operators.

### Laboratory Work №3. Operators of Context Retrieval. Operators of Distance Between Words.

**Task 1.** With the help of the program "Poshuk-META", to find out who is the author of the given quotations:

1. The best mistake is the one made while studying.
2. Mathematics should be studied at least for the fact that it puts mind in order.

### Task 2. To enter the suggested queries:

1. *physical culture, "physical culture"*;
2. *computer games, "computer games"*.
   To analyze the numbers of documents found.

### Task 3.

1. To find documents containing the words *internet, technology, access*.
2. To find documents containing the words *internet, technology, access*. The text fragment, where the key words occur, must not exceed 10 words.
3. To find documents containing the words *internet, technology, access*. The text fragment, where the key words occur, must not exceed 5 words.
   To analyze the numbers of documents found.

**Laboratory Work №4. Operators Limiting the Area of Retrieval by Certain Fields of Web-documents.**

To find with the help of the program "Poshuk-META":

1. documents the titles of which contain the word *enactment*;
2. documents the titles of chapters of which contain the word *legislature*;
3. documents the titles of chapters of which contain the word *law*.

Concluding tasks:

1. To check if there is information of your native town in the retrieval base of the program "Poshuk-META"?
2. To check if there is information of the educational institution you'd like to study at after leaving school in the retrieval base of the program "Poshuk-META"?
3. To check if there is information about your favorite singer (music group, actor, football-player) in the retrieval base of the program "Poshuk-META"?

We suggest such time plan of work with this program: 2-3 lessons – for learning of theoretical material, and 4-7 lessons – for carrying out of the laboratory works. A number of lessons depends on the level of pupils' efficiency (for example, demonstrations may be considered or not).

# 4  Results of the Pedagogical Experiment

The program "Poshuk-META" was introduced into the process of studies at some secondary schools in Ukraine. The introduction was accompanied by questioning the 284 pupils took part in the experiment.

The study has shown that: the majority of the people questioned considers the internet as an additional source of information (87%), but most respondents prefer entertaining kinds of resources (84%). Among other materials, pupils mentioned database of reports as absolute leaders in the list of interest. But electronic libraries are used only by 8% of the respondents. An important result of the survey is the fact that almost 98% of pupils think that the skills to realize information retrieval in the internet will be necessary for them in future studies and professional activity.

The question of search systems the pupils use was important for carrying out the experiment. Figure 2 shows the distribution of the rating of popularity of search systems before and after learning the theme "Studying of Information Search Systems of the internet".

Before studying the theme 29% of the pupils questioned couldn't name any information search system. After studying only 2% of pupils were ignorant. It should also be mentioned that after studying the theme the number of pupils who know and use in their work not one but some search systems got increased. It is underlined by the decrease of the percentage of popularity of Rambler and increase of the rating of search systems studied in the theme: <META> – from 5 to 22%, Yahoo! – from 6 to 9%, Yandex – from 11 to 12%, Google – from 9 to 16%. The data given show that most pupils prefer Russian search systems and Russian-language internet-resource.

The reasons for this are insufficient knowledge of English and underestimation of the development of the Ukrainian-language content of the internet. The authors set before them a task to attract pupils' attention to the Ukrainian-language segment of the internet and to show the great potential of the English-language resource. As the data given show they managed to do it to a certain extent.

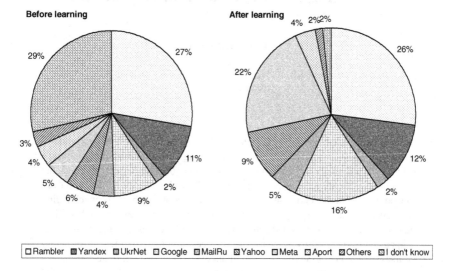

**Fig. 2.** Distribution of the rating of popularity of search systems

Application of the computer program "Poshuk-META" in the teaching process was effective and expedient.

## 5 Conclusion

The skills to appreciate information from the point of view of its authenticity, accuracy, adequacy for the solution of the concrete information task are formed either in the process of learning of internet search systems or in the process of the retrieval activity under the teacher's supervision. The skills to carry out information retrieval in the internet intensify pupils' cognitive activity, raise the level of their information culture.

## References

1. Выготский Л.С. Собрание сочинений: В 6-ти т. – Т.3. – М.: Педагогика, 1983. – 368 с. (Vygotsky L.S. Complete works: In 6 vol. – Vol.3. – Moscow: Pedagogics, 1983. – 368 p.).
2. Бабаева Ю.Д., Войскунский А.Е., Смыслова О.В. Интернет: воздействие на личность // Гуманитарные исследования в Интернете / Под ред. А.Е. Войскунского. – М.: Можайск-Терра, 2000. – С. 11-39. (Babaeva Y.D., Voiskounsky A.E., Smyslova O.V. The internet: influence on a person // Humanitarian researches in the internet / Edited by A.E. Voiskounsky. – Moscow: Mozhaisk-Terra, 2000. – pp. 11-39.).
3. Арестова О.Н., Бабанин Л.Н., Войскунский А.Е. Мотивация пользователей Интернета // Гуманитарные исследования в Интернете / Под ред. А.Е. Войскунского. – М.: Можайск-Терра, 2000. - С. 55-76. (Arestova O.N., Babanin L.N., Voiskounsky A.E. Internet users' motivation // Humanitarian researches in the internet / Edited by A.E. Voiskounsky. – Moscow: Mozhaisk-Terra, 2000. – pp. 55-76.).

# Why Teach Introductory Computer Science? Reconciling Diverse Goals and Expectations

Jürg Nievergelt

Informatik, ETH, CH-8092 Zürich, Switzerland
jn@inf.ethz.ch

**Abstract.** Introductory computing courses emerged during the sixties, under a variety of designations such as "programming" or "automatic computing", offered to university students in a broad range of disciplines. Whereas the concept of a "first course in computer science" survived four decades, and even moved to the high school level, its goals and contents have been changing excessively, and have not as yet reached a stable state. We review the historical development of typical introductory CS courses and analyze the forces that shaped them. Inspired by more mature sciences, and the way their introductory courses evolved over centuries to simultaneously meet distinct expectations, we argue that an introductory CS course should address three goals: the development of skills in programming some simple system, appreciation of intellectual achievements, and the role of information technology in society. Although this requirement may be considered overly ambitious, we aim to show that it can be achieved if issues are presented in terms of well-chosen examples rather than in a general, abstract manner.

R.T. Mittermeir (Ed.): ISSEP 2005, LNCS 3422, p. 92, 2005.
© Springer-Verlag Berlin Heidelberg 2005

# Teaching: People to People – About People
## *A Plea for the Historic and Human View*

Laszlo Böszörmenyi

University Klagenfurt, Austria
laszlo@itec.uni-klu.ac.at
https://www.ifi.uni-klu.ac.at/ITEC/Staff/Laszlo.Boszormenyi

**Abstract.** The importance of the historical and human aspects of the didactics of informatics is discussed. The threefold human aspects of teaching: by, for and about people is explored. Using the example of the notion of the procedure, the potential of the historical discussion is investigated. A strengthening of the historical and human view is required both in university research and in the curricula of the informatics education at both secondary and university levels.

## 1 Introduction

Informatics is a complex science, with roots in formal mathematics, in cybernetics and system sciences, in electrical engineering, in economical and social sciences, in language theory, and so on. It has applications in virtually all areas of life. This fact alone should be sufficient motivation for great care in the teaching of the subject - far more care than, alas, is presently the norm.

Informatics education is dominated by the idea of teaching young people how to do things: how to program, how to use various tools and environments, how to design. The educational process is not designed to engender understanding. In a world where more and more people use more and more "things" with less and less understanding about how these "things" fit into an overall context, something more is needed in our syllabuses.

It is here that informatics could enable a certain kind of learning which is not possible with any other discipline: the building of a bridge between abstract and real. One component of this bridge is the relationship between a technology and the people and historical context which gave rise to that technology. Although perhaps an oversimplification, we can say that the subject of any education is the human mind and that any education can and should present people, humanity, and some part of the real world. This is particularly important in today's increasingly virtual world and consequently, in the way we teach informatics.

Teaching itself is a process which involves people – teacher and pupil – and its subject should include those people who contributed, changed the course of development, have been instrumental in deciding what would be imposed upon the given world, why, when and within which context. This would argue for, amongst other things, the inclusion in any informatics syllabus of an historical and human reflection on informatics. This is of course not only a question of good will but also of knowledge and of an understanding which is as yet immature. This is an exiting research field, offering beautiful, stimulating and challenging research works.

## 2  Human Aspects of Informatics Education

### 2.1  The People We Teach

No one thinks – at least I hope so – that we teach gymnastics in our schools because we find it especially important that our children learn to turn a perfect somersault. The purpose of teaching gymnastics is much rather to keep children healthy and to help them to find their delight in the proper movement of their bodies and in the discipline that is necessary to do active sports. In the case of music, it might be an important secondary aim that children learn a certain basic repertoire of well-known music pieces, extracted from their own traditional music as well as from international classical music. However, it is clear in this case as well, that the primary goal is to develop a special capability – that of enjoying music – and thus again making the children healthier, in this case especially in their souls. At a competition of school choirs, we are not so much interested in the number or length of the pieces the children sing, but rather in how clean they sing, how well they keep the rhythm, and how much joy they find in their own music. Even though this capability may be very different in different children, studies have shown that every child has a certain ability for music and that this can be extensively developed. In an experiment in Hungary, a few seemingly "untalented" children were integrated into special music classes – with such success that after a few years these "untalented" children could no longer be distinguished from the other, presumably talented, children.

The primary goal of good teaching is always the development of capabilities. Moreover, I dare to add rather provocative statement that proper development of capabilities makes children healthy, whereas the failure to develop and nourish hidden capabilities leaves children sick and impoverished. This is precisely what makes teaching so difficult, what makes it a real art: the teacher is supposed to recognize *hidden capabilities* of the children.

In the case of science it seems to be less obvious that the primary goal of teaching is less the transfer of a certain amount of knowledge than, as with to music or gymnastics, the healthy development of the soul and the spirit. Ironically, even in the domain of religion, a given church often finds it more important to teach specific dogmas than to develop the religious talents of the children. Maybe this explains why some children who initially relate to spiritual issues and ceremonies, after an exposure to formal religious education in the school, become skeptical and mistrustful of religion. And in mathematics we often teach theorems and lemmas and even their proofs, but we rarely bother to discuss how it was that the author of the theorem ever came to the given idea. This is absent not only in teaching; the scientific community itself largely refuses to deal with the issue of how we come to our ideas. As Dijkstra put it [1]:

*"Mathematical <u>results</u> are published quite openly and are taught quite explicitly; but how mathematics is <u>done</u> remains largely hidden. To publish besides the results the way (and the order!) in which they were reached, to mention blind alleys as well, to mention whether the solution was found in three months or twenty minutes [...] all this is regarded as 'unscientific', and therefore, 'bad style'. (Just try to include such remarks in your next publication: if the referees don't object to them, the editor will!)"*.

In religion and in mathematics, historical and human aspects get short shrift: in informatics these issues are completely ignored. We are preoccupied with rather secondary didactical issues such as 'should we start teaching programming with the object-oriented approach or in a rather traditional way' and similar matters. Although these questions are interesting, they cannot be answered properly if we are not able to ask and answer the primary question: What kinds of capabilities the teacher of informatics be trying to find, develop and enhance? Other questions, such as those of methods and of proper age, can hardly be discussed without the context which this question pre-supposes.

Any discussion on didactics of informatics should give serious attention to this one basic issue; otherwise, we run the risk of doing something that leaves our children sick and impoverished rather than healthy and rich in spirit.

## 2.2 The People Who Teach

Even though no proof is necessary that not only children and scientists but also teachers are human beings, it is more than worthwhile to say a few words about the human side of teaching. E-learning is a very popular buzzword. The idea of using the computer to help learning is almost as old as the computer itself. And many would agree that the computer is an excellent educational aid. However, many proponents of e-learning go much further. Even while emphasizing that they do not to want to eliminate human instructors, they usually want to minimize the human teaching resource as much as possible. Another new-old trend is to use modern media to create "super courses", the idea being that best experts of a certain field create super panels of such a course, which becomes thus the "best possible course". The sad point is that people working on such courses are not only ignoring their own, maybe less well-known, colleagues, but more importantly they ignore the most important aspect of teaching: and this is the human communication between teacher and pupil. The role of a teacher, especially in informatics, must go further than just transporting knowledge. It is the teacher who carries the responsibility of providing context to the student, of building bridges between the abstract and the real.

In a recently held workshop in Switzerland[1], secondary school students were invited to participate, alongside adult professionals who had a hobby-level interest in the PC, in a robotics workshop. Teams were built with one adult and one or two teenage 'experts'; the latter were confident of their PC prowess and regarded the adults as their students and protégées. At least initially! The children were indeed speedy in building a robot and in handling the initial programming and setting their

---

[1] Conducted and reported by Dr. Ann Dünki (Dünki & Co, Switzerland).

robots on the floor. But then came some very interesting interactions, and actually the most significant learning experience.

The robot's wheels were driven by motors, and the programmer could vary the power that was exerted on the wheel drive. There were no commands that said 'turn left' or 'turn right'. In one team, the youngsters wanted their robots to turn – but did not know how to make this happen. One of the adults, an engineer by profession, told them to apply different levels of power to the wheel sets on each side: more power on the right, less on the left and the robot would turn left. Skeptical, they put the idea into action – and the robot turned. In another team, the robot was to give an acoustic signal for different situations and states. For this, a rudimentary set of sounds, or notes, were available and could be varied easily. These were O.K. but not exciting, until one woman, a music teacher, started writing out the notes for some well known melodies and had the youngsters click these into the program. Their robot instantly became much more human, and much more attractive.

*All the students benefited, but the girls blossomed. Too often, informatics is a cold study, leaving out any considerations of usefulness. Studies have shown that women, of all ages, tend to use computers to do things whereas men tend to focus on how the computer, or the program or the device, works. Women tend to reject this narrow space and to respond to informatics when it can be related to broader aspects of their lives.*

In each team, the secondary-schoolers discovered relationships between their abstract informatics and the real world; they saw that 'old-timers' somehow knew *what* to do, even if they did not know *how*. This could never happen in an e-learning mode, which by necessity is focused, convergent, limited in its breadth. Today we worry that the informatics teachers don't know enough informatics, that the children figure out the 'how-to' faster than their adult teachers, and based on such considerations we think that the teacher is expendable. But if the teacher goes, who will teach our budding programmers *what* to do? Who will provide them with context? Who will help them bridge their virtual toys back to a real world? Certainly not a computer!

If we recognize that some teachers and parents cannot, or will not, meet up with this massive challenge then it is good if we are alarmed, good if we feel called upon to do something. But surely not in a pure instrumental manner! No automata can provide the fuzziness, the breadth, the diversity and the divergence which is provided by the complement of teachers and parents which are part of a healthy and humanistic education. We can quote again Dijkstra [1]:

*"We have – despite what psychologists, pedagogues and the like may think – not the faintest idea how knowledge, insights and habits are transferred."*

If we don't know how children learn, we had better provide them with a large learning environment.

## 2.3 The People We Teach About

In literature we deal with the actual works of excellent authors. Even if the children learn little about the life of Shakespeare or Goethe, by reading their works they gain a personal relation to them. After a while, a good student will never confuse Goethe with Hölderlin, later on not even with Schiller. Similarly, a student who has developed a musical talent will quickly be able to distinguish Bach from Mozart, and later even from Händel. The pupils understand – even if the teacher does not say this explicitly – that the oeuvre of Goethe would not exist without a certain person, called Goethe. If he had not lived and worked then we just wouldn't have Faust, no matter how sad this would be.

In the case of natural sciences and mathematics – as partly touched already – this is different. Even if children learn the names of the most well-known scientists, the scientific facts are taught as if they were independent of the human spirits who discovered them. It is of course obvious that the law of gravitation was in effect before Newton defined it. However, people did not know this. The world has been really changed by Newton's formal observation. It is not as if, prior to Newton, objects were flying above the ground; but Newtonian physics opened entirely new ways of scientific thinking and technique. (By the way, it might have closed some other ways as well, as Goethe worried; Goethe criticized Newton in a rather novel way, in a debate which today is mostly forgotten.)

It may make little sense to philosophize about whether or not, had Newton never existed, another person would have discovered the law of gravitation. The heart of this consideration is that even "objective" science is made by subjects – there is no other choice. This fact does not make science subjective; correct scientific results are customarily proved by others. The important implication is that science is a creative human act which occurs within a particular historical context and that the destiny of science and the world depends very much upon the extent to which we realize this. Some people assume that science is in its last phase and could soon run dry; that man's contributions have all been made. If we believe this, then we teach dogmas, complex yet static 'truths'; we teach how to do something but not what we should do, or why; we teach young minds to move around in a complex structure, but give no hint as to how such a complex structure could be created in the first place.

We teach the "best of breed" method as if this 'best-ness' were dictated by some higher power, or perhaps grown in the field like a plant. And simply dropping a few famous names does not change anything. Rather, the teaching of informatics should include a strong emphasis on studying the road, the development of a certain idea, the roles of certain people, the context and drivers that catapulted certain ideas into the forefront (and left others by the wayside). Kristen Nygaard, the inventor of what we call today object-orientation, wrote [5]:

*"We teach students very little about the production of new knowledge, and many believe that important new ideas somehow descend upon us through 'inspiration'. It is true that you may get euphoric when something suddenly is understood or created in your mind. I remember very, very clearly the exact moment, around two o'clock in the night at the desk in the bedroom at Nesodden, January 1967, when the concept of 'inheritance' (or classes and subclasses) had been created. I realized immediately that this was the solution to a very important problem Ole-Johan Dahl and I had been struggling with for months and weeks. I also realized that the solution introduced for the first time in a programming language a strong and flexible version of the notions*

*of generalization and specialization, with all the power embedded in those concepts. And sure enough, inheritance has become a key concept in object oriented programming, and thus in programming in general. But was it created at that desk, at that moment? Yes and no. Yes, because the idea was not there before two o'clock. No, because in my opinion it could not have been created without all the previous weeks, with discussion after discussion producing only half-baked solutions. Through that work Ole-Johan and I had built up: (1) a large amount of information useful in blocking unpromising avenues, (2) understanding of what criteria a solution would have to satisfy, (3) visualization of what the implementation problems would be, (4) families of mental models that could be used for analysis of ideas."*

Our pupils need to learn such things. I do not plead for replacing formal definitions and programming practice with interesting stories about great computing scientists. But I do plead that we provide an integrated view of the ideas, their time and place in history, and the thinking processes pursued by the creators of these ideas. Only this will lead to understanding. Friedrich Dürrenmatt, a well-known Swiss author, wrote a wonderful satirical drama, The Physicists. The story takes place in a madhouse and involves three physicists. One of them tells us:

*"A machine only becomes useful when it has grown independent of the knowledge that led to its discovery. Hence today any fool can make a light bulb glow – or an atomic bomb explode."*

### 2.3.1 An Historical Side-Product

Interestingly, the historical approach has numerous didactical advantages. If we introduce new ideas in their historical sequence, then we usually provide a stepping stone towards understanding. It does not mean of course that we should follow the steps of historical development in a dogmatic way – no approach is good enough to be followed dogmatically. However, where we have difficulty in deciding upon a workable sequence, it turns out that history can often advise. Maybe the historical advice is: do *not* follow the historical time line in the given case, because it was too complicated or too much influenced by unscientific – political, economic etc. – factors. More often, the advice will be to introduce the new ideas in their historical sequence.

Mathematics in general is taught in this way. Very roughly, we tend to start with the Greek mathematics and come only later to the more modern issues. The Lobachevsky-Bolyai geometry may include the Euclidian one, but – hopefully – nobody thinks to start with the former in the secondary schools. Similarly, object-oriented programming includes procedural programming, but we do not have to conclude that therefore we have to start teaching programming with object-orientation. Actually, we may assume that there must have been good reason that object-orientation, although introduced by Nygaard and Dahl in the late sixties, took roughly twenty years until it was generally understood by a broad audience. This opens at least the question as to whether it is a didactically good idea to start with this obviously not too simple approach. Or take the following example: Parallel programming includes sequential programming, but it is very likely that is better to start with sequential programming – as it happened indeed historically.

# 3   The History of a Simple Notion: An Example

In the following section I give an example of how the historical view could work, and of how exciting the story of a basic and well-known notion is. Obviously we cannot recount such stories for every new concept or idea. But it would be advantageous if the teachers possessed a wealth of such historical anecdotes from which to draw. The historical view could be an essential part of the informatics didactics education at the universities. In this example the center of interest is not a great computing scientist, but a simple notion. This might appear as a contradiction to the thesis before that teaching is always about people. However, the history of a notion is always a history of the persons who worked on it – and this is exactly this interaction between subject and object, between process and product of thinking that makes history so fascinating.

## 3.1   The Notion of the Procedure

Nowadays, many universities and schools start teaching programming with the programming language Java. Java is certainly a clean and good language and even if it has some weaknesses, it is by far the best among the "popular" programming languages (such as Fortran, Cobol, C and C++). My basic criticism of using Java as a first-course language is that a number of basic programming concepts are supported only in an indirect way, and thus the language suggests a limited view of programming (see more in [18]). The notion of a module arises only as a special case of a class, the notion of a procedure as a special case of a method, and the notion of a constant as a special case of a variable. This has a certain mathematical beauty, but makes initial understanding difficult. As if my mother, instead of saying: "Please bring a chair to the table", had said "please, send a message to an instance of the class chair, which is a subclass of class furniture, to be brought to the very instance of the class table, being also a subclass of class furniture." I doubt that I could have ever learned to speak in this way.

A negative consequence of starting with Java can be – if the teacher follows too much the notion suggested by the language – that the pupils do not even learn the notion of a procedure, only that of a method. This would be, however, very regrettable, which becomes obvious, if take a look at the history of both notions.

The procedure in informatics has two roots: the mathematical function and the algorithm.

As computers were originally intended to be pure "computing" – actually deciphering – machines (as opposed to "controlling" machines as we mostly use them today), the need for expressing mathematical functions arose very early. Unfortunately, the digital computer does not fit the needs of classical, continuous functions very well. But, as history tells us, a way was found to describe such functions as a sequence of operations: as an algorithm [15]. Even though in introductory courses we love to teach the famous and ancient Euclidean algorithm to compute the greatest common divisor, the algorithm represents a relatively new (medieval) branch of mathematics, one which for many years was not particularly well respected. The early algorithms addressed such issues as just doubling a number, and later on general multiplication and division. During a certain medieval period, addition and subtraction are said to have been taught at German universities, but in order to learn multiplication and division an Italian university had to be visited. The real significance of algorithms was only recognized in the 20<sup>th</sup> century, with the age of computers. Starting with the historic work of Alan Turing on computable numbers [2], algorithms become the central issue in automated computing. A short definition could be: An algorithm is a precise, unambiguous specification of a finite, effective *procedure*. This is where the computer term *procedure* comes from. An effective procedure consists of a sequence of individual steps, each describing a single operation. See more e.g. in [15].

Procedures appeared from the very beginning in programming languages – already in the first practicable higher level programming language, FORTRAN. Syntactically the procedure is similar to a mathematical function: it has a name, and parameters in parenthesis, such as *sin(x)*. Moreover, and here we see a difference from the usual mathematical view, it has a body (enclosed between { and } in the "C-family" and between the keywords BEGIN and END in the "Algol-Pascal-family"). The procedure body contains an algorithm that computes some desired result step-by-step. The procedure is consequently a named algorithm, computing some function value, or performing some desired side effect. These are the most essential characteristics of the procedure.

Another aspect is that, in its relation to other programming language constructs, the procedure can be treated as a *constant*. Once defined, it can be used as often as required; each time called, it computes the function value by applying the same algorithm to the arbitrary input parameters. Some languages, such as Mesa or Modula-3 [15] express this aspect in their syntax as well. In Modula-3, e.g. CONST N = 3 means that the value 3 is assigned to the name N for the entire scope of N. Similarly, in the declaration PROCEDURE F(x: INTEGER): INTEGER = BEGIN ... END F; the "=" sign indicates that the algorithm between BEGIN and END is permanently assigned to the function name F, wherever F is known.

In 1971 Niklaus Wirth introduced the Pascal programming language [3], with a concise type system. Its predecessor, the Algol-60 language [4], contained only predefined types, with the one exception being the **array** construction, which could be regarded as a type constructor (the Algol report does not use this notion yet). Pascal goes much further, it introduces a number of *type constructors* and, and this is an integral part of the whole sense of Pascal, it allows the definition of procedure types. A procedure type declaration specifies only the head of the procedure. Variables of a certain procedure type can be declared, and actual procedure values (constants of further variables) can be assigned at run-time. This is what is well-known as *dynamic binding* of procedures. E.g. the call on *f(x)* may mean either *sin(x)* or *cos(x)*, depending on the question if an assignment f:= sin resp. f:= cos was executed before. Note that, no matter how important this issue is, it has a secondary importance in understanding what a procedure is.

More or less parallel to the development of Pascal, Kristen Nygaard and Ole-Johan Dahl developed the programming language Simula-67 (as a successor of Simula I, a successor itself of Algol 60); this was the first object oriented language. Indeed,

Simula-67 contained all essential features of present object oriented languages, except one feature: that of encapsulation also known as information hiding. This was not interesting for Nygaard and Dahl at that time: the idea of classes and inheritance was born in searching for useful notions for modeling (simulating) real life objects and not in searching for solutions to the software crisis. Even though Dahl worked a lot on the theory of structured programming [7], the idea of information hiding or encapsulation was developed later by David Parnas – and then enjoyed a hearty initial reaction of total rejection [8].

The essential idea of object orientation is that simulated objects are described with the help of a hierarchical classification scheme. General features are described in classes near to the root of the hierarchy. The more specific an issue is, the further it is from the root. E.g. a convertible could be described as a special case of an automobile, which again could be described as a special case of a vehicle etc. Subclasses inherit data and behavior of the super-classes and can extend, and even to a certain extent modify them. The idea was really revolutionary at the time of its birth, and the authors, Nygaard and Dahl, were aware of the significance of the idea of inheritance, or "prefixing" as it was originally called, even if they could not begin to imagine the enormous influence this idea would later have on a vast number of subsequent programming languages. As Nygaard put it [9]:

*"Usually a new idea was subjected to rather violent attacks in order to test its strength. The prefix idea was the only exception. We immediately realized that we now had the necessary foundation for a completely new language approach ..."* .

Simula-67 allows one to declare a procedure as *virtual*. This is a restricted form of dynamic binding. In Pascal, the dynamic assignment of procedure values to procedure variables is fully under the control of the programmer, which is flexible, but error-prone. Simula-67 and the following legion of object oriented languages prefer this restricted dynamic binding, which is nowadays well-known under the name *method overriding*. Dahl describes the original concept in the following way [10]:

*"If a procedure P is specified as **virtual** in a class C the binding scheme is semi-dynamic. Any call for P occurring in C or in any subclass of C will bind to that declaration of P which occurs at the innermost prefix level of the actual object containing such a declaration (and similarly for remote accesses). Thus, the body of the procedure P may, at the prefix level of C, be postponed to occur in any subclass of C. It may even be replaced by more appropriate ones in further subclasses. This binding scheme is dynamic in the sense that it depends on the class membership of the actual object. But there is nevertheless a degree of compiler control; the access can be implemented as indirect through a table produced by the compiler for C and for each of its subclasses."*

An interesting extension of this story is that Niklaus Wirth (who, incidentally, resisted the idea of object orientation for quite some time) made an effort in the middle of the eighties to find the absolute minimal programming language support for object orientation. In the Oberon language [11] he implemented sub-classing with the help of so-called extendable records. Methods and method overriding were simply implemented by record fields of type procedure. This worked of course, but was error-prone, because a programmer might have assigned a wrong procedure – or even none! – to a procedure-type field. Therefore, he and Mössenböck later on extended the language by type-bound procedures (i.e. methods) in Oberon-2 [12, 13]. Nevertheless, we can learn much from the minimalist approach of Oberon. The following anecdote, recorded by Stephan Gehring, may help to understand this [14]:

*"In a small lecture hall [...] late 1988 [...] Niklaus Wirth [...] explained that not only had they developed a new computer, but also an operating system and a new programming language named Oberon. He placed a slide on Oberon onto the slide projector, exposed the top four lines and said: «These are the features that we added to Modula-2». He then uncovered the rest of the slide, about a dozen more lines, and said with a triumphant smile: «And these are the features that we removed from Modula-2! »"*

### 3.2  Short Moral of the Long Story

Virtual procedures or methods, procedure types and variables, issues of method overriding and method redefinition [15] etc. are all issues pertaining to the static, dynamic, or semi-dynamic (as Dahl called it) binding of procedure values (i.e. code) to variables denoting an action. No matter how interesting these issues are, it is probably wiser to concentrate first on the essence of the procedure, and come only later to the exciting story of binding.

The second and maybe more important lesson we can learn from this story is that one single notion can lead us into unexpected new corridors of informatics. Actually, I had originally planned to give several such examples and was then surprised to see how long my story of a single notion has become. And it could be of course much longer.

## 4  Summary and Further Work

Teaching informatics is teaching a way of thinking and understanding. I have tried to show that such education must address much more than digital dexterity skills. In an increasingly abstract world, I have contended that informatics education could be the vehicle for providing a bridge to reality, a context for understanding; and that the historical aspects of informatics could be an essential part of such an educational process. This paper is at most a first attempt in this direction. It rather formulates the questions than answering them. Most of the work is still to be done.

I have argued that universities which address the didactics of informatics should pay more attention to the historical and human issues as is currently the case. Moreover, they should devote more research effort to a most interesting and central issue: Why do we teach informatics, what capabilities do we wish to awake in the pupil? The leitmotif for such research could be, and this should not surprise us:

Broad education is the basis of any good teaching, including
the teaching of informatics.

# Acknowledgements

My thank goes to Dr. Ann Dünki for her encouragement, for the careful reading, and for her invaluable support by critical remarks and excellent extensions.

# References

1. Dijkstra, E.W.: Homo Cogitans, Personal Note EWD533, November 1975
2. Turing, Alain: On computable numbers with an application to the Entscheidunsproblem. In London Math. Soc., pages 230–265, 1936.
3. Wirth, Niklaus: The programming language Pascal. Acta Informatica, 1(1):35–63, 1971.
4. Naur, P (as editor, coauthors: J. W. Backus, F. L. Bauer, J. Green, C. Katz, J. McCarthy, A. J. Perlis, H, Rutishauser, K. Samelson, B. Vauquois, J. H. Wegstein, A. van Wijngaarden, M. Woodger): Report on the algorithmic language ALGOL 60, 40 p., Regnecentralen 1960; Acta Polytech. Scand. 284; Numerische Mathematik 2 (1960), pp.106-136; Comm. ACM 3, 6 (June 1960), pp. 299-314.
5. Nygaard, Kristen: "Those Were the Days"? or "Heroic Times Are Here Again"?, The Scandinavian Journal of Information Systems, 8(2), 1996
6. Dijkstra, Edsger Wybe: Craftsman or Scientist?, Personal note EWD480, 1975 (The manuscript was published as pages 104-109 of Edsger Wybe Dijkstra, Selected Writings on Computing: A Personal Perspective, Springer Verlag, New York, 1982)
7. Dahl, Ole-Johan; Dijkstra, Edsger Wybe; Hoare, C. A. R.: Structured Programming, Academic Press, 1972
8. Parnas, David: The secret history of information hiding, In Software pioneers: contributions to software engineering, Ed. Manfred Broy and Ernst Denert, Springer-Verlag, 2002
9. Nygaard, Kristen and Dahl, Ole-Johan: The Development of the SIMULA Languages, ACM SIGPLAN Notices, 13(6), pp. 245-272, 1978
10. Dahl, Ole-Johan: The Birth of Object Orientation: the Simula Languages, June 2001. In From Object-Orientation to Formal Methods, Essays in Memory of Ole-Johan Dahl, Series: Lecture Notes in Computer Science , Vol. 2635 Owe, Olaf; Krogdahl, Stein; Lyche, Tom (Eds.) 2004, X, 389 p.
11. Wirth, N: The Programming Language Oberon. Software – Practice and Experience 18(7): 671-690, 1985.
12. Mössenböck, H. und Wirth, N: The Programming Language Oberon-2, ETH Zürich, Institut für Computersysteme, Oktober 1993.
13. Mössenböck, H.: Objektorientierte Programmierung in Oberon-2, Springer-Verlag, Berlin, 1993.
14. Gehring, Stephan W.: Learning the Value of Simplicity, In The School of Niklaus Wirth, Böszörmenyi, Laszlo; Gutknecht, Jürg; Pomberger, Gustav (eds.) dpunkt.verlag, 2000.
15. Böszörmenyi, Laszlo; Weich, Carsten: Programming in Modula-3 - An Introduction in Programming with Style Springer Verlag, Heidelberg 1996.
16. Böszörmenyi, Laszlo: Informatik in der Schule (in German), In: Erziehungskunst, Februar 1997.
17. Böszörmenyi, Laszlo; Podlipnig, Stefan: People Behind Informatics – In memory of Ole-Johan Dahl, Edsger W. Dijsktra and Kristen Nygaard, Klagenfurt, 2003.
18. Böszörmenyi, Laszlo: Why Java is not my favorite first-course language? Software - Concepts & Tools (1998) 19: 141-145

# Preparatory Knowledge: Propaedeutic in Informatics

Susanne Loidl[1], Jörg Mühlbacher[1], and Helmut Schauer[2]

[1] Institute for Information Processing and Microprocessor Technology (FIM),
Johannes Kepler University Linz, Altenbergerstr. 69, A-4040 Linz
{loidl, muehlbacher}@fim.uni.linz.ac.at
[2] Department of Informatics (IFI), University Zurich,
Winterthurerstr. 190, CH-8057 Zurich
schauer@ifi.unizh.ch

**Abstract.** In the recent past a number of concepts have achieved prominence in the quest for basic principles of informatics with long-term validity. Particularly at schools providing an all-round education, it makes sense – and is necessary – to concentrate on basic concepts. The fact is that strictly product-related knowledge is inadequate, and in some cases already obsolete before pupils leave school. A more systematic grasp of these concepts and their interrelations is therefore not just desirable, but essential. Some of these "unchanging values" in informatics are briefly introduced here, and it is shown how they can be, first, made more comprehensible by means of applets, and second, put to work in teaching right now, in conjunction with eLearning.

## 1 Introduction

In the recent past a number of concepts have achieved prominence in the quest for basic principles of informatics with long-term validity – and these should be playing an increasing part in the curricula of schools providing an all-round education; the concepts in question are briefly introduced and discussed here (this paper is a shortened version of [6]; see also [3]). Examples of such concepts are: abstraction, particularly in connexion with modelling and recursion, differing forms of notation (with a clear distinction between syntactic and semantic aspects), or distinctions between static/dynamic and local/global aspects also appear important. Again, special properties of relations, such as transitivity, symmetry or reflexivity, and (say) the difference between identity and equivalence, are of primary significance in informatics. The examples selected and given below (see also [10] and [12]) are intended to show how and (especially) which concepts can be conveyed.

The issue of how far procedural or object-oriented programming should be included in formal education is not discussed here. While programming is an excellent training in algorithmic thinking, it does require a certain amount of practice. The latter counts as a skill, and its status and scope are bound to depend on the individual type of school and the educational goals the school pursues.

R.T. Mittermeir (Ed.): ISSEP 2005, LNCS 3422, pp. 104–115, 2005.

## 2    Examples of Basic Concepts in Informatics

Let us consider a typical task in information processing: determining the mass x of an unknown object by means of a balance. To analyse this task, we start by constructing a **model** [2] (Fig.2).

### 2.1    Modelling, Abstraction, States

Modelling involves **abstraction**: certain aspects of the task are deemed to be relevant, and are taken into account in the model, while other aspects are treated as irrelevant and thus ignored. What is deemed to be relevant or irrelevant is of fundamental importance, and depends on the purpose of modelling. Here we ignore the size, shape and colour of the unknown object, for instance, and consider the balance only at rest, with three possible results of weighing: the mass of the object in the left-hand pan can be less than, equal to or greater than the sum of the masses of all the weights in the right-hand pan. This last point illustrates the distinction between **static** and **dynamic** aspects of modelling and the concept of a **state** which a system can be in. A system of this kind, that can be in various defined states and that switches from one to another as a result of defined **events**, is called an **automaton**. If every subsequent state is uniquely determined by the current state and the event in question, the **automaton** is **deterministic** and its behaviour can be forecast. Gambling machines are typically non-deterministic. If we consider placing a weight in a pan as an event, our model of a balance is then a deterministic automaton. If we permit the removal of weights previously placed, a change of state can be reversed. Changes of state can thus be **reversible** or **irreversible**. In the case of computer applications, any action that can be reversed by means of **undo** is an example of a reversible change of state.

A further important aspect is the **accuracy** of a weighing procedure. For instance, we can decide in favour of a discrete model with integer weights, with which the mass of the unknown object can be ascertained only as a whole number, while leaving it open whether the weights are specified in grams, kilograms, etc. With the distinction between **discretely** and **continuously** variable values we have another concept basic to informatics.

Another key aspect of modelling is deciding what is rigid about the model and what can be altered. For example, a given set of weights could be prescribed, or the choice of weights could be left open. Again, the balance beam could be supported at its midpoint in all cases, or the point of support could be shiftable, to permit a free choice of leverage. Which the **parameters** of a model are, and which quantities are treated as **constant** and which as **variable**, are thus also fundamental issues. Alan Perlis [9] put this very neatly 30 years ago in the remark "One man's constant is another man's variable".

One special aim in the balance example, going beyond modelling as a function of the level of abstraction selected, is a discussion about the purpose of the resulting model. For mathematicians the equation $x*a = g*b$ suffices, where g is the weight used to determine x and a and b are the beam lengths. This presupposes that the aim is to model a mechanical balance, for a weighing device in which (say) the extension of a spring as a function of the weight applied is used to measure mass involves a different equation.

Informatics specialists using integer weights (here their order of magnitude plays a part) need to take into account both the resulting "inaccuracy u" of the balance and the process of the balance coming to rest; in the model they will therefore start from an inequation $|x*a - g*b| < u$, or regard the equation as satisfied once the angle $\alpha$ is less than an $\varepsilon$ adapted to the purpose of weighing. So a discussion of the balance example can well lead on in the classroom to a discussion of the difference between formal, mathematical modelling and the sort of modelling typical of the engineering sciences. Interpreting the findings obtained from a model will also need discussion.

The following key properties of models can thus be discussed: Completeness (in terms of the purpose intended), freedom from contradictions (consistency), fidelity to the original and the associated interpretation of the data provided by the model.

The metamodel for discussing modelling is shown in Fig 1.

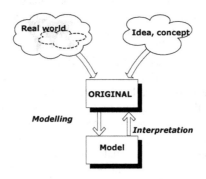

**Fig. 1.** Metamodel of the modelling process

On top of this, for informatics specialists the weighing procedure leads directly to the concept of an algorithm.

## 2.2 The Concept of an Algorithm

No doubt about it, the concept of an algorithm is fundamental to training in informatics. As indicated initially, we shall not comment on programming in a programming language, although programming is naturally the special procedure for informatics specialists to formulate algorithms. At this point we are more concerned with the concept of an algorithm independently of the software context.

Let us consider the sequence of actions that are performed when an object is weighed by means of a balance or a model that mirrors its behaviour. For instance, we can place weights in the pan or remove them completely at random, until the balance is in equilibrium. Apart from the fact that this procedure takes time, it comes to an end only if the mass x of the object can be represented as the sum of a subset of the available weights.

So let us search for a directed procedure that determines the mass x of the object in as small a number of weighing operations as possible. This leads us to the concept of an **algorithm**. If the individual steps are to be performed in a particular order, the algorithm is called **sequential**. Algorithms in which the individual steps can be performed in any order, or even simultaneously, are called **parallel**. For example, several weights can be placed or removed simultaneously, and thus parallel; on the other hand the individual weighing operations are performed sequentially. The distinction between sequential and parallel procedures is also of great importance in informatics – we need only think of data transfer via serial or parallel interfaces, say.

As formulated here, the examples belong to the class of **iterative** algorithms. Going further, we come to the issue of **recursion**. Often a recursive approach yields a simple solution to a problem. "Recursive" means "with self-reference". Recursion occurs whenever something refers to itself.

Traditional examples of recursion, such as the Fibonacci series: $Fib(n) = Fib(n-1) + Fib(n-2)$ with $Fib(1) = Fib(2) = 1$ or n factorial: $n! = n*(n-1)!$ with $n>1$ and $1! = 1$, are to be found both in informatics teaching and in mathematics teaching.

However, we are more concerned with recursive thinking, the recursive description of observations and the use of recursion to solve problems. Here comprehensible, concrete tasks and examples adapted to the year/level in question must be found.

An initial, straightforward example of recursion from everyday life is a tree. Let us imagine a cross-section through a tree-trunk and examine the growth rings that have formed around the central pith. A tree one year old has one annual ring surrounding the pith. In the general case the cross-section of a tree-trunk consists of the outermost ring surrounding the cross-section as it was one year earlier. And this recursive perspective continues until the "abort criterion" is satisfied, when the pith is reached!

The following example does cause a certain surprise in class (in our experience), when one explains a succinct way of describing a queue of people waiting ahead of a cash desk in a supermarket: a queue Q of persons P is either empty (an empty queue) or consists of a person P followed by a queue Q. If one points out at the same time that one ca abstract from a "person P" to any object, and introduces a non-existent "empty" object ε in analogy to the empty set, one gets the pure concept of a queue!

By comparison, describing a queue iteratively takes much more doing. It depends on the educational goals the school in question pursues, and on the year/level in question, whether one then decides to tackle the next step towards EBNF (Extended Backus Naur Form) by means of the following example, which is also excellent training in thinking: how do we describe how a train is put together?

To put it simply, a train consists of an engine E at the head, followed by at least one coach C. The recursive description focuses on "how is a train put together". We can write: train = ET and T = C | CT. For practice one can then derive train = ECC, train = ECCC, train = ECCT etc. and recall the situation with the queue for comparison: Q= ε|P|PQ.

## 2.3  Time Complexity

Let us try to estimate the effort involved in our weighing algorithm. With a purely trial-and-error approach the mean number of weighing operations is proportional to the number of all possible subsets of the weights. If the number of weights is n, the number of all subsets of these weights is equal to $2^n$, so the mean effort increases exponentially with n. The reason for this unnecessarily great effort is that with a purely trial-and-error approach weights are selected for the next operation independently of the unsuccessful previous tries. No use is made of the information whether the object was lighter or heavier than the sum of the weights selected for these tries! Actually, the largest weight value tested that was lighter than x forms the lower limit, and the smallest weight value tested that was larger than x forms the upper limit, of an interval that the value x to be found must lie within. The strategy behind an optimized weighing algorithm can only be to halve this interval at each weighing operation, by comparing x with the arithmetical mean of the interval limits. If x is lighter than this mean, the latter becomes the new upper limit; if x is heavier than this mean, the latter becomes the new lower limit. x has been found when it equals the mean or the interval has been reduced to 1. Since each weight is placed only once, the effort (number of operations required) is in **linear** proportion to n. This optimized algorithm is thus much more efficient than trial and error. In connexion with the time needed to perform an algorithm one speaks of **time complexity**, a fundamental concept in informatics. Other key issues in connexion with the concept of an algorithm include the question of whether an algorithm holds, whether a problem is decidable, computable, etc. We return to these questions later.

### 2.4 Number Systems, Coding

Since the number of weighing operations required is a function of the number n of weights, the question arises of whether the number of weights can be reduced without restricting the range of weight values that these can represent. With a conventional set of weights with the eight values 1, 1, 2, 5, 10, 10, 20, 50 for instance, all integer weight values within the interval 0 to 99 can be represented. This choice of weights is

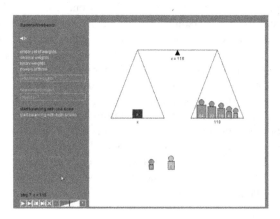

**Fig. 2.** Picture of a model of a mechanical balance, as an example of modelling and binary coding (with the weights 32, 16, 8,4,2)

obviously inspired by the decimal number system. Interestingly, the sequence 1, 2, 5, 10, 20, etc. has the original property that for each pair of numbers in sequence the first value is the integer half of the second value (the sequence 1, 2, 5, 10, 20, etc. corresponds to the values (rounded to integers) in the European Standard sequence E3, which assigns three logarithmically roughly equidistant values to each decade).

The sequence of powers of 2 1, 2, 4, 8, 16, 32, 64, etc. also adheres to this principle; with the corresponding binary set of weights with the seven values 1, 2, 4, 8, 16, 32, 64 all integer weight values within the interval 0 to 127 can be represented. Although a binary set of weights of this kind is not a standard product, it is superior to the decimal set of weights.

Fig. 2 shows the result of a weighing operation using a binary set of weights. The weights placed in the pan correspond exactly to the positions of the ones in the binary coding of x.

## 2.5  Decidability, Computability, NP Complete Problems

In connexion with questions such as whether an algorithm holds, i.e. whether we are dealing with a decidable, computable problem, a tractable problem etc., the favourite objection is that such questions are far too complex, go beyond schools' educational targets and should be reserved for the sphere of tertiary education. In this section we want to show that simple examples that can be formulated intuitively really exist and can be used to introduce these topics in informatics in secondary schools.

At the same time there must be a strict requirement that informatics should be taught only by people with a relevant qualification! We accordingly take it that the discussed topics are already known, and concentrate on the issue of satisfactory didactic treatment.

We start by considering whether everything that occurs to one can be subjected to algorithmic treatment, and thus ultimately to programming.

The halting problem is a good example of a problem that is easy to grasp: can one define an algorithm that decides, for any algorithm whatever (!), whether it completes after a finite number of steps or not? Depending on what the pupils already know, this problem is fairly easy to describe verbally: imagine someone sitting at a PC, waiting some time for results and becoming increasingly worried about whether the program currently running just takes a considerable time or whether a bug has crept in and the best thing would be to abort it. This leads to the wish for a test program that can decide in advance whether the program in question will ever complete and provide results. One can then point out that theoretical informatics delivers the conclusion (which pupils might not have expected) that tasks do exist that are not computable, i.e. not programmable, and that the halting problem is an example of such a task. At the same time the pupils are confronted with a good reason why informatics investigates its own basis in theoretical informatics.

At the next stage it can be assumed that from now on only computable problems will be examined in detail. Here they are very simple, instantly comprehensible tasks such as sorting a finite set of numbers etc. At the same time the requirement should be to perform such tasks in the most efficient way possible, i.e. to search for good algorithms – "good" can be defined as minimizing run time. To illustrate what counts as a good or a less good algorithm, let us take n = 7 integers, order them graphically, first as a linear list and then a binary search tree, and now ask how many comparisons are needed to find out whether an integer x is *not* among the 7 numbers selected; this provides a preliminary justification for the subject "Algorithms and data structures". If a link to mathematics is to be developed here and the pupils have the necessary basic knowledge, the binary search resulting from this example leads to logarithms to the base 2, $\log_2$ n. The next question is how the number of comparisons increases if one selects 2n rather than n numbers.

At the next stage a particularly impressive example is used to make it clear that time-consuming problems cannot be solved simply by technical progress – acquiring a faster computer. To illustrate this phenomenon, the puzzle problem discussed in detail below can be presented; it is easy to explain:

We consider a very small jigsaw puzzle, measuring 5 by 5 pieces. All the pieces are different, but should yield the picture intended, if they are put together correctly.

First of all one must ask the didactically central question whether the problem is soluble at all (computable), i.e. whether it can be solved with the 25 pieces given. If we recall that children can perform this task before they start going to school, there does not seem to be much of a problem. However, it is clear that a computer will need an algorithm: before tackling the puzzle problem, we must find out whether it is computable! A simple brute-force algorithm supplies a positive answer:

- Number the pieces from 1 to 25.
- Arrange all pieces in a sequence. We thus obtain all n! sequences of the n (= 25) numbers.
- For each resulting sequence, check whether it solves the puzzle.

In the worst case it takes n! tries to find the correct sequence!

At this point, faithful to the principle of interdisciplinary teaching, we can introduce the concept of permutation, and use a few examples to derive the number n! of permutations of n numbers, or even repeat the definition n! = n(n-1)! (with a glance back to recursion).

If we omit rotations – determining the number of possibilities could get us into didactic difficulties –and use a computer performing 1 billion checks per second, we get the following figures: Placing: $25! = 1,55*10^{25}$ seconds, i.e. $\sim 4,9*10^{11}$ years. That is still 15 times as long as the time that has elapsed since the original big bang! It is didactically effective to get the students to give an intuitive estimate of the time required first.

Two lessons emerge from this: acquiring a faster computer does not help at all, and we need to start hunting for a better (good) algorithm.

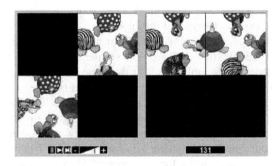

**Fig. 3.** Puzzle problem simplified with 2x2 pieces

At this point it is up to the teacher to convince the pupils that procedures for solving the puzzle problem within a realistic length of computing time are known, e.g. by using structural data about the edges of the individual pieces to get to a solution.

However, a discussion about this leads straight to the issue of NP complete problems, though we must be aware that this topic can be mentioned only verbally and in simplified form. But even at this level it is perfectly suitable for awakening pupils' curiosity, and thus getting them interested in the science of informatics.

The following selection of examples has worked well in practice: one starts with the Travelling-Salesman-Problem (visiting n towns without visiting any of them more than once), which can be explained graphically without difficulty. It is also easy to show that this problem is computable: the approach is to list all permutations of the n towns and to check for each permutation whether it satisfies the criterion for a round trip. In secondary education one then has no choice but to point out that, interestingly enough, (1) for large n no method of solving the problem in a realistic length of time has yet been found, and (2) theoretical informatics provides the following remarkable statements: (a) there is reason to suspect that no algorithm exists to solve the problem, and (b) according to the state of science it will never be possible to prove that the suspicion voiced in (a) is correct.

The next step is to remind the pupils that, if their school has a large number of classes and teachers, the timetable they get at the beginning of the school year is unlikely to be definitive – instead, it will be a compromise (method of successive approximation), since the task to be performed is defined as follows: obviously no teacher can teach in two classes simultaneously, but he or she should a continuous succession of lessons with no gaps, and the sequence of subjects per schoolday should make sense for each class.

The remarkable thing is that the same suppositions apply in the case of this so-called timetable problem as with the Travelling-Salesman-Problem: if n (the number of teachers) and m (the number of classes) are very large, trial and error will not lead to a satisfactory result. Oddly enough, though, if a good (polynomial time bounded) solution were found, it would follow that a good solution in the same sense existed for the timetable problem, and it would make sense to go on hunting for one. The converse also applies: if a proof of statement (a) were found for the Traveling-Salesman-Problem, we would know that no solution existed for the timetable problem, either. The argument also applies in the other direction: if it can be proved that no tractable solution exists for the timetable problem, then none exists for the Travelling-Salesman-Problem.

The following selection of examples has worked extremely well in the classroom: one presents the timetable problem verbally only, and then goes on to the so-called clique problem as a further instance of an NP complete problem. It is very easy to illustrate this by drawing a graph [11] with 5 nodes and 8 edges (Fig 4), with no need for previous knowledge in mathematics.

As with the Traveling-Salesman-Problem, there is an opportunity here to return to the concept of a model: here the nodes correspond to persons, and an edge is drawn if a special relationship exists between two persons. A subset of nodes and edges is called a clique if an edge exists between every pair of nodes.

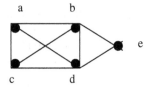

**Fig. 4.** Graph with 5 nodes and a clique of four defined by a, b, c, d

In our experience classwork is enhanced by a discussion of this issue, together with a reference to the fact that more than a thousand problems equivalent to the two presented here are known [1]. Here Informatics teachers are confronted with the same didactic problems as their colleagues in the natural sciences, who are obliged to draw attention in their teaching to any number of unresolved issues. In our view it is didactically worthwhile to point out the limits of a discipline without explaining the underlying formal basic principles.

As a special aid in connexion with this topic, a study guide has been added to the eLearning version of the preparatory course in informatics [10]– see section 3.2.

As regards, first, the exact definition of "tractable" by means of "big" O notation with a polynomial to describe run-time complexity and, second, the definition of "computable, but intractable", we advise against tackling this in secondary education. Even if familiarity with polynomials can be assumed, the definition of O(f(n)) for time complexity is hard for pupils to grasp and should not be thrust upon them.

### 2.6  Information, Language, Alphabet

The **representation of information** by a code, and the distinction between the form of this representation and its significance, i.e. between **syntax** and **semantics**, are further basic concepts in informatics and imply the definition of information in contrast to **data** and **knowledge**. The concept of **language** is closely linked to syntax and semantics; this includes programming languages, since syntax is a set of rules for constructing words, plus the rule that only words constructed in this way belong to the language. Semantics defines the meaning of these **words** in a language.

Then again, language involves the concept of an **alphabet**, since a language consists of a set of words over the alphabet, while an alphabet is defined as a set of symbols drawn from a supply of signs.

While presenting the concept of the syntax of a language, one is bound to raise the issue of how to describe syntax. This leads us on to "metalanguage", and we recall that when we were discussing models we referred to a metamodel, as diagrammed in Fig. 1. And we also briefly referred, in our treatment of recursion, to EBNF, a concept of a metalanguage to describe syntax.

It seems clear, though, that while there are no didactic snags involved in presenting the concepts of an alphabet, a code and formal languages in secondary education, given their direct relevance to practical work (programming languages), one runs up against the limits of what is feasible in the case of metalanguages such as EBNF. If one decides to avoid programming languages altogether as instances of formal languages at this stage, possible alternatives are: the rules for writing syntactically correct mathematical formulae or musical notation. The latter is particularly suitable, inasmuch as it includes semantic annotations (volume: piano, forte; tempo: presto, etc.)!

## 2.7 Relations

Of course a **classification** of data with respect to their properties, their **structure** and their **relations** belongs to the concepts of long-term validity with which properties such as **symmetry** or **equivalence**, and thus **equivalence classes**, can be explained.

The list of concepts given here is purely exemplary and anything but exhaustive; it is meant to encourage further discussion. However, our aim is to show that in the context of all-round education informatics teaching must be concerned not with technological artefacts, but with concepts of long-term validity, and can at the same time be organized to link up with other subjects (here with mathematics); this also applies in reverse.

# 3  Ways of Putting the New Media to Work

From the various figures it is already clear to what extent the new media and eLearning can help to represent these "unchanging values" in informatics more effectively. At FIM and also at IFI eLearning has been an important issue for years now; at FIM the first steps in this direction were taken 20 years ago, when CBT (Computer-Based Training) courses (concerned with programming, operating systems etc.) were developed and offered as an enhancement of traditional teaching.

## 3.1  What Has Been Developed

From the focus on eLearning several tools have taken shape; these have been in use in teaching for some years now. In particular, FIM has developed the WeLearn.Framework, which is constantly being enlarged in scope; it currently comprises the components, such as an open, easy-to-use eLearning environment (WeLearn) of universal applicability; didactic models for use at universities, in schools and in adult education; various tools and courses (in particular to implement our ideas about introducing students to informatics) to enhance teaching in the final years of secondary education.

Here we draw attention to [5],[8] and [10]. One study [7] has investigated how well the learning material and the learning environment provided were accepted.

## 3.2  "Propaedeutic in Informatics"

A key element in realizing our ideas about introducing informatics consists of specially prepared teaching and learning material available to students both via the WeLearn platform and on CD. "Propaedeutic in Informatics" is an introductory course for informatics students held by FIM at the JKU Linz. It regularly takes place in the winter semester; and involves blended learning [4] as a didactic model: here lectures and phases of self-organized study alternate. In the summer semester the subject matter is treated again, for the benefit of working students, other latecomers and interested pupils in the final years of secondary education (see below); in this case, though, the course consists of a kick-off meeting followed exclusively by distance learning.

This course is provided not only at the JKU, but also – with a different setting – at the University of Zurich, where students of business informatics are familiarized with the topics discussed here, using the same electronic material. Parts of it have also been successfully incorporated into an academically oriented course at the FH Vorarlberg.

The electronic material currently available comprises:

- A study guide: guidance for self-organized study and an explanation of parts of the subject matter, presented in the form of a dialogue between youngsters, and aimed particularly at pupils in the final years of secondary education
- The entire study material in the form of illustrated, partly interactive HTML pages
- The study material in full as text, also available as printed lecture notes
- The full set of transparencies for individual lectures
- Applets, on the basis of which students can carry out experiments and simulations and thus penetrate the subject matter. The applets discussed in chapter 2 are included here.

As regards teaching in secondary education, the following should be borne in mind:

Parallel to the above forms, the electronic material is also issued to secondary schools, where it can be used for teaching informatics/in preparation for Informatics A level (see below). Secondary-school teachers with a teaching qualification in informatics use the eLearning material (available on CD) in class, or have installed their own WeLearn server, via which they not only make the study material available but also help their pupils with queries, by means of newsgroups. Attention should be drawn to the following rule at the JKU Linz: Students commencing a degree course in informatics at the JKU after passing Informatics A level need not attend the preparatory course in informatics, provided that the subject matter for A level roughly corresponds to the scope of the basic principles presented in this paper.

## 4  Conclusion and Outlook

People often say we live in a particularly fast-moving age – and this is especially true of the still young discipline of informatics. If we date the breakthrough in informatics to the 1960's, its history goes back less than 50 years, compared with a few thousand years in the case of mathematics. Informatics has developed extremely rapidly; particularly in the software field, the number of products available goes up by leaps and bounds, while their half-life diminishes dramatically. It thus seems logical and necessary to concentrate on the basic concepts, particularly in the field of secondary education. The fact is that purely product-related knowledge and skills in the narrow sense are inadequate, and in some cases already obsolete before pupils leave school. A more systematic grasp of these concepts and their interrelations is therefore not just desirable, but essential.

# Literature

1. Garey M.R., Johnson.D.S.: Computers and Intractability: A guide to the Theory of NP-Completeness, W.H. Freeman, San Francisco, 1979
2. Hubwieser P.: Modellierung in der Schulinformatik. LOG IN 19, Heft 1. S.24-29, 1999
3. Informatik als Grundbildung; Informatik Spektrum, Band 27, Heft 2-4, 2004
4. Loidl, S.: The Beautiful but challenging World of Elearning. In Auer, M. E. and Auer, U., editors, International Conference on Interactive Computer Aided Learning, The Future of Learning, Villach Austria, Kassel university press 2004, ISBN 3-89958-089-3
5. Loidl, S., Sonntag, M.: Using metadata in creating offline views of e-learning content; in: Auer, M., Auer, U. (Ed.): ICL; Learning Objects and Reusability of Content, Kassel university press 2003
6. Loidl, S. Mühlbacher, J, Schauer, H.: Preparatory Knowledge: Propaedeutic in Informatics, Propädeutisches Informatikwissen, http://welearn-lavista.fim.uni-linz.ac.at/ (english/german), 2004
7. Mühlbacher, J., Mühlbacher, S.C., Loidl, S.: Learning Arrangements and Settings for Distance Teaching/Coaching/Learning: Best Practice Report. In Hofer, C., Chroust, G. (Ed.) IDIMT – 2002
8. Paramythis, A., Loidl, S.: Adaptive Learning Environments and e-Learning Standards; in: Roy Williams (Eds.): Proceedings of the 2nd European Conference on e-Learning, Glasgow, 2003
9. Perlis, A.J.: Epigrams on programming. SIGPLAN Notices, 17 (9),1982
10. Propädeutikum aus Informatik, http://welearn.fim.uni-linz.ac.at, 2004
11. Rosen, K.H.: Discrete Mathmatics and its Applications, 5th Edition, McGraw-Hill, 2003
12. Schauer, H.: Langlebige Standards in einer schnelllebigen Welt, CD Austria, 5/2004

# A Pragmatic Approach to Spreadsheet Training Based Upon the "Projection–Screen" Model

Karin Hodnigg

Klagenfurt University, Institut für Informatiksysteme, Austria
karin@isys.uni-klu.ac.at

**Abstract.** Spreadsheets are part of the educational syllabus of instruction for secondary schools in Austria. They are mainly taught using applications, disregarding the fact that building spreadsheets is programming. But the programming nature of spreadsheets is undeniable. Data in cells is interconnected with a rather sophisticated formula language. Since the spreadsheet paradigm differs from common procedural or object-oriented paradigms that students may already be aware of, teaching spreadsheets is a complex task. Moreover, the data flow paradigm is a concept foreign to students or trainees.

Lack of proper paradigms or computational models even complicates the situation. Is there a so called spreadsheet didactics - and if not, how should it look like? Should teachers train spreadsheet applications or insist on building models before implementing? How should they consider the spreadsheet programming viewpoint - without students scaring away and without loosing the spreadsheet's charm since they are said to be easy to use? This paper presents the main problem fields, presents a didactical model, and finally presents some rather pragmatic advice on how to teach spreadsheets.

## 1 Introduction

Spreadsheets emerged in the late 1970's, with the first systems still looking like a common paper spreadsheet, where values and simple sum formulas could be put into. Things developed quite quickly, offering more than only two columns (or five in VisiCalc, respectively) to the user, with more elaborate functions, from text interface to the modern click and point (and drag-and-drop) interface of modern spreadsheet systems. Today the user is confronted with an enormous amount of rows and columns, a huge amount of sometimes very complex functions, tools and features. In our terms, but although the application environment has grown, little has changed concerning the very basic concepts.

Spreadsheet education is mainly based upon Microsoft's spreadsheet system "Excel". Students are taught to first input values, then formulas and then using the functions and features Excel offers. More precisely, problems and their solution space is reduced to features of the spreadsheet system. While teaching application specific features is convenient, it is in fact problematic, since this didactical approach implies training an application, not teaching programming.

R.T. Mittermeir (Ed.): ISSEP 2005, LNCS 3422, pp. 116–129, 2005.

Due to its simplicity, end-users tend to see "Excel" as just another office application. But the intuitive use of such applications where typing some values, building some sums is sufficient for most first results conceals the fact that building a spreadsheet is programming. Even without specific training, every user who can generate spreadsheets for the own domain. This ease of use (identifying what to do and how to do it) contributed to the sheets enormous success. We find various definitions of spreadsheets: One rudimentary, but basic definition declares the main objective of spreadsheet programs as *"manipulation and presentation of data found in tabular form"* [Fil98]. However, the fact that this idea dominates leads us to the fact that teachers have to insist on a clarification: Building a spreadsheet means programming. Generally, students are not confronted with any kind of data dependency paradigm, thus training the spreadsheet paradigm with its data referencing mechanisms is - in an non–obvious but nevertheless dangerous manner - full of pitfalls.

In this paper the notion of spreadsheets will rely on the "original paradigm", that is spreadsheets are functional programs in a tabular layout. Procedural extensions, such as VBA in Excel will not be considered. As already mentioned above, the elaborates of spreadsheet users are referred to as spreadsheet programs.

## 1.1   Business Relevance

Why should spreadsheets be taught? When talking about the importance of spreadsheets, the main issue is its common use:

- **Spreadsheets have great impact on business decisions.** Spreadsheets applications are to be found on nearly every desktop computer [Cle03]. Besides the very popular *Microsoft Excel*, one could imagine *OpenOffice*, *KCalc* or *Gnumeric*. Researches agree on the fact that a huge number of business decisions are based on information derived from spreadsheets. In [BCP+03], the authors insist that *"many [business decisions] are much more serious, affecting significant financial decisions and business transactions"*.
- **Spreadsheet systems are easy-to-use.** The success of spreadsheet systems is based on a rather simple, declarative formula language. End user programming is made possible without high development costs. Since spreadsheet applications already provide a simple model, the spreadsheet user can fit the problem into the cell matrix rather than building a new model from scratch. Thus, it is commonly believed that training efforts compared to conventional programming are remarkably reduced.

Hence the assumption that the spreadsheet language is a "programming language for the masses" [Mostöm, 1998] seems to be justified. The complexity of spreadsheets is underestimated, though.The implementation of spreadsheets is largely left to the "spreadsheet programmer". But one may not forget that spreadsheets are often used to solve very complex and evolving problems. Since quality is one of the main issues in spreadsheet research, one must consider a range of problem areas solely generating from the special nature of spreadsheets.

## 2   Didactical Considerations

If teachers and trainers are challenged to explain what spreadsheets are, the answer depends on grade of preparatory training in class. Explanations ranging from rather simple models ("cells are kinds of connected calculators") to sophisticated essays concerning data flow or graph reduction paradigms. All of these answers have their relevance - but none of them really fits.So, how do spreadsheet users work? Data and references to cells are put into the spreadsheet according to a mental model[1] or according to layout considerations[2]. This mental model is based upon more or less profound reflections on the problem spreadsheet users try to solve.

But in fact, spreadsheet users (students as well as teachers and/or trainers) do not consider themselves being programmers. [Cle03]. Since they do not see their work as software, they shy away if training is based upon the "programming approach". End users suppose that spreadsheets loose their charm of being "easy-to-use" and "easy-to-learn" if they talk about programming and not about using "Excel". Excel, though a brand name is quite often used as generic name for spreadsheet systems.

Spreadsheet development is often treated very informal despite the fact that *"many applications are large and complex, and development often involves interactions among multiple people"* [Pan00]. In [Pan00], [Cle03] and [CHM02] two different types of spreadsheet applications are clearly identified: On one hand, the short living, "scratch pad" use of spreadsheets, on the other hand, the long living problem modeling. Evolving problems lead to change requests to a spreadsheet. This spreadsheet program maintenance is commonly handled by mostly local and therefore dangerous adaptation to the new requirements. The maintainer' mental model may differ from the implemented model, though. The spreadsheet model the users have in mind is adapted - mostly without regarding further adaption needs or possible inconsistencies in the spreadsheet program. This is another issue spreadsheet training has to deal with.

A spreadsheet development process model and a quality assurance process are approaches already proposed (see [RPL89],[BBN03], [RB00]). But they are not commonly accepted among the spreadsheet community. Spreadsheets have to be treated as software - since the impact on business decision cannot be estimated high enough, spreadsheets have to fulfill high quality requirements. If the development process of spreadsheets cannot be influenced (due to the fact that end-users are unwilling to follow a structured software development process), serious verification and auditing strategies on spreadsheet programs have to be provided. Training must provide a deep insight into the spreadsheet paradigm (its strength, but also its weaknesses and pitfalls) to overcome these shortcomings.

---

[1] In the following referred as *spreadsheet model.*

[2] *"[Spreadsheet programs] are even special programs from the perspective that the placement of code is dependent on the layout of the result."* [ACM00].

## 2.1    Spreadsheet Characteristics

The spreadsheet paradigm relies on n-dimensional[3] presentation of data. There is a range of properties which are provided by spreadsheet applications to support the spreadsheet programmer.

- **The Tabular User Interface**

  Organizing data in cells, rows and columns, can help users to map their spreadsheet model into an already given and sophisticated framework rather to invent a new one bottom-up [Cle03], e.g. object-oriented or rule-based. The grid of a spreadsheet program can therefore be filled with data values, labels or formulas to solve the problem the end-user has.

- **Locality**

  Spreadsheet programmers tend not to think in global terms. Rather, they reduce the enormous complexity of their business problem by considering each cell being independent. Therefore, they concentrate on a very localized view. Training should incorporate this fact because scope is a fundamental concept to be grasped.

- **High-Level Constructs**

  The formula language is high-level and contains simple control constructs, e.g. the *if*-clause. It offers a number of arithmetic, financial, statistical and logical functions. Combining these constructs and displaying their intermediate results ends up in the very high expressivity of spreadsheets while not loosing simplicity.

- **Learning Rate**

  To start with a first useful spreadsheet program, only sparse knowledge of spreadsheet application specific constructs and spreadsheet paradigm is needed. As experience grows, the programmer acquires new constructs and uses them incrementally.

Combining an expressive high level programming language with a "powerful visual format" for data organization and display [NM90], spreadsheet applications provide a solid user programming environment. Thus, the strength of spreadsheets is characterized by Nardi and Miller [NM90].

1. **A limited set of high-level, task-specific operations**
   The declarative and expressive formula language impacts the modeling of spreadsheet programs.
2. **A strong visual format**
   The second major spreadsheet application element is the data layout. The tabular layout supports the solution of three crucial problems
   (a) *viewing data*, (b) *structuring data* and (c) *displaying data*.

---

[3] With n=2 for tabular layout or n=3 for possible further layout of data, e.g. data cubes.

## 2.2    Definitions on Spreadsheets

But to simplify further reading, some basic definitions are briefly reviewed.

A **cell address CA** is an n-tuple. In common two-dimensional spreadsheets, the *cell* address is a pair (row, column) that denotes the cell's location in the two-dimensional matrix. A *value* v is an element drawn from the set of values V = {Numbers} ∪ {Strings} ∪ {Error} ∪ {Undefined}.

A **spreadsheet S** consists of a set of cells. A *cell C* is represented by a triple $(ca : CA, v : Value, f(< arguments >) \Rightarrow Value)$, *ca* is the unique cell address, *v* is the value that is displayed. The value *v* results from formula evaluation *f* with $v = eval(f)$. In case of f being degenerated to a constant, *eval(f)* yields the identity of this constant.

Arguments to *function f* can be either constants or cell referencing functions. A *cell referencing function cref(src : CA, id : CA)* returns the value associated with the cell at address $src \oplus id$. *src* is the recipient cell's own address, *id* added for relative references.

The **spreadsheet formula language** is the basis for expressing formulas f. f is defined as $f(< arguments >) \Rightarrow value$. *f* is specified by a string, starting with "=" followed either by a function or by an operation either on constants or on cell references. Constants are not considered as input for the formula as there is no need for evaluation of a constant value unless the formula itself is (re-)evaluated.

A **spreadsheet program** is defined as a subset of the spreadsheet, containing all non-empty formula cells and cells that are absolutely referenced. Relatively referenced cells are only part of the spreadsheet program if they contain a formula. If they contain constants, they are considered as input cells. A **spreadsheet instance** then is the union of a spreadsheet program and its input data.

## 2.3    Graphical Representation

Cell references represent the data flow of a spreadsheet program. When building a conceptual model of a spreadsheet instance, a data dependency representation intuitively comes to mind. Cells are interconnected by references and information is passed on from one cell to another. Cell references represent the arcs where data flows. Different representations and different aggregations have been proposed to visualize data flow in spreadsheet programs. Some common ways to express these are:

- **Data Dependency Graph (DDG)**
  Every (defined or "content bearing") cell (of interest) in a spreadsheet is represented by a vertex, and relations between cells are represented by (directed) edges. This graph represents data dependencies between cells, as shown in Fig. 1 on the next page.
- **Set Relation Graph (SRG)**
  The Set Relation Graph is used to summarize the data dependency graph, since a look-up from a higher level may be of interest. In a set relation graph vertices are put into blocks or areas to visualize their dependency to other blocks.

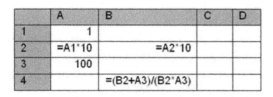

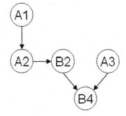

| | A | B | C | D |
|---|---|---|---|---|
| 1 | 1 | | | |
| 2 | =A1'10 | =A2'10 | | |
| 3 | 100 | | | |
| 4 | | =(B2+A3)/(B2'A3) | | |

**Fig. 1.** A Data Dependency Graph Example

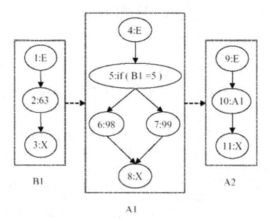

**Fig. 2.** A Cell Relation Graph example

- **Cell Relation Graph**
  Rothermel et.al. [BCP+03] define a cell relation graph that illustrates both cell execution paths and cell relationships. Entry and exit points are specially marked, the formulae (and their inherent control flows) are depicted, as illustrated in Fig. 2.

Representing a spreadsheet as data dependency graph serves a dual purpose. On one hand it is the basis for computing the evaluation sequence. On the other hand it might enhance the users conceptualisation of what was pinned down by a set of otherwise independent formulas that contain only references to their direct arguments. However, data flow semantics is not in all cases an appropriate model for spreadsheet semantics.

## 3    The Spreadsheet Paradigm

Generally, we agree on the fact that a spreadsheet program is software. If the very base of spreadsheet systems is considered, programming will be met. Data in cells is interconnected and modified to gain more information. Filby's definition above meets the definition of programming in this particular way. In [KCK+01],

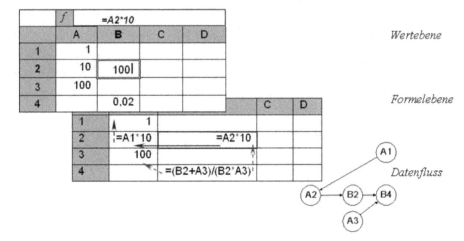

**Fig. 3.** The Spreadsheet Three Layer Concept

Burnett et. al. state that spreadsheets *"are not just mechanisms for organizing and displaying data: rather, they are programs that use formulas to transform inputs into outputs."*

According to [EM94], or more detailed to [Cle03] and [CRBK98], a spreadsheet is a matrix of cells with addresses that uniquely identify them. Every cell can contain a value or a formula. Formulae representing the *formula layer* compute their result values generally on the values of one ore more other cells. The value based upon the formula evaluation is displayed for every cell. This is the the so-called *value layer*. The formula can be either a built-in, application internal function or a *user-defined algorithm*, hiding behind a (probably misconceived) static value on the *formula layer*. The inherent nature of these two layers is one reason for the complexity of the spreadsheet paradigm.

Mittermeir et.al. [CHM02] and Panko [Pan00] emphasize Sajaniemi's statement that *"Computations in spreadsheets are hard to grasp and consequently many errors remain unnoticed. The problem with hidden errors lies in the invisibility of the structure of calculations"*[Saj98]. So let us take a closer look at the nature of spreadsheets and spreadsheet applications. In Fig. 3 (based upon Igarashi, [IMCZ98]) a model for the spreadsheet layer concept is shown, where arcs in the "formula layer" visualize data dependencies.

The tabular layout is augmented with a visual formula language. The invisibility of formulas and their immediate evaluation is probably one of the strongest ideas of spreadsheets. The invisibility of data flow causes cognitive overhead, since a spreadsheet user has to (iteratively) click into a cell, understand the formula and recognize all references[4] to get an overview over the spreadsheet model behind the spreadsheets. If a spreadsheet user wants to fully understand the (trivial) computation of cell B4 in Fig. 3, he/she has to analyze first the cells

---

[4] And recursively the formulas in these "referenced" cells, the transitive closure.

B2 and A3. Since B2 contains another computation based upon cell A2, cell A2 needs to be understood. A2 then references cell A1 that holds a constant. To understand how a computation in a spreadsheet program works, all transitively dependent cells have to be analyzed.

On the other hand, the concept to hide complexity eases the implementation. On the other hand, it complicates the comprehension of the "mental model". Characteristically for spreadsheets, there is no formal model and/or specification, but we may refer to a "mental model", the spreadsheet model, that builds the basis of the spreadsheet program. It is a fact that spreadsheets are poorly documented. Although there are some slightly helpful tools to visualize "relations" between cells, it is a non-trivial task to understand a spreadsheet program. Lack of a specification and lack of adequate documentation is a major software engineering issue.

## 4    A Computational Model

One is tempted to ask, whether there is such a thing as a "spreadsheet language" and if so, what this language might be. For a given product, it makes no difference, whether one types $= IF(A1 = B1; ...)$ or $= WENN(A1 = B1; ; ...)$. Likewise, it makes no difference, whether this command has been typed in, selected by mouse click from some panels, or copied and then edited from a cell holding a similar formula. The clue is that the system provides the concept of case discrimination and this concept is presented in different linguistic forms to the user.

But the differences in the linguistic form are rather shallow and users have to develop a conceptual model resting on the concepts behind the functions implemented in various spreadsheet products. Since all of these functions rest on common mathematical concepts, users must not be blamed if they assume that the sheet behaves in exactly the way they expect these mathematical functions to behave. The functional programming paradigm clearly contrasts "conventional" programming. The spreadsheet language is highly declarative as it "emphasizes on the evaluation of expressions" [Montigel, 2002] and is mathematically traceable.

Spreadsheet languages focus on spatial relations of data, not on the temporal sequence. Nonetheless, the spreadsheet development process has some specialties that influences the resulting spreadsheet. The drag-and-drop approach of inputting formulas and then dragging them over a (geometric) row or column area to do incremental or similar computations result in a geometric pattern. This specific pattern influenced by the spreadsheet application. Different spreadsheet system implementations provide different heuristics for these copy-and-paste/drag-and-drop editor operations[5]. Whether the value of a constant is increased, when a formula is dragged over a cell range, or not, is part of the spreadsheet language. However, defining all components of a spreadsheet language as such is still a "hot topic" in the spreadsheet community.

---

[5] For a detailed discussion, please see [HK04].

Spreadsheets do not lack control flow, a rather difficult programming concept, "it is just conceptually simple" [NM90]. The programmer can only specify control flow on the cell level with *if*-clauses. The absence of an explicit control flow is one of the strengths of spreadsheet programming as simplicity is a main success factor. The user stated formulas contain an *implicit* flow of control as any cell can reference any other. Dependent cells are immediately adapted when a value in a related cell changes.

Thus, the immediate feedback encourages *a style of trial and error, cutting and pasting, copying and modifying* [ACM00] in the development process. Users can simply and immediately check whether the cell value corresponds to the value they expected. Spreadsheet systems are easy to use but implementing "good" spreadsheet programs is not simple! Even so, formal methods and a software methodology is not part of the training. It is probable that rigorous formal methods would be misplaced in spreadsheet training since we are talking about end user programming. However, training has to be based upon the "right" paradigms and models.

## 4.1   Established Paradigms

How to teach spreadsheets? Is there a possibility to rely upon an already established paradigm in spreadsheet training? The graphical representation as discussed above leads us to the assumption: We have data dependencies - why not taking the data flow paradigm? Moreover, we have a graph representation - why not taking the graph reduction paradigm? Both paradigms seem to fit - but they are slightly different [HK04]. In fact, they differ enough to cause misconceptions about spreadsheets.

- **Different Semantics**
  Data flow does not fit, since in a spreadsheet program, nothing flows. Graph reduction would correspond to the evaluation of a formula's result, but differs in other aspects.
- **Persistence of intermediate results**
  Neither graph reduction nor data flow corresponds to the persistence of intermediate results. Evaluation is a non-destructive operation, the input values (and immediate results) persist. A spreadsheet program does not define one distinctive result, moreover, intermediate results are visible to the user.
- **Incorporation of loops**
  A very obvious difference is the incorporation of a loop concept in both the discussed paradigms. Loops, however, are totally foreign to the traditional spreadsheet paradigm[6].
- **Interactivity**
  The second major difference is the immediate feedback - and the interactive evaluation process. Neither graph reduction evaluation strategies nor data flow evaluation expresses the power of spreadsheet evaluation. Changes in a

---

[6] Although spreadsheet applications support the notion of circular references, this is more a dangerous and confusing issue.

spreadsheet program are immediately propagated through the program to keep the program consistent.

To a spreadsheet developer who starts from scratch, development of a spreadsheet is much like building a house with cells being bricks that have to be placed somewhere upon a sheet. The data dependencies on such a sheet leads us to a notion of interdependent calculation devices. If neither graph reduction semantics nor data flow semantics work, we have to take a closer look at the kind of interdependency.

## 4.2    Scope and Visibility

The interactivity of the spreadsheet evaluation process then seems most important, since this is a foreign concept to both paradigms. Interactive evaluation means that as soon as a cell has changed, its dependent cells change, too. This immediate change propagation when a cell "looks" at cells it is referencing, motivates a notion of observer and observed cells. According to the observer pattern common to programmers (for a detailed discussion please see [Lar02]), one has to imagine a network of cells that observe ("look" at) their referenced cells.

Fig. 4 revisits our small data dependency example. Let us take a closer look at cell *B2*. To compute the result of its formula, a cell has to "look" at all cell it references. B2, for example, has to see A2. Since A2 references A1, A2 has to see A1 and transitively, B2 "sees" A1. So in a spreadsheet program, an implicit visibility order is given. B2 does not explicitly look at cells that it is not referencing. This concept of visibility is not supported by any of the paradigms presented above, so **visibility** must be added to the visualization of a common "interconnected rubber band calculators" spreadsheet conception.

On the other hand, cells that are referencing B2 should not be visible to B2 since we do not allow circular references: B2, for example, cannot reference B4 without building the very dangerous construct of a circular reference. According to the simple brick model, a brick rests upon underlying bricks but cannot rest upon bricks that lies upon it. Another peculiarity has to be considered: A cell *c* can be referenced from a cell anywhere on the sheet, except cells that are somehow transitively referenced by this cell *c*. This concept of global **scope** is the second main idea of the now presented "projection-screen" model.

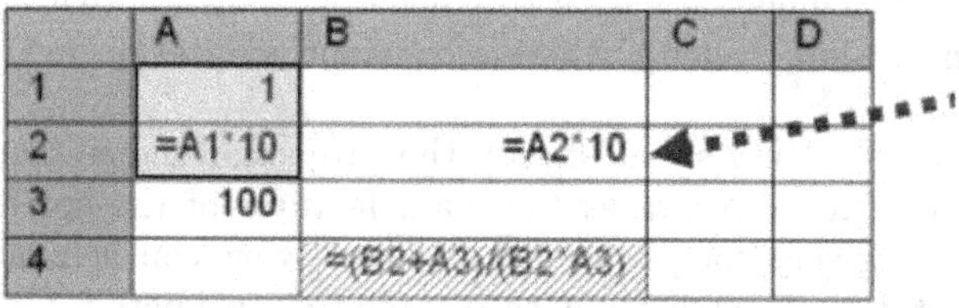

**Fig. 4.** Scope and Visibility Example

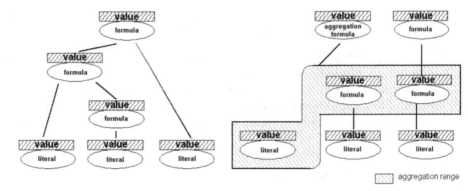

**Fig. 5.** Projection-Screen examples

### 4.3    The "Projection–Screen" Model

In this context, it makes sense to treat a cell as a kind of projection-screen device that "reads" the values of its source cells (cells it is referencing), calculates its result according to its formula and represents the result on its screen. This result then can be read by any other cell, that is not part of the calculation process so far (since this would represent a circular reference). With this notion, aggregative formulae (with range references A2:A10) can be visualized by "spotlights", comprising all cells that are source for the aggregative formula. Fig. 5 shows how such a network of projection-screen devices could look like. The first example is a short (two-level reference) formula, the second one describes an aggregative and non-aggregative formula.

As presented in [HK04], there are some common "patterns" that can be found in spreadsheet programs. These patterns result from the cut-and-paste and drag-and-drop development of spreadsheets and may be a good basis for spreadsheet training.

### 4.4    The Pragmatic Spreadsheet Training

Some ideas presented in this paper are now condensed in a rather informal, pragmatic approach on spreadsheet education. The pragmatic nature of this last section arises from the necessity of being more general since the notion of "constant change" is native to education. This approach should reflect the school and training reality, where a constant adaptation to the student's needs is necessary.

To train students spreadsheets, the projection-screen-model could be very helpful, since it incorporates the main features of the spreadsheet paradigm, without being very complicated. The simple view can help students to develop a notion of data dependency with regards to immediate feedback. Students can simply understand how cells can be interconnected. Changes in a spreadsheet program can result in changes anywhere on the sheet (immediately). To avoid that this fact remains unnoticed, the projection-screen model is very helpful.

Students have some kind of interactive network in mind rather than a "static" data graph where evaluation takes place after everything is defined.

1. **It is simple, but building a spreadsheet implies programming**
   Students should be aware of what they are doing and that they are implementing programs. Incremental learning is a very strong fact, but to shape the opinions right away from the beginning is useful, when complex problems have to be solved later on. To build a theoretical basis using the projection-screen model would make sense. The basic ideas of spreadsheet programming are explained with this model as well as the fact that students are programming when using a spreadsheet system.

2. **Be aware of what spreadsheets are (and what they are not)**
   A spreadsheet application offers a huge amount of different features. It is very important that students comprehend the limits of spreadsheets. E.g., those are reached when iterative computation is needed where the number of iterations varies. The projection-screen model could be very helpful for emphasizing the main program concept. Students should be aware of computation "outside" the cells, e.g. with *VB-Scripts* or *Makros*. These values are constant values, they do not adapt and are therefore very dangerous since they miss an adaptivity which is not obvious.

3. **One step after another - solution cell by cell**
   Beginners tend to "overload" a formula, with several functions within a single cell. To stay comprehensible, it is reasonable to produce more intermediate results. One formula for one purpose. Students should be urged to reduce the formula complexity and use some common spreadsheet program patterns as presented in [HK04], since referring to established patterns can ease the understanding of spreadsheet programs.

4. **Document it!**
   Documentation of a spreadsheet is very important due to an inevitable maintenance process. Nevertheless, the task of documentation is neglected. Reuse and maintenance of spreadsheets thus become very complex. To train that documentation in a spreadsheet program is necessary and meaningful may have an impact on this obvious deficiency of current spreadsheets programs[7].

5. **Thus, think before you do it!**
   As with most modeling languages, the projection-screen model provides one main benefit: "Think, before you do it."' To analyze a problem before simply typing a formula that could match is badly needed. Instead of just trying to solve a given problem, students have to model their problem with a rather simple framework. The main issue here is: *"Think more global when modeling, but solve problems local when implementing it!"*

Learning needs problems. Thus, teachers as well as trainers do have to think of appropriate examples (transcending the common "'Open file, change cell $Xn$"'-approach). Concrete modeling of a spreadsheet program, handling the complex

---

[7] Labeling cells areas is (not yet) part of the projection-screen model, but would be an interesting research topic.

nature of the spreadsheet paradigm has to be taken into account if new examples and solutions for spreadsheet education are provided.

## 5    Conclusion

This paper presented ongoing work on spreadsheet training efforts. Spreadsheet training is necessary, but contends with some basic difficulties. To be able to put spreadsheet training on a fundamental basis, this paper first presented some major problem areas and already proposed definitions and visualization concepts. To meet training requirements, a proper definition and a delimitation of the spreadsheet paradigm is essential to provide a appropriate didactical model.

I do not claim this approach to be complete, but it should be useful for spreadsheet education to depart from pure application training towards a more sophisticated and elaborate view on spreadsheet programming. Spreadsheet training should be handled with the same carefulness as teaching any programming language. As the proposed model deals with main spreadsheet issues, it inspires much confidence that it will be helpful in classroom situations.

## References

[ACM00]   Yirsaw Ayalew, Markus Clermont, and Roland T. Mittermeir. Detecting errors in spreadsheets. *EuSpRIG 2000 Symposium - Spreadsheet Risks, Audit and Development Methods*, 2000.

[BBN03]   Daniel Ballinger, Robert Biddle, and James Noble. Spreadsheet structure inspection using low level access and visualization. In *Proceedings of the Fourth Australian user interface conference on User Interfaces 2003 - Volume 18*, pages 91 – 94, 2003.

[BCP⁺03]  Margaret Burnett, Curtis Cook, Omkar Pendse, Gregg Rothermel, Jay Summet, and Chris Wallace. End-user software engineering with assertions in the spreadsheet paradigm. *International Conference on Software Engineering 2003, Portland, Oregon*, 2003.

[CHM02]   Markus Clermont, Christian Hanin, and Roland Mittermeir. A spreadsheet auditing tool evaluated in an industrial context. *Proceedings of the 3rd Annual Symposium of the EuSpRIG*, 2002.

[Cle03]   Markus Clermont. *A Scalable Approach to Spreadsheet Visualization*. PhD thesis, University of Klagenfurt, 2003.

[CRBK98]  Ed Huai-Hsin Chi, John Riedl, Phillip Barry, and Joseph Konstan. Principles for information visualization spreadsheets. *IEEE ComputerGraphics*, 18(4):p.30–38, August 1998.

[EM94]    Skip Ellis and Carlos Maltzahn. Collaboration with spreadsheets. *Journal of the Brazilian Computer Society*, 1(Special Edition on CSCW):pp.15–23, 1994.

[Fil98]   William G. Filby. *Spreadsheets in Science and engineering*. Springer, 1998.

[HK04]    Clermont M. Hodnigg K., Mittermeir R. Computational models of spreadsheet devlopment: Basis for educational approaches. *Proceedings of EuSpRIG 2004*, 5:p.153–168, 2004.

[IMCZ98]    Takeo Igarashi, Jock Mackinlay, Bay-Wei Chang, and Polle Zellweger. Fluid visualization of spreadsheet structures. *Proceedings of the 1998 IEEE Symposium on Visual Languages*, 1998.

[KCK+01]    Vijay Krishna, Curtis Cook, Daniel Keller, Joshua Cantrell, Chris Wallace, Margaret Burnett, and Gregg Rothermel. Incorporating incremental validation and impact analysis into spreadsheet maintenance: An empirical study. In *Proceedings of the International Conference on Software Maintenance*, November 2001.

[Lar02]    Craig Larmann. *Applying UML and Patterns*. Prentice Hall, 2002.

[NM90]    Bonnie A. Nardi and James R. Miller. The spreadsheet interface: A basis for end user programming, 1990.

[Pan00]    Raymond Panko. What we know about spreadsheet errors. *Journal of End Users Computing's Special Issue on Scling Up End User Development Volume 10, No. 2, Spring 1998, p. 15-21*, 2000.

[RB00]    Vaclav Rajlich and Keith Bennet. Software maintainance and evolution: A roadmap. In Anthony Finkelstein, editor, *The future of Software Engineering*, 2000.

[RPL89]    B. Ronen, R. Palley, and H. Lucas. Spreadsheet analysis and design. *Communications of the ACM 32 (1)*, pages p. 84–93, 1989.

[Saj98]    Jorma Sajaniemi. Modelling spreadsheet audit: A rigorous approach to automatic visualization, 1998.

# A Strategy to Introduce Functional Data Modeling at School Informatics

Markus Schneider

Institut für Informatik,
Technische Universität München,
Boltzmannstraße 3, 85748 Garching, Germany
`markus.schneider@in.tum.de`

**Abstract.** Having analyzed standard applications by use of object oriented modeling in the 6th and 7th grade functional data modeling is the first topic to be discussed in the 8th grade of the mandatory subject informatics at the Bavarian Gymnasium. First, the data flow modeling technique is introduced and the resulting data flow models are implemented on spreadsheets maintaining the geometrical structure of the diagrams. Yet the first data flow models show the necessity to introduce the concept of functions in full strength. In contrast to the mathematical way the concept of functions is introduced informally using graphical concepts. In a second phase the data flow models are transformed to one complex term. Exemplarily an appropriate algorithm to perform this transformation is presented. Boolean functions and conditional expressions deepen the modeling technique and introduce further central concepts of informatics. Conditional expressions are discussed as functions of arity 3 modeling again commonly known structures. Finally iterative calculations are simulated using a step by step strategy.

## 1 Introduction

Some reader may wonder why functional data modeling opens the mandatory subject informatics in the 8th grade, since until now the so called classical way was favored, i.e. the teaching of some "hard" programming skills, namely imperative-like control structures. Moreover, one will be reminded through the attribute "functional" to the paradigm of functional programming. Will be recursion the content of the 8th grade? Not to raise such fears one has to emphasize that functional modeling is a pure sequential modeling technique. Only the causal structure and the functional data flow of a context can be represented; recursion or loop-like structure cannot and should not be modeled.

On the other hand, a new empirical study on the learning process of students at university level [5] has shown that students have lowest problems with the functional modeling technique but greater problems with imperative one. So it is obvious to start yet at school with functional data modeling (evidentially, without the concept of recursion). Recently P.Hubwieser [4] has presented the basic principles of functional data flow modeling for the 8th grade. The present paper deals with the details of this

R.T. Mittermeir (Ed.): ISSEP 2005, LNCS 3422, pp. 130–144, 2005.

concept and offers a strategy to teach functional data modeling. The strategy results from an experimental course carried out from May 2004 to July 2004 in the 9th grade of a Gymnasium near Munich.

The first chapter presents the technical elements of data flow modeling and the transformation of a model to spreadsheet applications. The second chapter, a more mathematical one, introduces the general concept of functions informally using graphical means. Afterwards the third chapter deals with the algorithm to compress the data flow diagram to one term and give heuristics to implement the term in concrete spreadsheet applications. The fourth and fifth chapters on Boolean functions and the conditional expression deepen the concepts discussed so far and introduce at the same time central elements of informatics. The sixth and last chapter discusses problems demanding iterative strategies.

## 2  Data Flow Modeling and Spreadsheets

Data flow modeling is one of the central abilities to be taught in the 8th grade in Informatics according the new curriculum of the Bavarian Gymnasium. Similar to the suggestion of Hubwieser [4] we use simplified data flow diagrams containing the following elements: Data storages represented by rectangles, data flows represented by arrows and data transforming processes represented by ellipses.

### 2.1  An Introductive Example

Introducing new modeling techniques at school, one has to show students the benefits resulting from such a technique. Therefore one has to choose examples of which the term structure is not obvious but of which the data flow is of intuitive evidence. This seems to be a contradiction. But this is not the case: Often students have the raw idea to solve algebraic problems, but they cannot transform their idea to term structure. We illustrate this by an example:

*Dr. Mabuse has bought an apartment for 140 000 Euro. Having a capital of 70 000 Euro he borrows the half of this amount from a credit institution with an interest rate of 8% per year. Renting the apartment, he wants to finance the credit, i.e. to pay the interests. Calculate the monthly rent (obviously exclusive of heating) for the apartment*

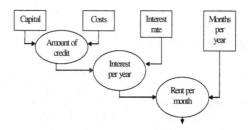

**Fig. 1.** The Data flow diagram of the introductive example

This problem is simple but complex enough not to apply some predefined formula. To manage such problems, data flow modeling acts as a mediator between the contexts formulated in natural language and algebraic expressions. First we establish the data flow diagram as shown in Figure 1. Up to now, no algebraic elements are used. The diagram shows only the data flow and the causal relations between the objects to be calculated.

Next, the transformation processes will be modeled in detail using standard mathematical functions (Figure 2); finally the resulting detailed model can simply be projected to spreadsheets as shown in Figure 3.

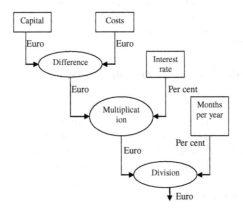

**Fig. 2.** The detailed model of the introductive example

| | A | B | C | D | E |
|---|---|---|---|---|---|
| 1 | Capital | | Costs | | |
| 2 | | | | | |
| 3 | | = A1 – C1 | | Interest | |
| 4 | | | | | |
| 5 | | | | | |
| 6 | | | = B3*D3 | | 12 |
| 7 | | | | | |
| 8 | | | | = C6/E6 | |
| 9 | | | | | |
| 10 | | | | | |

**Fig. 3.** The implementation of the model in figure 2

The detailed model in Figure 2 contains a non standard element: The arrows are labeled with the formats of the data elements. This technique has tried and tested in practice and it has been turned out that these annotations are of great importance for the transformation process from data flow model to spreadsheet implementation. The students are forced to model the various formats and the adjustment of the format can be embedded in the automatic transformation process from data flow model to spreadsheet implementation. For standard spreadsheet applications this adjustment is really necessary, since most operations are polymorphic and incorrect formats results in subtle behavior. Moreover, this technique prepares the concept of the signature of a function discussed below.

A hint ought to be made with respect to the naming of the transformation processes: The above figure uses the identifiers `Difference`, `Multiplication` and `Division`. Some reader may ask why standard binary operations have not been used. The answer will be given in the next chapter where we present an algorithm to compress a data flow diagram to one single term. The use of binary operations would make this algorithm more complex.

## 2.2 The Learning Targets

Analyzing the above example one recognizes the learning targets of the first phase:

- Students get to know the data flow diagram as a technique to model the functional behavior of problems from the everyday life and they are able to apply this knowledge.
- Students are able to transform data flow models to spreadsheet implementation maintaining the geometrical structure of the diagram, i.e. they will not derive compressed terms. This transformation will be done in the following way:
  - Data elements and transformation processes correspond to spreadsheet cells.
  - Transformation processes correspond to functions or binary operations, often introduced with an "="-sign.
  - Arrows correspond to references inside functions.
  - The format of the cells has to be adjusted according to the annotations of the arrows.
- In the first phase we do not discuss the compressed term structure of the whole problem. Instead we transform the data flow diagram intuitively to the spreadsheet as shown above. So we avoid the discussion of the problem of binary operations and their corresponding prefix-notation. This will be the topic of the next section.

## 2.3 Further Examples

Evidently, the data flow modeling technique described has to be deepened by suitable examples. The introductory example mentioned above illustrates basic conditions for suitable problems:

- The problem should be embedded in everyday contexts, so that no standard mathematical formula can be applied.
- The term representing the solution of the problem ought to contain the standard functions of spreadsheet applications.

Considering the current curriculum of Bavarian Gymnasia (secondary schools), tasks like the following are conceivable:

- The so called "text-problems" ("Textaufgaben" in German), where the formal structure of the solution is not obvious, but the data flows are of intuitive evidence (standard mathematical textbooks offer numerous examples),

- Percentage and interest calculations as shown above,
- Calculation of the mean value by explicit means,
- The simplification of expressions containing fractions; i.e. these expressions have to be simplified using addition, subtraction, multiplication and division. Here the greatest common divisor (or the lowest common multiple) plays an essential role,
- The areas (volumes) of figures (bodies) composed by standard geometric figures (bodies).

## 3   The Concept of Functions

According to the current mathematic curriculum of the Bavarian Gymnasium functions are discussed in the middle of the $8^{th}$ grade. As shown in the previous section, data flow modeling uses this concept from the very beginning in this grade. Moreover, this modeling technique works with functions having arbitrary arity. Therefore, the concept of function has to be introduced yet in the informatics course. It is enough, though, to introduce this concept in an informal manner, since the formal discussion of this concept lies beyond the scope of school mathematics and (evidently) of school informatics.

### 3.1   Functions of Arity 1

Text books on school mathematics define the function (evidently the function of arity one) as "a map from some set $D$ to another set $I$ which associates each element of $D$ a unique element of $I$" (see for example Barth et al., [1]). The interpretation of this definition by a suitable data flow diagram results in the one given in Figure 4.

**Fig. 4.** The data flow diagram of a function having arity one

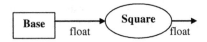

**Fig. 5.** A concrete example of function having arity one

The basic idea for the introduction of functions in informatics is to describe a function as graphical concept. Therefore, a function is defined as a process which transforms each element of the data type D to a unique element of data type I. Evidently, at school one should proceed in an inductive manner and discuss known functions like `square` or `clean`. These functions have data flow diagrams like shown in Fig. 5.

Having introduced functions of arity 1 as graphical objects the functional behavior of such objects may be characterized textually in a second step using signatures, e.g. `square (base: float): float`, which is very close to the mathematical way of function definition. Moreover, the signature smoothes the way to the syntax of the function call which is nothing than a textual representation of the data flow diagram (without data types).

## 3.2 Functions of Arity 2

Having introduced the principals of functions of arity 1, it is natural to proceed with functions of arity 2 using functions like

```
power (base : float, exponent : nat ) : float,
gcd (arg1 : nat, arg2 : nat ) : nat,
concatenate (text1 : string, text2 : string) : string.
```

It is helpful to start with functions having prefix-notation. The data flow diagram of such a function suggests the definition of a function of arity 2 as a process which transforms two arbitrary elements of the data types $D_1$, and $D_2$ to a unique element of the data type $I$ (figure 6).

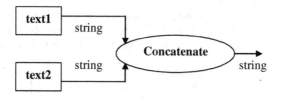

**Fig. 6.** The data flow diagram of a function having arity two

Again, the structure of the function call is just the textual representation of the data flow diagram resulting from the signature by dropping the data types. To avoid confusions about the order of the arguments inside the function call we use the convention that the order of arguments corresponds to the graphical order from left to right.

*Binary operations and prefix-notation*
Introducing the concept of functions in such a manner, we have no problems with binary operations and their interpretation as functions of arity 2, since the function is introduced primarily as a graphical concept, whereas the binary operation is a concept of the implementation. Performing this purely syntactical conversion students recognize intuitively the equivalence of functions having arity 2 and binary operations. In contrast to the data flow diagram and its textual representation the implementation is application-specific and some applications offer several implementation possibilities: For example in Microsoft-Excel, the exponentiation can be implemented both as the term x^y and `power(x;y)`; similarly, the addition in the standard form A1+B1 can be also expressed in the form `sum(A1;B1)`.

### 3.3 Functions of Arity Zero

Functions of arity zero ought to be discussed carefully since some standard spreadsheet functions seem to have arity zero but in fact they use hidden variables. For example the standard spreadsheet operations `today()` or `random()`: The result of these functions depends on the date in the case of the operation `today()` or some other influences (state of the computer, etc.), i.e. we have global, hidden variables, which determine the result.

In contrast the function `Pi()` is a function of arity zero; constant data defined in a data flow diagram can also be interpreted as function of arity zero. Though the number π will formally be introduced yet in the 9th/10th grade, most students know this number informally and the comparison of the functions `today()` or `random()` with the function `Pi()` may be instructive for the students. However, the interprettation of data elements as function of arity zero is perhaps to abstract.

## 4    From Data Flow Diagram to Compressed Terms

Yet in the first phase of data flow modeling some students will intuitively compress some parts of the data flow diagram to one expression, since this shortens the implementation process. This chapter deals with the formal way to compress a data flow diagram to one single term. Discussing the data flow diagram for addition of fractions we illustrate the principal way. For brevity we restrict ourselves to the data flow diagram describing the calculation of the numerator of the result (shown in Fig. 7):

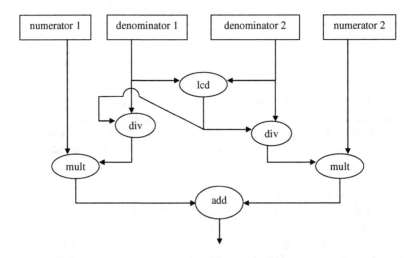

**Fig. 7.** Addition of fractions: The calculation of the numerator

We derivate the structure of the compressed term using a "bottom up" strategy. The outermost function is the function "`add`" in the last (5) row of the data flow diagram. So we have initially the textual representation

```
add( ? , ? ).
```

Were the question mark denotes the result of the inner function calls. The arguments of the function `add` are the elements of the fourth row and one gets:

```
add( mult(?,?), mult(?,?)).
```

Inserting the arguments of the function `mult` results in

```
add( mult(nominator1,div(?,?)),
     mult(div(?,?),nominator2)).
```

Translating the remaining graphical elements, we get finally:

```
add( mult(nominator1,
          div(lcd(denumerator1,denumerator2),
          denumerator1)),
     mult(div(lcd(denumerator1,denumerator2),
          denumerator2))
          nominator2)).
```

Initially, the term presented is nothing than a textual representation of the data flow diagram. To implement this term into a concrete spreadsheet application it has to be adjusted to the respective application. Dependent on the application, some parts of the term have to be translated to infix-notation or to special function-identifiers. Best, one starts with the innermost terms, i.e. with the function `div` in the above example and proceeds outwards. So, one gets first:

```
add( mult(nominator1,
          lcd(denumerator1,denumerator2)
          /denumerator1))),
     mult((lcd(denumerator1,denumerator2)
          /denumerator2))),
          nominator2)).
```

After two further translations we finally have:

```
(nominator1*(lcd(denumerator1,denumerator2)
/denumerator1))
+((lcd(denumerator1,denumerator2)/denumerator2)*
nominator2).
```

The application-specific term presented here is suitable for standard application as Microsoft-Excel for example.

## 5   Boolean Data Types and Boolean Functions

Some reader will wonder why to discuss Boolean expressions and functions? What is the benefit of such a unit, since this topic has disappeared yet from some curricula in mathematics? On one hand, the Boolean data type is a fundamental data type in informatics appearing yet in simple expressions containing relational operators like "=", ">" or "<". On the other hand, the conditional expression, which will be discussed later, contains Boolean functions as a central element.

Sometimes, the discussion of this topic at school is carried out abstract emphasizing primarily the mathematical relevance. But as the some textbooks on formal logic (see. for example R. Winter, [6]) show, this must not be the case: Taking statements and contexts from everyday life, students realize that Boolean functions are a natural element of our communication. As outlined above, one has to start with examples were the mathematical solution is not obvious but were the model contains standard Boolean functions of spreadsheet applications.

What class of problems might be suitable? Standard spreadsheet operations offer some Boolean functions: the logic standard operations and the polymorphic Boolean functions: greater, less, equal. The last three functions work both on numbers and strings. Since the lexicographic order ought to be well known to students on an informal level (telephone book, class list, etc.) problems based on the lexicographic order seem suitable to introduce the concept of Boolean functions.

## 5.1 Boolean Data Types

First of all the concept of Boolean data type has to be introduced. This can be done analyzing some simple statements, i.e. sentences which are either true or false:

- In an encyclopedia the name "Radlbacher" is found first, the name "Wastlhofer" behind.
- The name "Häberle" is equal to the name "Häfele".

To delimit the concept of statement from other structures one ought to compare this statements with other grammatical structures, for example with questions like "What is your name?" or with orders like "Write down your name!"

Modeling the data flow of the above statements one gets the data flow diagram shown in Figure 8:

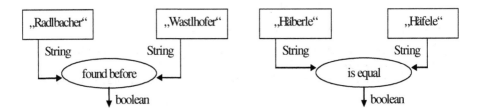

**Fig. 8.** Examples to motivate the use of boolean expressions

Interpreting these statements as functions they have a result value which is either true or false, i.e. the result value is of the Boolean data type. Therefore, we define Boolean functions as transformation processes of arbitrary arity and Boolean result values.

To implement the above examples we turn to the textual representation:

- foundBefore("Radlbacher", "Wastlhofer")
- isEqual("Häberle", "Häfele")

Implementing these terms, the students are really surprised recognizing that the somehow cryptic functions `foundBefore` and `isEqual` are represented by the common "<" and "=" operators. Beside, the teacher has the possibility to deepen the structural similarity between the lexicographic order and the order over numbers.

Obviously the strategy presented could be carried out using numbers instead of strings. But then one has the problem to motivate the data flow modeling: Starting with expressions like "3 is less than 4", one has no necessity to model the data flow, since the final term is evident.

### 5.2   Complex Boolean Functions

Having introduced the basics of Boolean data types, one continues with complex Boolean functions. Again, we discuss problems based on the lexicographic order and combine them with the standard logic operations `and`, `or`, `not`.

Suitable problems may look like the following:

- Give the data flow model of a function, which determines if two names are different.
- Give the data flow model of a function, which determines if your name is found in an encyclopedia between the two names "Dimpflmoser" and "Schlotterbeck".

Solving these problems one gets the following data flow diagrams:

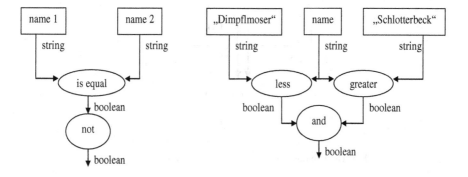

**Fig. 9.** Two examples of complex boolean functions

Without efforts, the logic operators `not`,  `and` are introduced in a natural way. The transformation of the data flow diagrams to compressed term and finally to application specific form is straightforward and will not be discussed here. Having implemented the models one ought to analyze the semantic of the standard logic functions in detail.

## 6   Conditional Expressions

The conditional expression is a central control structure in Informatics. In this unit students get to know the conditional expression as a function of arity 3, having a

Boolean function as the first argument and two other expressions with identical data type as second and third expression.

Though possible, it is not recommendable to begin with pure mathematical examples. Instead one might begin with an analysis of common conditional sentences, like the following rule applicable an hot pre-summer day:

> *If the temperature at school exceeds 30° at 10 o'clock, the instruction terminates at 11 o'clock, otherwise instruction happens according to class schedule.*

The Raw analysis of this sentence shows that a conditional sentence contains three parts:

- The condition, prefaced with "if"; this condition is either `true` or `false`.
- Two consequences; the first is carried out, if the condition is true, the second otherwise (sometimes the second alternative is omitted).
- Therefore, the modeling of conditional sentences with conditional functions results in a function having 3 arguments:
- A Boolean function.
- Two functions with arbitrary but identical result-data type; the first function is called, if the condition is true, the second otherwise.

Therefore, we get a function with a data flow diagram as shown below in figure 10.

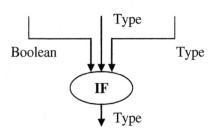

**Fig. 10.** The data flow diagram of the conditional expression

The signature of such a function has the structure:

```
If (condition: Boolean,
    true-function: TYPE, else-function: TYPE): TYPE
```

were `TYPE` denotes an arbitrary data type.

Since conditional sentences on everyday contexts cannot be implemented via spreadsheets, more formal examples (but not necessary mathematical ones) have to be used. Here we present the problem to compare three strings with respect to their lexicographic order and to calculate the "greatest" among them. (It should be mentioned that this example is too complex as unproductively example at school. Instead one ought to proceed step by step and discuss first the analogue problem for two strings.)

The solution of this problem cannot be modeled using one conditional expression. Instead, one has to nest two conditional expressions. The considerations concerning data flow diagrams of conditional expressions suggest the model shown in Figure 11: First, two strings are compared and the greater one is returned; afterwards this result is compared with the third string in the same manner.

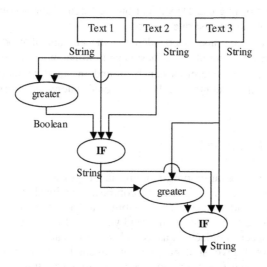

**Fig. 11.** The data flow diagram to calculate the "greatest" of three strings

As above the compressed term is calculated using the "bottom up" strategy. Translating the outermost conditional expression we get:

```
If(greater(?,text3),?, text3)
```

Now, the question marks have to be substituted by the term

```
If(greater(text1,text2), text1, text2).
```

So we get:

```
If(greater(If(greater(text1,text2),text1, text2),
               text3),
      If(greater(text1, text2),text1, text2), text3)
```

Finally this implementation independent term ought to be prepared for specific implementation:

```
If((If(text1>text2), text1, text2)>text3,
               (If(text1>text2), text1, text2), text3)
```

Translating the data flow diagram to term structure, it is important to mind the order of the arguments. As above, we have the convention that the graphical order of arguments (left to right) corresponds to the textual one.

The example illustrates a specific feature of functional modeling: There is no possibility to store a result. For example, the term (If(text1>text2), text1, text2) has been used two times and it has been calculated two times. This is due to the fact that functional modeling lacks the concept of variables.

Finally, we present some possibilities to deepen conditional expressions:

- Calculation of interest: Dependent on the "sign of the account" the sign and the value of the interest rate changes.
- Discount calculations: Dependent on the amount of products bought one gets a specific discount. Here, nested conditional expressions can be used
- Further ideas for exercises can be found in standard school-textbooks on informatics in the context of the conditional statement (for example: Fuchs et al., [3]).

## 7 Iterative Calculations

Standard courses on imperative programming languages at school contain a chapter discussing loops as a central element. In contrast, functional data models are pure sequential structures and we have no possibility to model loop structures. Instead, such calculations have to be carried out step by step performing the various iterations explicitly. With respect to didactical aspects this is no disadvantage: The step by step calculations discussed give students the fundamental experienc to recognize the necessity of loops as an efficient tool to model repetitive structures.

A treasure of ideas on iterative calculations with spreadsheets can be found in Dopfer G., Reimer R., [2]. Unfortunately, some interesting examples like Heron's algorithm to calculate the square root of a number, or the algorithms to approximate the number $\pi$ cannot be used due to curricullary conditions. Some other examples, however, like the one on the greatest common divisor or interest calculations with regular (or irregular) payments are undoubtedly applicable.

Though the cited textbook of Dopfer G., Reimer R. presents valuable ideas, these ideas have to be designed for functional data modeling. In the sequel, we illustrate the principal strategy discussing the step by step calculation of the greatest common divisor:

Yet in the 5th grade students learn Euclid's algorithm to calculate the greatest common divisor of two natural numbers. Obviously, the algorithm used here ought to show a non-recursive structure like the following:

*Euclid's algorithm to calculate the greatest common divisor of two natural numbers a and b, gcd(a, b):*

1. Let $a_1 = a$ and $b_1 = b$;
2. If $a_1$ equal $b_1$, then $a_1$ is the gcd(a, b) and the algorithm terminates
3. Calculate $a_2$ and $b_2$ as follows:
   If $a_1 > b_1$, then $a_2 = a_1 - b_1$ and $b_2 = b_1$, otherwise $a_2 = a_1$ and $b_2 = b_1 - a_1$;
4. If $a_2$ equal $b_2$, then $a_2$ is the gcd(a, b) and the algorithm terminates
5. Calculate $a_i$ and $b_i$, for $i > 2$ analogous until $a_i = b_i$; then gcd(a, b) = $a_i$.

The data flow model (Figure 12) for this algorithm is developed in two steps: First one ought to model the global data flow to calculate the various values $a_i$ and $b_i$. This initial model is shown on the left side of Fig. 12. The second step deals with the data flow model to calculate $a_{i+1}$ from $a_i$ and $b_i$. This model is given on the right side of the figure. It shows the details of a transformation process from the left side (colored ellipse).

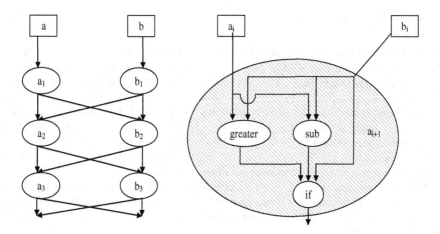

**Fig. 12.** Data flow diagrams to calculate the greatest common divisor of two numbers

The implementation of this model proceeds analogously: First, the global model is transformed to the spreadsheet maintaining the geometrical structure. Afterwards, the detailed model has to be compressed to one term and inserted into the respective cells (Figure 13).

|   | A | B | C |
|---|---|---|---|
| 1 | $a_1$ | | $b_1$ |
| 2 | | | |
| 3 | | | |
| 4 | = If(A1>B1; A1-B1; A1) | | = If (A1>B1; B1; B1 – A1) |
| 5 | | | |
| 6 | | | |
| 7 | = If(A3>B3; A3-B3; A3) | | = If (A3>B3; B3; B3 – A3) |
| 8 | | | |
| 9 | | | |

**Fig. 13.** The implementation of the data flow diagram in figure 12

Abstracting from this example, one recognizes the well known structure of loops: The detailed (inner) model corresponds to the body of the loop, the global or outer model to the various iterations. But in contrast to loop or recursive structures, the user himself decides whether the algorithm terminates after a certain step or not.

Further topics for exercises:

- The calculation of roots by nested intervals,
- Growth or decay-rates
- Interest calculations with regular (or irregular) payments; (see P. Hubwieser, 2004 for the basics of such exercises).

## 8  Final Remarks

To my knowlede the only official publication on functional data modeling at school is the one of P. Hubwieser (2004) [4]. Based on this publication the author of the present paper has taught functional data modeling from May 2004 to July 2004 in the $9^{th}$ grade of a Bavarian Gymnasium near Munich. The experiences made there are already incorporated into the strategy presented. But nevertheless, we have great lack of suitable material. Since the mandatory subject informatics starts in 2006 with functional data modeling in the $8^{th}$ grade, it is really urgent to continue the phase of material development. Teachers and scientists ought to conceive and evaluate examples and problems on functional data flow modeling.

A central problem omitted here concerns the methodology of. teaching functional data modeling: The method of project based teaching, a central element of informatics at school, should be integrated into the course strategy by the development of suitable worksheet sequences.

Apart from the topic discussed here the mandatory subject informatics of the Bavarian Gymnasium offers teachers and scientists numerous fields to work on such as data bases, imperative programming, and automata to mention only three topics of similar urgency. These topics ought to be addressed from interested scientists.

## References

1. Barth F., Federle R., Haller R., 1996: Algebra 8, Ehrenwirth Verlag
2. Dopfer G., Reimer R., 1995: Tabellenkalkulation im Mathematikunterricht, Klett-Verlag
3. Fuchs M. et al., 1994: Einführung in die Informatik, Klett-Verlag
4. Hubwieser P., 2004; Functional Modeling in Secondary Schools using Spreadsheets; in "Education an Information Technologies" of the Official Journal of the IFIP Technical Committee on Education, Vol. 9, Nr. 2
5. Schneider M., 2004; "An Empirical Study of Introductory Lectures in Informatics Based on Fundamental Concepts" in "Informatics and Student Assessment" Lecture Notes in Informatics, Vol. 1
6. Winter R., 1996: Grundlagen der formalen Logik, Verlag Harri Deutsch, 1996

# Informatic Models in Vocational Training for Teaching Standard Software

Siglinde Voß

Department of Didactics of Informatics,
Technical University of Munich,
Boltzmannstr. 3,
85748 Garching, Germany
siglinde.voss@web.de

**Abstract.** Users of current software are faced with ever rising requirements as these tools are subject to more and more changes. These tools, which are getting more and more complex, can only be used efficiently, if users are capable of an abstract and structured approach. In further education, it is necessary to sustainibly develop training-concepts that will give them skills irrespective of special software.

Informatic models have proven to be suitable to teach document structures which will be of long-term use. So users will no longer be dependent on the knowledge of the ever-changing surface they will rather help them to understand the working of modern software-systems.

Based on didactics of informatics the following text will present approaches for assorted contents in the context of training Microsoft®Word and gives information on two courses conducted in companies and the experiences made.

## 1 Modeling in Informatics Education

If you follow the discussion about the didactics of informatics of recent years[1], you can observe that the topic of "Modeling" in teaching informatics is often discussed widely. Emphasing an information-centered approach, Hubwieser [2] has developed a teaching-concept which stresses informatic modeling when teaching informatics at grammar schools in Bavaria.

For 11- and 12-year-old pupils (form 6 and 7), he suggests an object-oriented modeling or analysis of standard software which enables students to work with an underlying inner structure of the documents when changing them and this will make them independent of the fast-moving user-interface of the respective tool. [3]

At Bavarian grammar schools these aspects are part of the curriculum of the subject "Natur und Technik" (nature and technology) with the subgroup informatics which has been obligatory for all students in form 6 and 7 since September 2004. [4]

---

[1] Brinda summarizes current results and the present state of research in the area of object oriented modeling [1], p. 15ff.

R.T. Mittermeir (Ed.): ISSEP 2005, LNCS 3422, pp. 145–155, 2005.
© Springer-Verlag Berlin Heidelberg 2005

Even at a number of Bavarian "Realschulen" (English equivalent: secondary modern school) the classical subject "text processing" is replaced by a subject called information technology that has been enlarged by contents of informatics. This development clearly shows that knowledge about informatics is necessary for a long-term learning of word processing: If students just know how to work with the user-interface, they will find it much harder to apply their knowledge to similar systems.

## 2   Object Models can be Used to Explain and Illustrate Informatic Phenomena in Word Processing

Although office users today do not generally have basic knowledge in informatics, corresponding models can be used to explain and illustrate the effects of word processing software. This could be observed in vocational training courses conducted by the author.

The graphic representation of these models is drawn upon representations as they can be found in the informatic text book for form 6/7 of Bavarian grammar schools such as [5], [6] or in UML-syntax such as in [7] and [8].

But the level of abstraction must be lowered accordingly. That's why the author decided not to describe generally valid connections for example with the help of class diagrams. Instead, object diagrams are used to illustrate relations of objects in concrete documents.

Class- or object-cards were employed to list the attributes and operations of individual objects. Having this piece of information the user can assess which options of structuring he has or doesn't have in connection with individual objects in a document.

Sequence diagrams were used to illustrate the dynamics. They are suitable for the representation of the exchange of messages between the existing objects after an operational command of the user.

Finally state-transition diagrams clarify that objects do not always behave in the same way; it depends what state they are in at present. For example certain operations of objects possible cannot be called upon, if single attributes adopt certain values.

## 3   Carrying Out Two Vocational Training Courses

In January/February 2004 and in June/July 2004 the author conducted a vocational training course for office users for employees of a smaller company - both were planning to introduce the participants to "Word" and also deepen their knowledge.

In the first case there were five, in the second six participants whose background was differing widely concerning school and professional training. The course in both cases took place weekly for five consecutive weeks; each session lasting for three hours. Following topics were covered:

- Session1: Basics

> Formatting characters, paragraphs, sections; the simple structure of documents and object connections

- Session 2: Graphics and tables:
>    Pixel- and vector graphics; embedded and linked graphics; forming tables, sorting contents

- Session 3: Format styles:
>    Creating character- and paragraph-styles and assigning them to characters and paragraphs; creating new styles based on already existing ones; adapting document templates for personal usage

- Session 4: Text fields, cross references:
>    Positioning and connecting text fields, creating cross references with the help of hyperlinks; adding references into strings and graphics;

- Session 5: Headers and footers:
>    Inserting text and graphics in headers and footers; using different headers and footers in a document;

The typical approach in a lesson consisted of explaining and illustrating the relevant aspects with the help of graphic models. In addition the whole process was demonstrated on the software used. It was absolutely necessary for the users to practice for themselves on their own computers immediately afterwards. When the participants had questions or problems, the author only used the models taught in her explanations. The user interface was not referred to.

The advantage of this approach among others was that the same model could be used for both courses, although two different versions of MS-Word (MS-Word®97 and MS-Word®XP) were taken. Even if the user interfaces shows a number of differences, the structure of the documents hasn't changed decisively by the replacement of MS-Word®97 of MS-Word®XP.

Of course the participants had to be shown which buttons, menus etc. had to be used, so that the object structure of the given model could be implemented. But this was not among the syllabus of the course. As both groups used different versions of MS®Word and in addition every tool in most cases offers different ways to achieve the same aim, the participants were allowed to choose the operations which they liked best.

# 4  Examples of the Realization of Single Contents

## 4.1  Topic "Basics – Inserting Columns"

One of the aspects of the first unit was arranging text in various columns. The structure of the document can be presented by the class diagram shown in Fig. 1.

Every text document contains at least one section which is subdivided by exactly one columngrid including at least one column. Every section contains at least one paragraph which can contain any number of characters.

### Classroom Approach

In lessons the class diagram was not referred to. Instead, the students were confronted with a concrete example of a document and its respective object diagram.

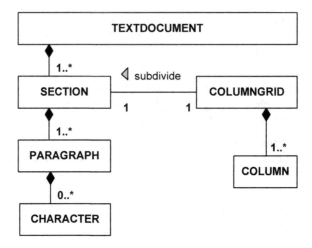

**Fig. 1.** Class diagram of a simple structure of a text document

At this point the students already knew that one section can contain several paragraphs. The item "column grid" and "column" were new. The arrow representing the association "subdivides" shows that the column grid subdivides the section (not just the paragraphs).

The example in Fig. 2 shows the standard situation. The text document contains exactly one section with a column grid, which contains only one column:

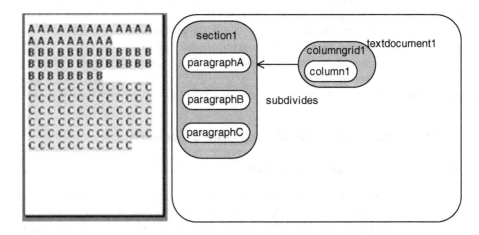

**Fig. 2.** Example of a text document containing one section and the corresponding object diagram

If you want to arrange the text in the different paragraphs in various columns, you have to insert two additional sections, as can be seen in the following object diagram:

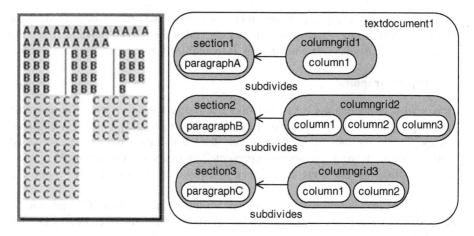

**Fig. 3.** Example of a text document containing three sections with various column grids and the corresponding object diagram

Each section has its own column grid; the latter is automatically assigned, after the user has created a new section. For example, after you have created section3, the column grid is immediately assigned to it. If the user inserts an additional column, the width of the column is automatically adjusted after the operation.

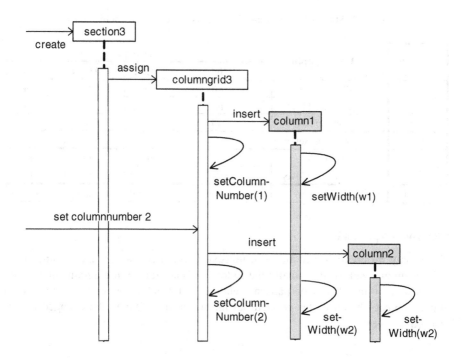

**Fig. 4.** Sequence diagram

The (simplified) sequence diagram (Fig. 4) shows the process described above and is to clarify to the participants of the course that they do not have to create the column grid themselves. It immediately is available after the creation of a section.

## 4.2  Topic "Graphics"

Object in text documents do not always behave in the same way. For example some operations of a graphic object can be called upon only in certain circumstances. To clarify these correlations, one uses a dynamic model, the so-called state transition diagram. States are represented by ovals, the transitions by arrows. The transition of one state to another is caused by an event, for example a command of the user.

A graphic is in a certain state, depending on the attribute values of the graphic. In this respect attributes can be seen as variables. State transitions are caused by altering attribute values.

In this case, the author has only worked with variable states relevant for the model. For example not all four attributes for text space (at the right, left, above, below) can be altered. This depends on the value of the attribute "textwrapping". The corresponding attribute "value" then is nil.

If we take these five attributes into consideration, we can make out seven states altogether:

**Table 1.** States of a graphic-object and its respective attribute values

| State | Textwrapping | Textspace | | | |
|---|---|---|---|---|---|
| | | Right | Left | Above | Below |
| z1a | likeCharacter | nil | nil | Nil | nil |
| z1b | inFrontOfText | nil | nil | Nil | nil |
| z1c | behindText | nil | nil | nil | nil |
| z2 | aboveAndBelow | nil | nil | not nil | not nil |
| z3a | likeBorder | nil | not nil | nil | nil |
| z3b | likeBorderCover | not nil | not nil | nil | nil |
| z4 | rectangular | not nil | not nil | not nil | not nil |

**Classroom Approach**

If you only differentiate according to textspace which can be changed, some states can be summarized, so that finally the following state-transition diagram can explain the most important behavior patterns relating to the adjustment of textspace of a graphic object (the attributes crossed out mean that these cannot be changed in this respective state):

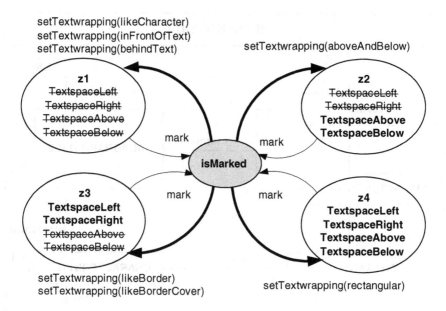

setTextwrapping(likeCharacter)
setTextwrapping(inFrontOfText)
setTextwrapping(behindText)

setTextwrapping(aboveAndBelow)

setTextwrapping(likeBorder)
setTextwrapping(likeBorderCover)

setTextwrapping(rectangular)

**Fig. 5.** State-transition diagram

## 4.3  Topic "Format Styles"

If you include format styles, the object structures of text documents will increasingly get more complex and manifold. Even if you restrict yourself to character- and paragraph-styles the class diagram (Fig. 6) shows that in this case already four different kinds of correlations are possible:

The most important format styles are paragraph-styles. The latter possess paragraph attributes to format paragraphs assigned but also character attributes, with which they format the whole set of characters (the so-called charactercollection) included in the paragraph.

On the other hand, character styles can format single characters of the character collection if wanted, that means that certain character values can be allocated to chosen characters.

Occasionally you want to create a new paragraph- or character style which only differs minimally from a given format style. In this case this format style can be used as a basis for a new one. The relation *isBasedOn* expresses this option. If a format styles attribute value is not defined explicitly which means that the value is nil, the format style will select the corresponding value in the basis and pass it on.

Finally, the user can select one paragraph style in a given paragraph style which will be relevant for the formatting of the next paragraph. The corresponding relation is called isNext. In most cases thus a certain paragraph is related to itself.

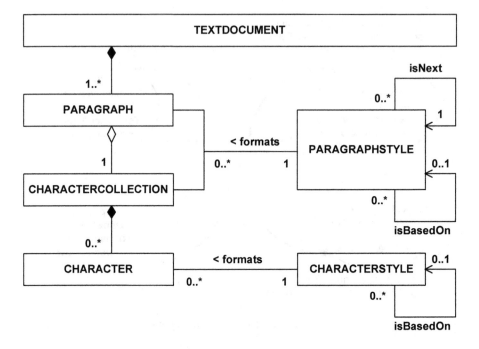

**Fig. 6.** Class diagram of a text document format styles included

## Classroom Approach

This time the participants of the course also get to know concrete case examples. Here, *paragraphstyleB* is to be created on the basis of the given *paragraphstyleA*. *Paragraph1* then is to be formatted with *paragraphstyleB*. The structure of the finished text document is represented by the follow object diagram:

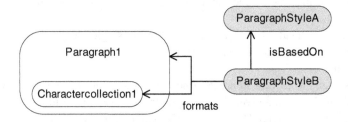

**Fig. 7.** Object diagram with one paragraph formatted by paragraph-styles

As paragraphstyleB is generated from another one, it is not necessary that it defines all the attribute values. Here the attribute values were specified as shown in Fig. 8:

The user now formats paragraph1 with the help of paragraphstyleB by marking paragraph1 and finally selecting paragraphstyleB. So, paragraph1 and its character collection1 receive all attribute values of paragraphstyleB which are defined there.

| ParagraphStyleA | | ParagraphStyleB | |
|---|---|---|---|
| FontType | = Arial | FontType | = Courier |
| FontSize | = 12pt | FontSize | = 10pt |
| FontColor | = black | FontColor | = nil |
| isBold | = no | isBold | = nil |
| isItalic | = no | isItalic | = nil |
| Underline | = no | Underline | = nil |
| ... | | ... | |
| IntendationLeft | = 0 | IntendationLeft | = nil |
| IntendationRight | = 0 | IntendationRight | = nil |
| SpacingBefore | = 0 | SpacingBefore | = nil |
| SpacingAfter | = 0 | SpacingAfter | = nil |
| Alignment | = left | Alignment | = justified |
| LineSpacing | = single | LineSpacing | = nil |
| ... | | ... | |

**Fig. 8.** Object cards listing attributes and their values

All other attribute values, which are defined in paragraphstyleB are requested by paragraphstyleB and delivered by its basis paragraphstyleA. The following sequence diagram illustrates this process:

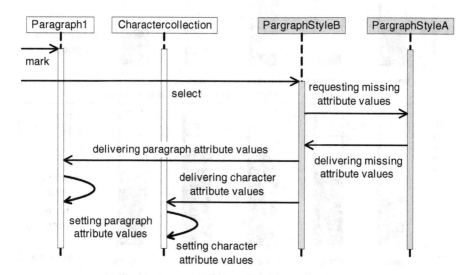

**Fig. 9.** Sequence diagram which illustrates the exchange of messages between various objects by applying paragraphstyleB to paragraph1

After the single processes have finished the listed attribute values as shown in the following object cards have been allocated to paragraph1 and charactercollection1.

| Paragraph1 | |
|---|---|
| IntendationLeft | = 0 |
| IntendationRight | = 0 |
| SpacingBefore | = 0 |
| SpacingAfter | = 0 |
| Alignment | = justified |
| LineSpacing | = single |
| ... | |

| Charactercollection1 | |
|---|---|
| FontType | = Courier |
| FontSize | = 10pt |
| FontColor | = black |
| isBold | = no |
| isItalic | = no |
| Underline | = no |
| ... | |

**Fig. 10.** Object cards of paragraph1 and charactercollection1

## 5  Appraisal

With the help of two questionnaires immediately before and after the course the author wanted to find out whether the participants benefited from the course.

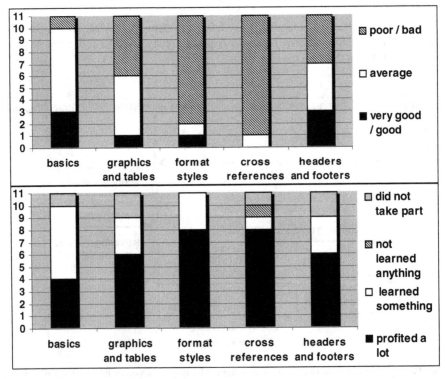

**Fig. 11.** Appraisal of the participant´s knowledge before the course (above) and learning progress after the course (below) dependent on the respective lesson item

In the first questionnaire the participants among other things were asked how they assessed their own knowledge and their skills (*very good, good, average, poor, bad*) in five contents (Fig. 11, above).

After the course they were asked to comment on the progress they had made. This time they could tick off three options: *profited a lot, have learned something, did not learn anything* (Fig. 11, below).

Although at the beginning a number of participants considered themselves as very good or good in six cases altogether, in three of these cases they stated that they had profited a lot, in other three cases they stated that they had at least learned something, in two cases, people did not take part at the specific lesson.

Also, in six of eighteen cases where participants considered their own knowledge in the different fields as average, they could profit a lot, in six cases they could learn something and in two cases, they did not take part in the specific lesson.

At least, in 29 cases people stated before the course that their knowledge in the respective fields was poor or bad. Later, in 21 cases of them, participants said they had profited a lot, in five cases people at least admitted that they had learnt something. A single person stated that he had not learnt anything. In two of these 29 cases, people did not participate in the relevant lesson.

Nearly all the participants have observed learning progress within all five ranges. So it is possible that informatic concepts can indeed help people to learn intensive word processing.

# References

1. Brinda T.: Didaktisches System für objektorientiertes Modellieren im Informatikunterricht der Sekundarstufe II. Dissertation, FB Elektrotechnik und Informatik, Universität Siegen, 2004
2. Hubwieser, P.: Informatik am Gymnasium. Ein Gesamtkonzept für einen zeitgemäßen Informatikunterricht. Habilitationsschrift, Fakultät für Infromatik, Technische Universität München, 2000
3. Frey E., Hubwieser P., Humbert L., Schubert S., Voß S.: Informatik-Anfangsunterricht. In: LOG IN 21 (2001) 1, S. 20-32
4. Staatsministerium für Unterricht und Kultus des Landes Bayern (Hrsg.): Lehrplan für die Klasse Informatik im G9 (10.09.2004)
   http://www.isb.bayern.de/gym/informat/lehrplan/inf-6.pdf
   Fachprofil informatik (10.09.2004)
   http://www.isb.bayern.de/gym/informat/lehrplan/i-fachpr.pdf
5. E. Frey, P. Hubwieser, F. Winhard: Informatik 1. Objekte, Strukturen, Algorithmen. Ernst Klett Verlag, Stuttgart, 2004
6. Siglinde Voß: Informatik in der 6. Jahrgangsstufe. In [10]
7. Balzert H.: Lehrbuch der Software-Technik; Heidelberg, Berlin; Spektrum, Akad. Verl. Bd. 1. Software-Entwicklung, 2000
8. Oestereich B.: Objektorientierte Softwareentwicklung: Analyse und Design mit der Unified modeling language; München, Wien: Oldenbourg, 2001
9. Voß S.: Objektorientierte Modellierung von Software zur Textgestaltung. In: [11]
10. ZBORNIK RADOVA (Hrsg.), SAVREMENE INFORMATICKE I OBRAZOVNE TEHNOLOGIJE I NOVI MEDIJI U OBRAZOVANJU, Sombor 2004
11. Hubwieser, P. (Hrsg.): Informatische Fachkonzepte im Unterricht. Köllen, Bonn, 2003

# Evolving Boxes as Flexible Tools for Teaching High-School Students Declarative and Procedural Aspects of Logic Programming

Bruria Haberman[1] and Zahava Scherz [2,*]

[1] Computer Science Dept., Holon Academic Institute of Technology, and
Dept. of Science Teaching, The Weizmann Institute of Science,
Rehovot 76100, Israel
bruria.haberman@weizmann.ac.il
[2] Dept. of Science Teaching, The Weizmann Institute of Science,
Rehovot 76100, Israel
zahava.scherz@weizmann.ac.il

**Abstract.** During the last decade a new computer science curriculum has been taught in Israeli high schools. The curriculum introduces CS concepts and problem-solving methods and combines both theoretical and practical issues. The Logic Programming elective module of the curriculum was designed to introduce to students a second programming paradigm. In this paper we describe how we used *evolving boxes*, when teaching abstract data types (ADTs), to introduce the interweaving declarative and procedural aspects of logic programming. The following types of evolving boxes were used: (a) black boxes that could be used transparently, (b) white boxes that could be modified to suit specific needs, and (c) grey boxes that reveal parts of their internal workings.

We conducted a study aimed at assessing students' use of ADTs. The findings indicated that the students demonstrated an integrative knowledge of ADT boxes as programming tools, and employed unique autonomous problem-solving strategies when using ADTs in programming.

## 1 Introduction

During the last decade a new computer science curriculum has been taught in Israeli high schools. The curriculum introduces CS concepts and problem-solving methods independently of specific computers and programming languages, along with the practical implementation of those concepts and methods encountered in actual programming languages [5, 6]. One elective module of the curriculum- *Logic Programming*, was designed to introduce a (second) declarative programming paradigm.

Logic programming (LP) enables programmers to concentrate on the declarative and abstract aspects of problem solving, and usually liberates them from dealing with

---

* Corresponding author.

R.T. Mittermeir (Ed.): ISSEP 2005, LNCS 3422, pp. 156–165, 2005.

the procedural details of the computational process. However, sometimes the procedural aspects of logic programming, besides the declarative ones, are also encountered, especially when manipulating compound data structures. Therefore, it is important to use suitable instructional tools to teach the interweaving declarative and procedural aspects of programming. One way that this can be accomplished is by using *evolving programming boxes*.

We developed a two-stage "Logic Programming" course, implemented in the Prolog programming language, which was designed for high-school students. One main goal of the course was to expose students to different aspects of logic programming and to enhance their problem-solving and design skills in the context of the LP paradigm. The 90-hour basic module was designed, as part of the CS curriculum, for beginners and covers the following topics: introduction to propositional logic and predicate logic, including logic programming, data base programming, compound data structures, recursion, lists, introduction to abstract data types (ADTs), and basic methods of problem solving and knowledge representation. The 60-hour advanced module, designed for advanced students who had already learned the basic module, introduces advanced methods of problem solving and knowledge representation, advanced generic abstract data types, and advanced programming techniques [11].

Being a declarative language, logic programming is suitable for knowledge representation and content formalization [16]. Abstract data types are considered as useful tools for CS problem solving and knowledge representation [1]. Since logic programming abstracts the manipulation of compound data structures by hiding procedural aspects and details of their implementation [2], it is convenient for implementing and utilizing abstract data types; hence, it is a suitable programming environment for teaching the notions of ADTs [11].

The abstract data type, which is discussed in both modules of the "Logic Programming" course as a recurrent CS concept, is introduced to students as a *mathematical model with a set of operations* [1]. *Specification* of an ADT is achieved by formally and verbally defining its use as a model and its operations. *Implementation* of an ADT is achieved by means of the logic programming language by formulating rules to define general predicates for each of the specified ADT operations. The actual implementation of an ADT is achieved by creating a black box. The *use* of an ADT for problem solving is done by defining problem predicates using predefined general predicates.

Here we present how we used evolving programming boxes to gradually introduce ADTs as flexible problem-solving and programming tools. We demonstrate how evolving boxes may be employed to foster students' ability to organize declarative and procedural programming knowledge. We employed our instructional approach to teach declarative and procedural aspects of logic programming. However, these tools can be adopted to introduce similar aspects of any programming paradigm.

## 1.1  Evolving Programming Boxes

In this section we describe three typical types of evolving programming boxes that can be used in different layers of abstraction.

***Black Boxes:*** A black box is a fully implemented component with predictable functionality and pre-defined interface. Every black box has two components: (a) an interface visible to the user, which describes the implemented operations; in the context of logic programming, each general predicate is characterized by its name, its arguments, its meaning, and assumptions that relate to the way the predicate should be invoked during a programming process; (b) An implementation component that encapsulates the details of how the operations (general predicates in the case of logic programming) were implemented.

The underlying idea of using black boxes, according to the information hiding principle, is that the end-user is only permitted to know what the black box does, and is not allowed to know how the operation is done. Accordingly, the end-user does not need to know how predefined operations are implemented within the black box. The access to source code is therefore denied, and the use of black boxes is done by transparently invoking the encapsulated predefined operations to define new operations.

***White Boxes:*** Black boxes are ready for use without modification but cannot be customized to satisfy the requirements of a particular application. In contrast, white boxes are *visible* modules with accessible source code, and the user is supposed to read and understand thoroughly their internals, with the possibility of copying and modifying them to suit his needs.

Accessibility to the code has pedagogical as well as practical aspects. More specifically, it enables the student to learn and practice programming by: (a) understanding how a given code was implemented according to a given specification, (b) learning from examples how to create new and similar modules, (c) practicing debugging and modifying a given code to suit individual needs.

***Grey Boxes:*** When black boxes provide too little information and white boxes reveal too much, we need to go for a middle ground, which we termed grey boxes. A grey box reveals parts of its internal workings, not just the relations between the input and output. The information can become as detailed as necessary where needed. Revealing some internal information might also help the client (programmer) improve the performance of the complete system [3].

Black, white, and grey boxes are used in programming, especially in the development of object-oriented systems [7, 17]. White and black boxes are used to formally define behavioral compositions expressed via contracts [12].

Educators have stated that integrating black, grey and white boxes into the process of instruction has pedagogical benefits [7, 9, 11, 13, 15, 17]. For example, Eckstein [7] describes how various techniques emphasize different aspects of the architectural design of a framework, and how these techniques can be combined into a general paradigm for instruction. Specifically, she recommends integrating the following instructional methods: *black box teaching*, *white box teaching*, and *incremental teaching*, to explain a complex object technology-based framework by using smaller and simpler frameworks and patterns. She claims that in this way, the students become progressively more familiar with the context of the learned framework and its possibilities, and will recognize the overall picture and the functionality of the framework [7]. Haberman and Ben-David Kollikant demonstrated how black boxes can be utilized to introduce basic programming concepts to novices [9]. Haberman used black boxes to teach beginners how to use lists in Prolog, thus avoiding the burden of the implementation details, which were found to be very complicated [8]. Here we describe how we used evolving ADT boxes to emphasize the declarative and procedural aspects of logic programming.

## 2  The Instructional Approach

According to our instructional approach, we recommend that the ADT concept be gradually presented in 8 consecutive stages, as illustrated in Table 1. Stages 1-4 are designed for all students (beginners and advanced); we integrated them in the basic module of the logic programming course. We suggest that stages 5-8, which appear to be complicated [8], should be taught exclusively to advanced students. Accordingly, we integrated those stages into the advanced module of the course. Stages 1-3 deal with one specific type of problem solving, namely by using predefined tools to solve problems and to write programs. However, stages 4-7 deal with various aspects of implementation and with the development of new tools.

Stage 8 integrates both types of problem solving and provides a set-up for learning and using ADTs in the context of knowledge integration similar to the one described in [3]. We suggest that in order to foster integrative knowledge, besides learning new aspects of ADTs, students should progress in each stage, using all the tools and methods that they acquired in previous stages.   Next, we describe the activities associated with each stage.

**Stage 1 - Acquaintance with given specifications of ADTs:** Initially students become acquainted with the specification of generic abstract data types (e.g., lists, sets, multi-sets, trees, and graphs). Suitable examples of concrete problems should be used to illustrate the presented ADTs. Students should realize that the specification of an ADT is independent of the implementation (programming) stage, and of the programming environment.

**Stage 2 - Use of ADTs to solve a given problem:** Next, students should practice how to choose "known" ADTs to solve a given problem. For example, students should be able to determine that the *tree-* ADT is the most suitable one to present the family parenthood relationship between the females (or males), whereas the *graph*-ADT should be used to present that relationship between all the family members (without referring to a specific gender).

**Stage 3 - Use of ADT black boxes in programming:** One of our main pedagogical goals was to emphasize the declarative aspects of programming: To the end, the black boxes are presented in terms of *what they do* and not *how it is done*. In this stage, we emphasize the following declarative aspects: (a) the use of a black box is independent of its implementation and therefore does not require becoming acquainted with the implementation details; (b) the use of a black box binds to its interface. Moreover, the use of black boxes has declarative aspects in the sense that the definition of problem predicates is done declaratively in terms of general ADT predicates. For example, the definition of a student in a specific class is phrased as follows: "a person is a student in a class if he is a member of the list of students who belong in that class". However, procedural aspects must be also taken into account when using black boxes to implement declarations in order to accomplish a working program.

Accordingly, we suggest that at this stage students should practice using predefined ADT black boxes to write computer programs that solve given problems. Specifically, students are taught to define new problem predicates by transparently invoking predefined general predicates. In addition, ADT black boxes should also be used by students simply to define new general ADT predicates in terms of the predefined ones.

**Stage 4 - Specification of new ADTs**: At this stage the student plays the role of a consumer who specifies and orders a new ADT black box from his teacher. The teacher implements the required ADT according to the student's specifications in terms of a black box, which is then used by the student to write his program.

**Table 1.** Gradual presentation of the ADT concept

| Stage | Emphasized Aspects of programming | Target Population |
|---|---|---|
| Acquaintance with given specifications of ADTs | declarative | beginners and advanced |
| Determination of ADTs to solve a given problem | declarative | |
| Use of ADT black boxes in programming | declarative and procedural | |
| Specification of new ADTs | declarative | |
| Acquaintance with ADT grey boxes | procedural | advanced only |
| Manipulation of ADT white boxes | procedural | |
| Implementation of new ADTs | procedural | |
| Knowledge integration and autonomous problem solving | declarative and procedural | |

**Stage 5 - Acquaintance with predefined ADT grey boxes:** After students became familiar with the specifications and the use of ADTs, we suggest that they gradually learn how to implement an ADT according to its specifications. Initially, students become acquainted with the implementation of familiar ADTs. At this point the black boxes that have been transparently used in the previous stage become unfolded, i.e. the code within the black box is no longer hidden. Actually, at this point the black box becomes a grey box – visible yet *only read*, and the students perform operations such as reading the code, running the code and following up its execution in order to understand "how it works". At this stage students are also exposed to new procedural aspects of data implementation in terms of the language constructs (e.g., recursive data structures) and new techniques of data manipulation (e.g., recursive list processing).

**Stage 6 - Manipulation of Predefined ADT White Boxes:** At this stage the *read only* boxes turn out to be white boxes and the code becomes "more" accessible in the sense that it can also be modified. Here the following procedural aspects of programming are emphasized: students learn advanced programming techniques and efficiency aspects, and practice code debugging, code modification, and writing new code from scratch.

**Stage 7 - Implementation of New ADTs:** After becoming acquainted with the implementation of predefined ADT boxes, the students experience how to implement new ADT boxes according to a defined specification. At this stage they eventually become independent of the teacher in terms of supplying built-in programming tools. The following procedural aspects should be emphasized: (a) an ADT is implemented according to its specification; (b) the implementation of an ADT is encapsulated in terms of a black box; and (c) an ADT may have alternative black box implementations.

**Stage 8 - Knowledge Integration and Autonomous Problem Solving:** At this stage students make a significant step toward attaining proficiency, and they practice solving advanced and complex problems. To succeed in these complex missions, students need to understand how the problem-solving patterns that they have already acquired are connected to specific examples and to new problems; they also need to adapt their patterns to suit more complex situations [3]. Moreover, they have to integrate the knowledge that they have gained when learning, creating, and using ADTs in previous stages, and to successfully incorporate it into their solving-program processes.

On the one hand, the students start acting like autonomous standalone developers, reusing their own tools, and on the other hand, they experience sharing tools with peers and reuse others' tools. Actually, they employ ADTs to solve a given problem in the following process: They try to determine familiar ADTs suited for the given problem and use the relevant predefined black boxes. When the predefined ADTs do not suit their needs, they specify new ADTs from scratch or modify the specification of other ADTs, implement them in terms of black boxes, and then use them to develop their programs. The implementation of new black boxes is done based on the knowledge acquired when manipulating grey and white boxes.

# 3   Fostering Integrative Programming Knowledge

During the last few years, we have conducted an ongoing study aimed at assessing various aspects of students' use of ADTs in the Prolog environment: (a) one part of the study focused on students' strategies for using ADTs to develop Prolog programs [11]; (b) another part of the study focused on the role of ADTs in the project development process [15]; and (c) another part was concerned with students' views toward ADTs [10].

We found that students adapted various strategies for using ADTs, some of which proved that they correctly grasped ADT as a formal CS concept. Other students improvised alternative strategies, which indicated that their conception of ADT did not match the correct CS definition. Nevertheless, the use of ADTs for problem solving and knowledge representation helped many students to develop correct programs regardless of the strategies they used [11]. The findings also revealed that for most students, ADTs served as a project development organizer [15], and they mostly expressed positive attitudes toward ADTs as problem solving and programming tools [10].

Based on those findings, here we discuss the students' perception of ADT boxes from another perspective–the use of predefined modules of code as multifunctional components for composing and editing a program.

### 3.1 Students' Perceptions of ADT Boxes

We found that students had gained various perceptions of ADT boxes and of their role in programming. Figure 1 illustrates the types of boxes that reflect students' perceptions in terms of code transparency and accessibility. The less opaque the box is, the more it is accessible and changeable.

| Perception of box | Type of box | Associative activities |
|---|---|---|
| Sealed, inaccessible | Black Box | Transparent use |
| Visible, yet incomprehensible "Copy and paste" | Unfolded Grey Box | Code cloning (duplication) |
| Visible, comprehensible, yet unchangeable | Read Only Grey Box | Comprehension of implementation details |
| Problem-oriented "Cut and paste" | Flexible White Box | Deleting code, Asserting code |
| Generic Templates for defining new predicates | White Box | Code modification, rewriting, creating new boxes |

**Fig. 1.** Perception of ADT boxes

**Sealed inaccessible black boxes:** Beginners who had studied how to use ADT black boxes but were not acquainted with their implementation, perceive the boxes as an integral part of the programming language. Most of them consider the black box as a sealed entity whose content is inaccessible. They believe that it is impossible to examine the contents of the box or to change it; accordingly, they *transparently invoke* general predefined predicates in order to define new problem predicates. Most of the advanced students also use familiar generic black boxes transparently when defining new predicates, even though they have access to the context of those boxes and are familiar with their implementation. These students demonstrate the ability to decide when to use a predefined code as a black box or as a white box.

**Unfolded black boxes:** We found that students define problem predicates by cloning (non-transparently invoking) general predicates, and actually copy their implementa tion from the black box to the main program. Advanced students who are familiar with the content of the boxes usually use this strategy. Interestingly, we also found that some of the beginners used this strategy as well, even though they were not familiar with the box's implementation. They unfold the black box and reveal its code only for *copy and paste* purposes. Most of them do not try, nor do they demonstrate any willingness to understand the actual code inside the box. They just copy a selected part of the code and insert it, as is, in their programs. Actually, they perceive the ADT black box as a collection of predicates that can be duplicated and inserted in other programs. The findings indicated that these students are convinced that a correct program should contain all the definitions of the predicates involved. Moreover, they believe that copying the definition of the invoked general predicate contributes to a better understanding of the meaning of the newly defined predicates.

**Read only boxes:** We found that students use a white box as *read only* scaffolding tool for implementation purposes. They do not copy or rewrite definitions from the given predefined box. Instead, they first try to define problem predicates on their own, according to the conceptual patterns they had gained through the learning process and then check whether their definitions are compatible with those of the relevant general predicates in the box.

**Flexible problem-oriented white boxes:** Many advanced students perceive the predefined ADT box as a *flexible box* that can be reduced or expanded according to the problem to be solved. The reduction of the box is done by deleting redundant predicates. Students justify this approach by arguing that there is no point in overloading the computer's memory by the implementation of predefined predicates that are not used in the problem-solving process. The expansion of the box is accomplished by additionally implementing new, necessary general predicates that are used to solve the given problem.

**White boxes as tools for defining new predicates:** Many advanced students rewrite the definitions of general predefined predicates (instead of transparently invoking the general predicate) to define new predicates. Actually they use them as templates and rewrite their definitions by making small changes.

### 3.2  Construction of Integrative Knowledge

The findings of our study indicated that the students had constructed integrative declarative and procedural knowledge of ADT boxes, and they employed them in unique ways to develop programs. The use of predefined black boxes for ADT enabled them to concentrate on high-level cognitive tasks such as problem analysis, problem solving, and knowledge representation without the burden of knowing complex implementation details. In contrast, the white boxes enabled students to learn, through examples, how to implement ADTs according to a given specification, and to practice code reuse and modification. The students defined their own rules of using ADT boxes and demonstrated a variety of strategies of using them while writing their programs. Those who learned and comprehended the notions of the formal ADT concept, used it the way expert programmers do: They first try to determine the suitable predefined ADT for the given problem and then transparently use the relevant ADT black box. Only when the familiar predefined black boxes are insufficient to solve the problem, do they unfold a relevant box and make the minimal necessary changes, or specify and implement a new ADT. Once the new ADT box is implemented, they use it transparently as is common among professionals. In contrast, students who are immature, and are still in the middle of the learning process, interpret in their own way the roles of the ADT boxes. Some of them avoid using black boxes because they believe that the encapsulation of the general predicates they used reduces the meaning, clarity, and completeness of their programs. Others, although beginners, transparently used predefined black boxes, and temporarily avoided using them when they started learning about their implementation [11].

## 4  Conclusion

In this paper we demonstrated how evolving ADT boxes can be employed to teach the interweaving declarative and procedural aspects of logic programming. We believe that the suggested instructional model can be adopted to emphasize various aspects of any programming paradigm, and can also be used to guide the students toward proficiency in programming based on abstraction and code reuse.

We recommend that the suggested instructional model be employed while providing the students with an appropriate learning environment that promotes learning processes in the context of knowledge integration [4]. Various aspects of the learning concept should be introduced in different ways by repetition through simpler frameworks [7]. Scaffolding examples should be used to demonstrate the activities associated with each stage of the model; appropriate exercises and support activities should be developed to motivate students to use black boxes, comprehend the code of white boxes, reuse code provided by others, modify code, and choose the appropriate boxes to solve given problems. Moreover, in order to foster integrative knowledge, students should continue, in each stage of learning, to practice and meaningfully utilize the tools and the methods that they have previously acquired.

## References

1. Aho, A.V. & Ullman, J.D. (1992). *Foundations of Computer Science*, W.H. Freeman and Company.
2. Ben-Ari, M. (1995). *Understanding Programming Languages*. John Wiley.
3. Buechi, M. & Weck, W. (1997). A plea for Grey-Box components. *Workshop on Foundations of Object-Oriented Programming*, Zürich, September 1997 Available:http://www.cs.iastate.edu/~leavens/FoCBS/buechi.html
4. Clancy, M.J. & Linn, M.C. (1999). Patterns and Pedagogy. *ACM SIGCSE Bulletin*, 31(1), 37-42.
5. Gal-Ezer,J., Beeri, C., Harel, D., & Yehudai, A. (1995). A high-school program in computer science. *Computer*, 28(10), 73-80.
6. Gal-Ezer,J., Harel, D. (1999). Curriculum and course syllabi for high school CS program. *Computer Science Education*, 9(2), 114-147.
7. Eckstein, J. (1999). Empowering framework users. In *Building Application Frameworks: Object-Oriented Foundations of Framework Design*. Mohamed E. Fayad, Douglas C. Schmidt, and Ralph E. Johnson (Eds.). John Wiley & Sons, 505-522.

8. Haberman, B. (1990). Lists in Prolog. M.S. Thesis. The Weizmann Institute of Science, Rehovot, Israel. (in Hebrew)

9. Haberman, B. & Ben-David Kollikant, Y. (2001). Activating "black boxes" instead of opening "zippers" – A method of teaching novices basic CS concepts. *ACM SIGCSE Bulletin*, 33(3), 41-44.

10. Haberman, B. & Scherz, Z. (2003). Abstract data types as tools for project development – High school students' views. *Journal of Computer Science Education online*, January 2003. Available: http://iste.org/sigcs/community/jcseonline/

11. Haberman, B. Shapiro, E. & Scherz, Z. (2002). Are black boxes transparent? – High school students' strategies of using abstract data types. *Journal of Educational Computing Research*, 27(4), 411-236.

12. Helm, R., Holland, M. & Gangopadhyay, D. (1990). Contracts: Specifying behavioral compositions in Object-Oriented systems. In *Proceedings of the European Conference on Object-Oriented Programming on Object-oriented programming systems, languages and applications (ECOOP/OOPSALA)*. 25, Ottawa Canada, October 1990, 169-180.

13. Kiczales, G. (1994). Why are black boxes so hard to reuse? Invited talk, OOPSLA'94. Available: http://www.parc.xerox.com/spl/projects/oi/towards-talk/transcript.html

14. Resnick, M., Berg, R. & Eisenberg, M. (2000). Beyond black boxes: bringing transparency and aesthetics back to scientific investigation. *Journal of the Learning Sciences*, 9(1), 7-30.

15. Scherz, Z. & Haberman, B. (2003). The role of abstract data types in the project development process. Submitted to *Journal of Computer Science Education*.

16. Sterling, L. & Shapiro, E. (1994). *The art of Prolog* (2$^{nd}$ ed.). Cambridge, MA: MIT Press.

17. Warford, J.S. (1999). Black Box: A new Object-Oriented Framework for CS1/CS2. *ACM SIGCSE Bulletin*, 31(1), 271-275.

# The Role of ICT and Informatics in Austria's Secondary Academic Schools

Peter Micheuz

University Klagenfurt, A-9020 Klagenfurt, Austria
peterm@isis.uni-klu.ac.at

**Abstract.** Secondary academic schools in Austria provide students with a broad and extended general education. That is their mission. But although these schools consider it as one of their foremost tasks to impart knowledge, they also aim at providing students with other qualifications and skills. This paper describes the special and important role of Informatics and ICT on the lower and upper secondary level. Here an attempt is made to constitute the claim for the subject Informatics as part of general education from a scientific point of view. The recent and still ongoing shift of this subject from the upper level to the lower level secondary education caused some confusion about the allegedly different subjects such as introduction into Informatics, IT or ICT. In the perception of a broad public and even of teachers these terms mean almost the same thing. In this paper I suggest the acceptance of a broader view of the subject Informatics. Moreover an evaluation of all ongoing informatical activities at the secondary academic schools in Austria and subsequently the building of a framework of informatical competence for the whole scope of these particular schools is desirable.

## 1 Introduction

The question of how to deal with Informatics and later with ICT in education is as old as the introduction of computers and the internet in schools. Social and technologic developments, associated with an evident change from the industrial to the information and knowledge society, left their marks also in form of an enlarged offer of corresponding subjects in education. Governments have to facilitate the basic conditions that schools can provide their pupils and students with a modern education wherein Informatics and IT-relevant subjects play an important role. The importance and significance of the subject Informatics respectively ICT can be deduced from its weight in the timetables of all subjects in various types of schools. In this paper I will focus on Austria's secondary academic schools (allgemeinbildende höhere Schulen, AHS) and the relevance of this subject in these particular schools.

Secondary academic schools in Austria educate pupils in the age-groups 10 up to 18 years. About 30% of all primary school leavers in Austria attend academic secondary schools [2]. Compulsory education in Austria ends after 9 years of school attandance and after that about 40% are attending secondary higher schools. About 35% of these students are educated in the AHSes till the final exam ("Matura") [15].

R.T. Mittermeir (Ed.): ISSEP 2005, LNCS 3422, pp. 166–177, 2005.

Passing it is required for further study at university. The other 65% of the students graduate at vocational schools providing the students with reinforced technical and economic education. At the moment we can observe a growing tendency to attend vocational schools for various reasons. One reason could be, that in a technically and economically driven society, general education gets out of fashion. It also seems that the attraction of vocational schools correlates to a certain extent with excellent computer equipment and a wider offer of Informatics and IT-related subjects.

Some Austrian secondary academic schools in Austria reacted to this phenomenon with a reinforced offer of Informatics education and thus improved "customer retention". As an example, Fig. 1 shows very impressively the increase of the number of alumni in 1996 due to the new attractive subject Informatics in the school where I am teaching (Gymnasium Völkermarkt, Austria).

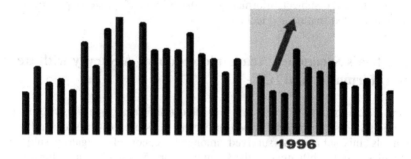

**Fig. 1.** Development of the number of alumni at the Gymnasium Völkermarkt

In 1996 Informatics in general was a real attraction. But this effect could not be maintained till today. Offering just Informatics does not guarantee to attract pupils any longer. 15 years ago introducing Informatics in the lower level of secondary education ago was quite unusual and innovative. Hence it was a distinguishing factor between competing schools.

## 2   About the Legitimation of the Subject Informatics in General Education

Besides the very pragmatical reasons for reinforcing Informatics at schools in order to attract pupils and to pretend progressiveness, there are other fundamental reasons which can be considered to legitimate this subject. Many computer scientists and teachers who are engaged in the field of Informatics didactics never end to demand an obligatory subject Informatics at schools. Especially in Germany and Switzerland we can find petitions for an establishment of Informatics in general education.

A widely accepted idea of general education which can be applied to the specific curricula at schools is due to Bussmann/Heymann [5]. Hubwieser [12] and Schwill [19] are adapting their ideas and deducing from them a viable legitimation for an independent subject Informatics as an indispensable part of general education. Another approach for the demand of imparting informatical competencies in schools by means of an independent subject can be found at [10]. There Friedrich refines the recommendations of the GI [20].

Another basic argument for the general character of the subject Informatics is found in [19]. There Schwill adapts the fundamental ideas of Bruner for the field of Informatics. Humbert [19] deduces the legitimation for this subject by a well-founded philosophical approach of (computer) science.

To round up the arguments which can be interpreted in a wider sense for an integrative but still independent subject Informatics the following position might be remarkable.

"If thinking about the next generation of computers and the generation after that", David Cliff predicts in [7] for the near future, "more immissions of natural systems and sciences into the field of Informatics and also into curricula are a consequence". Perhaps the amendment of secondary education in Bavaria points already in a direction where the subject Informatics in the 6th and 7th grade is part of a broader subject area called "nature and technics" [1].

## 3   Austria's Secondary Academic Schools – A Survey with Respect to Informatics and ICT

Is there a legitimation problem for the subject Informatics in Austria's secondary academic schools? Since 1985, when Informatics has been established in these types of schools, this subject has survived among the canon of obligatory subjects. But Informatics is only obilgatory in the 9th grades for 15 year old pupils for a two-hour lesson per week. The term "survival" is not far-fetched because in 2003 the Austrian ministry of education reduced the amount of lessons per week for all types of schools and for all age-groups by two. And for a certain time it was not clear that the compulsory subject Informatics would persist. Two hours of Informatics lessons per week in the 9th grade are assured and from the 10th to the 12th grade the subject Informatics can be chosen as elective. But this does not imply that Informatics and ICT are not present in the lower level of secondary academic schools. Quite the contrary, the Informatics/ICT scenery in Austria's secondary academic schools is for reasons of autonomous decisions made by the individual schools very alive and dynamic. As a consequence it is very inhomogeneous.

"In 1995 a fundamental school reform was started. It provided for autonomy of schools, giving them the possibility to develop their own characteristic school profiles and to establish areas of emphasis. In 1999 a new curriculum was introduced for the lower level of academic secondary schools and for general secondary schools. It consists of core and extension areas. On the basis of this curriculum, a new curriculum for the upper level was developed as well. It came into force in the school year 2004/2005. Another important step in this process of enhancing quality at school is the change from measuring input to measuring output. In this context, work is under way for establishing the educational standards for the fourth grade of primary school, general secondary school and academic secondary school. In this context it is also worth mentioning that the European Computer Driving License (ECDL) has developed into a best-practice model. Austrian pupils have passed a total of 320,000 individual modules since the year 2000. Thanks to the initiative "eFit Austria" schools are very well equipped with PCs. In Austrian secondary technological schools one PC is available for every four pupils. [2]"

This abstract of the recent report from Austria's Ministry of Education indicates five remarkable statements.

1. The autonomy of schools to alter timetables and introduce new subjects
2. New curricula
3. Change from input orientation to measuring output
4. Establishment of educational standards
5. Offering and support of the ECDL (and other IT-certificates)

These items have more or less important implications for the role of Informatics and ICT. They will be discussed in more detail in the next chapter.

# 4  Results of Autonomy in the Field of Informatics and ICT

Currently, there exist no comprehensive studies and statistics about the present realizations of autonomous initiatives in general. In consideration of thousands of schools this is not surprising. The more autonomy the less overview and vice versa. This includes also the fact that since 1992 [23] no nationwide empirically based study regarding Informatics and ICT in schools has been initiated.

Therefore, I am not able to quantify exactly the extent of Informatics and ICT in Austrians secondary academic schools. But I dare to give a qualitative overview due to informal surveys and reports.

At the lower level of secondary academic schools, autonomic decisions have already been made for some years. Although Informatics does not explicitly occur in the canon of obligatory subjects, there have been many initiatives in establishing Informatics in this age group. The 10-14 year old pupils today face a wide range of offer in the field of Informatics, which varies from school to school. In this spectrum we find courses for typewriting, word processing, courses preparing the ECDL, non-obligatory tutorials, and even not so few (in some federal states about 50%) obligatory lessons in Informatics which have been established at the expense of other subjects. Furthermore there are some models to integrate the computer and informatical methods in Mathematics, foreign languages or other established subjects such as Geography.

More than a decade ago this integrative approach was propagated and demanded by ministerial enactment. But in retrospective, one can state that this did not work in a satisfactory manner. The reasons were lack of appropriate standardized software, insufficient hardware at that time, and therefore, last but not least, the rather poor acceptance of the teachers involved. The situation in Germany was almost the same. The German initiative "ITG" (Informationstechnische Grundbildung) was doomed to fail for the same reasons.

In the meantime the conditions for ICT at schools have noticeably improved although they are far from being perfect. It is somehow remarkable but not astonishing that many secondary academic schools in Austria recognize the importance of introducing ICT or even Informatics at the exspense of other subjects.

Due to the ministerial strategy of extending autonomous facilities also to the higher level of secondary education it is, since this school year 2004/2005, possible to establish Informatics also as an compulsory subject in grades higher than 9th.

## 5 The European View

In [9] a comprehensive survey of "Key Data on Information and Communication Technology in Schools in Europe" is published. Many figures illustrate the state of the school computerization, the number of computers per student, and the teacher education which varies from country to country. In nearly all comparisons Austria is ranked above average. This study on ICT also deals with the broad range of curricular objectives in general lower secondary education. In detail the investigation revealed a wide coverage of the objectives: Learning the correct use of standard software (word processing, spreadsheets ...), learning the search for information, communicating via a network, using ICT to enhance subject knowledge, and developing programming skills.

It is remarkable that the last item "developing programming skills" can be found in this enumeration. The minor part of the European countries specifies programming skills for this level of education. This situation changes significantly when we consider the upper secondary level where only Belgium, Spain, France, Ireland, the Netherlands, and Norway do not mention "programming skills" in their ICT-curricula.

Comparing European educational systems is a very challenging task and for reasons of the vast variety very difficult. This task even gets more complicated in terms of IT-literacy, ICT and Informatics at schools. Whereas the term and the subject ICT is to a great extent unambiguous throughout Europe and its items can easily be subsumed (see above), this does not apply to the subject Informatics. Only in very few European countries such as Germany, Austria, Latvija, the Netherlands, there is a special subject called Informatics at all.

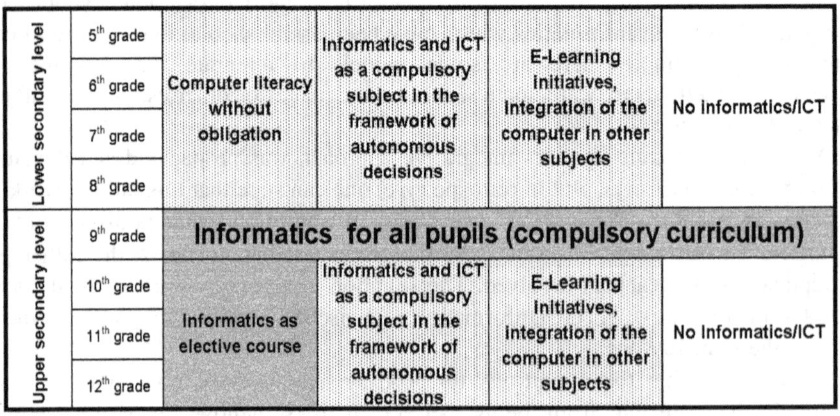

| | | | | | |
|---|---|---|---|---|---|
| **Lower secondary level** | 5th grade | Computer literacy without obligation | Informatics and ICT as a compulsory subject in the framework of autonomous decisions | E-Learning Initiatives, Integration of the computer in other subjects | No Informatics/ICT |
| | 6th grade | | | | |
| | 7th grade | | | | |
| | 8th grade | | | | |
| | 9th grade | **Informatics for all pupils (compulsory curriculum)** | | | |
| **Upper secondary level** | 10th grade | Informatics as elective course | Informatics and ICT as a compulsory subject in the framework of autonomous decisions | E-Learning Initiatives, Integration of the computer in other subjects | No Informatics/ICT |
| | 11th grade | | | | |
| | 12th grade | | | | |

**Fig. 2.** Spectrum of Informatics/ITC in the AHSes

A strong postulate for an independent subject Informatics has been published by Breier [3]: "We are deliberately breaking with the integration of computer science in affined subjects, recommended in the overall plan of the conference of federal states, as we take the view that the reasonable handling of information and information systems as well as the other cultural techniques, reading, writing and counting cannot be taught integrated in other subjects". In Germany there are still efforts to legitimate and establish Informatics as an obligatory subject also at a lower level, whereas in Austria the responsibility for an above-average provision of Informatics is delegated to schools.

For 20 years Informatics is a mandatory subject for all pupils in the 9th grade of Austria's secondary academic schools and an elective subject from the 10th to the 12th grade (see Fig. 2). In the late eighties and early nineties, when the computer played only a minor role in the secondary lower level, there was an implicit agreement on the content of this subject. At that time, computers with their limitations as informing and communicating tools were not appropriate for introducing ICT for all pupils.

But with the upcoming fascinating high potentials of multimedia and networked computers and with the ubiquitous presence of Informatics systems a veritable shift took place. It caused a partial relocation of Informatics from higher secondary level to lower secondary level. As a matter of fact over ten years ago, most of the pupils had their first experience with computers at school. In contrast, today pupils are already "digital natives" whereas teachers are "digital immigrants" [7].

In order to reinforce this statement, a recently accomplished study in 5th and 6th grades among the 10-12 year old pupils in secondary academic schools revealed that almost all have access to computers at home and nearly 70% to the internet. Moreover, amost all of them have already made some pre-experience with the computers at primary schools [16].

## 6   Can Informatics be Used as Generic Term for Computer Science, ICT and IT-Literacy in Schools?

Curricular school autonomy in Austria has made it possible to establish autonomous foci especially in the secondary lower level. The schools themselves are responsible not only for the altered timetables where Informatics and ICT figure to a various degree and in various forms. The spectrum ranges from a self-dependent subject Informatics to e-Learning initiatives and to carrying out interdisciplinary projects.

IT-competency at this level is varying from school to school and from federal state to federal state. This variety is also expressed by different synonyms and denotations for similar, if not the same, subjects. Within this scope we can find Informatics as well as information technology, introduction into Informatics, basic education in Informatics or even word processing and keyboarding.

Based on informal talks with colleagues I know that this situation is not really satisfying. But is this really Informatics what is taught at this level?

Hubwieser claims: "Unfortunately the term Informatics is misused for every activity with the computer. The spectrum reaches from a computer aided video course to elementary type writing on the keyboard" [12]. Like Breier, he also pleads for a fundamental informatical education beyond the mere training of computer skills.

Bavarian secondary academic schools are about to implement and realize Hubwieser's concept which focuses on six areas of computer education. There are designing graphics and editing text, arranging files hierarchically in file systems, achieving and transporting information by e-mail, linking extended amounts of documents into hypertext structures, extracting significant content out of the WWW, first steps of programming. Informatics is integrated in a subject area "nature and technics" in the 6th and 7th grade to the extent of one hour per week. It will be interesting if this approach of a conceptually well elaborated "real Informatics"-scenario at a comparatively early stage can hold its promises.

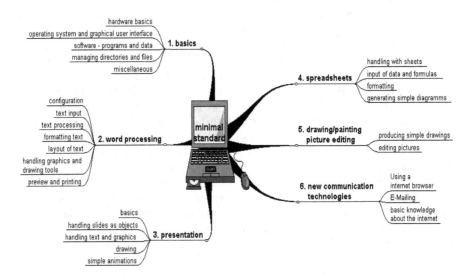

**Fig. 3.** Standardized learning objectives for 12 years old pupils in Carinthia/Austria

Another approach of introducing Informatics in the 5th and 6th grades is on the way in Carinthia/Austria where standards and concrete learning objectives have been worked out for nearly all the pupils. In cooperation with more than 2/3 of the secondary academic schools in this area, based on one-hour Informatics-education per week, learning objectives leading to the topics illustrated in Fig. 3. have been defined.

Unlike the Bavarian concept-based approach this is a pragmatical attempt to standardize the basic IT-skills and IT-knowledge of the pupils at an early age. They meet the "PISA-driven" shift from input orientation to measuring output. Maybe this collection of operationalized objectives could upset some didactics experts in the field of Informatics since it may be regarded as an adapted subset of the modules of the ECDL (European Computer Driving License). Is it justifiable to call this Informatics?

Historical reasons, a comparatively narrow interpretation, and concrete perception of Informatics as an independent subject in a few countries are certainly important reasons for separating the subject Informatics strictly from ICT. But this does not change the fact that even now the term and subject Informatics is not well known and accepted widely in the global (worldwide) educational context.

It is evident that Informatics at upper secondary level should meet higher demands than at the lower secondary level. But what prevents us to legalize something which seems to be colloquially already reality and to acquire a broader view on this term? In order to reinforce this let me quote Mittermeir ([14]) who pleads clearly when asking whether Informatics is a subject with strict borders or an area with open boundaries for the second aspect. "If Informatics lessons should be more than a mental exercise, teachers for Informatics should keep its borders open".

A traditional subject with a great affinity for Informatics is undoubtedly Mathematics. Nobody would be thinking of referring to this subject in school or in science by calculating or by geometry. Within the wide scope of this subject, contents such as calculating with natural numbers, algebra, geometry, analysis, and even the increasing use of calculators and CAS-programs have its place. Although every comparison has its limits and puristic teachers of Mathematics might not be amused when somebody puts Informatics at the same level as their fundamental subject, the idea of subsuming also ICT aspects into the broad term Informatics has a certain charm and is worth to be at least discussed.

The proverb "An error which is committed by many people is recognized as a rule after all." has no scientific foundations, but it should act at least as a stimulant in this discussion.

Informatical education takes place in various forms. These forms include not only the subject Informatics proper but also the increasing use of computers in other subjects. Computer, and, moreover, Informatics systems should be taught in an independent subject Informatics in order to provide informatical knowledge and skills as part of a redefined general education and of an extended cultural technique.

This measure guarantees a responsible, competent and interdisciplinary use of computers as a tool and as well as medium. The alternative of imparting informatical education integrated in other subjects, is reality in some schools and can be discussed, but it can by no means replace the substantial subject Informatics.

Many secondary schools in Austria did already react, others are aware of this and it is desirable that within the realm of autonomous decisions they maintain and establish Informatics preferably as an obligatory subject.

# 7 The 9th Grade: Informatics for All

Fig. 2 reveals that the only invariant within the wide scope of informatical education in the Austrian secondary academic schools in Austria, is the obligatory subject Informatics in the 9th grade. All the pupils have to pass it. Historically developed and emancipated from the subject "EDV" (electronical data processing), it has survived the recent amendment of the new upper level of secondary academic schools. Some years ago this subject represented for most of the pupils the first contact with a computer and a systematical introduction to something like Informatics. This has changed dramatically. Nowadays the differences between the informatical competence of 15-year-old pupils can be extreme even if they have attended the same school for four years. This is obviously an unsatisfying and untenable situation which has to be gradually improved.

The importance of this compulsory "sandwich"-subject Informatics in the 9th (see Fig. 2.) is due to the fact that it could exert a normalizing influence on the informatical education in the previous grades. To achieve this, however, we should first agree on minimal standards. Although the curriculum for this subject is extremely flexible [6] and obviously takes into account the big differences in the pre-knowledge of the pupils, measures should be taken to provide the pupils with a minimum of informatical competencies before they enter this grade.

An aspect to be taken into account is the influence of this subject with respect to autonomous decisions of pupils concerning further elective courses. It must not be underestimated that a poor informatical education at this level provides students with a wrong or false image of Informatics, and does not encourage them to choose this subject Informatics as elective course.

## 8  Is Informatics in the Grades 10 to 12 only for Specialists?

The desirable but only seldomly realized systematic education in Informatics already from the 5th grade on might suggest that the education for mastering most of the everyday tasks is completed after the 9th grade. Such a continuous education should guarantee to a certain extent a solid informatical fundament. Without doubt this could apply for a certain percentage of students in one age-group, but not for all. It is highly desirable that we encourage students to choose the subject Informatics above the 9th grade especially in a generally educating school. Economy and society needs people with a broad education and a profound informatical background. Therefore it is important to make efforts to maintain or even expand an attractive offer of Informatics in the 10th to the 12th grade also in general education.

However, recently accomplished informal surveys reveal a rather unpleasant picture. The attractiveness of the elective courses in Informatics which are provided from the 10th to the 12th grade is decreasing. One reason has been the overall reduction of two lessons per week last year at all levels and subsequently the restriction in choosing courses.

It can be estimated that this year about 20% of an age-group are choosing elective courses in Informatics. The percentage of schools which provide a reinforced education in Informatics with obligatory lessons at the upper secondary level is about 10% [20]. Field reports about the autonomous decisions of the schools in the upper secondary level do not exist by now because the reform is brand-new and therefore its implications are not transparent and noticeable yet.

Informatics at the upper level from the 10th to the 12th grade in the secondary academic schools should continue to be an attractive offer for interested students. But committing all the students to a special informatical education within a general education would go too far. However, from all students can be expected that they maintain their basic informatical competence, which they should have acquired by passing the 9th grade. This is not the case by now as a (unpublished) study conducted in Upper Austria 2003 has proved.

## 9 A Framework of Informatics at Secondary Academic Schools

Education in Informatics needs a solid and stepwise development with generous stages of exercising and consolidation. This is only ensured if a framework of realistic objectives for each level goes along with a sufficient amount of Informatics lessons and, desirably, with additional applications of the computer in other subjects.

Because of the fact that many pupils have already a certain pre-knowledge in using computers when they enter a secondary academic school it is advisable to start in the 5th grade. I recommend setting up informatical objectives for the lower level secondary education with a preliminary quasi-certificate at the "PISA"-age, when in Austria the pupils normally have accomplished compulsory school attendance.

On one hand, it is rather improbable that the Austrian Ministry of Education will discontinue autonomy and switch to central regulations regarding the organizational and curricular aspects. On the other hand, there is a strong demand for evaluation and output measuring. But what can be measured in the realm of Informatics when there are not even common objectives for the various levels?

Therefore, a generally accepted framework of informatical competencies as shown in [10] could be a good basis for a consistent guideline. At the lower level of secondary education, the syllabus of the European Computer Driving License [8] can serve as solid basis. Proper education should facilitate the requirements of the ECDL. But vice versa the ECDL should not dominate the Informatics education as a whole.

I can imagine that there is a high agreement on the common minimal objectives of Informatics instruction till the 9th grade. A framework for the further grades, where Informatics (in schools) is more and more regarded as a special branch of computer science, is much more difficult to build. There are unfortunately very few publications about what is really taught in Austria's secondary high schools at this level, but an informal survey reveals enormous differences regarding the teachers' interpretation of the curriculum of the subject Informatics. I suggest also for this level at least an informal agreement about minimal standards without thinking instantly of the EPAs ("Einheitliche Prüfungsanforderungen") in Germany.

If one takes a look at exemplary assignments of final exams in Informatics in Austria's secondary academic schools [20], it gets clear that the task of finding minimal requirements for that subject is not easy but nevertheless necessary and important. All students who are interested in these elective courses, should be informed about the contents and requirements when choosing the subject Informatics. Therefore, a mandatory basic framework beyond the very open Informatics curriculum is desirable. It would provide students and teachers as well with a basic orientation.

## 10 Conclusions

The situation of Informatics in Austria's the secondary academic schools differs widely. This is due to school autonomy in terms of curricula, hardware equipment, and, above all, the varying engagement of Informatics teachers. This leads to the undesirable effect of big gaps regarding the informatical competencies already at an early stage. This situation should be avoided by setting up a referential framework for informatical competencies for all levels in the secondary academic schools.

Standardizing measures should be taken as soon as possible in form of an independent subject Informatics for at least one hour per week for the lower secondary level.

Much importance should be attached to the $9^{th}$ grade where the subject Informatics is already established. Besides the standardizing effect on Informatics in the lower secondary level, this subject can encourage or discourage students from choosing Informatics further on. For the most part of the student population this grade is the tentative conclusion of a formal education in Informatics. After that students should be able to meet the average Informatics requirements in school and in everyday life. Although only a minor part of the student population decides to attend the subject Informatics further on, it should be a future challenge to define a sustainable framework for this age-group.

Finally, I suggest simplifying the terminology in the context of Informatics and ICT-related subjects especially in the lower secondary level. As Mathematics in schools covers the range from primitive calculating to abstract proving, I prefer the umbrella term "subject Informatics" for a wide range of informatical activities and contents. This includes the first systematic contact of pupils with computers as a subject-matter and the use of computers as a tool. In the upper secondary education this subject can and must be extended to more abstract concepts and to informatical methods as a precondition for software development and a deeper understanding of our digital world.

# References

1. Staatsinstitut für Schulqualität und Bildungsforschung, Bayerischer Lehrplan, http://www.isb.bayern.de/gym/nt/index.htm
2. Development of Education, Ministry of Education, Austria 2004, http://www.bmbwk.gv.at
3. Breier, Kretzschmar, Informatics in Mecklenburg-Western Pomerania: Overall plan for computer science education in general schools, SECIII, 2002, Dortmund
4. Bruner J.S., The process of education, Cambridge Mass. 1960
5. Bussmann, H. / Heymann, H.-W.: Computer und Allgemeinbildung, Neue Sammlung, 1987
6. BMBWK, Lehrplan Informatik Oberstufe, http://www.gemeinsamlernen.at
7. Boyle R., Proceeedings of the 9th Annual SIGCSE Conference (ITICSE) Leeds, ACM, 2004
8. OCG, Homepage of the ECDL in Austria, http://www.ecdl.at
9. Eurydice, Key Data on ICT in Schools in Europe, 2004 Edition, http://www.eurydice.org
10. Friedrich S., Informatische Fachkonzepte im Unterricht, INFOS 2003, GI-Ed., p.133f
11. Hubwiser P., Informatik als Pflichtfach an bayerischen Gymnasien, in Schwill, Springer, Potsdam, 1999
12. Hubwieser P., Didaktik der Informatik, Springer, 2000
13. Mittermeir R., Was ist Schulinformatik? In ME2001, Schriftenreihe Nr. 26, p. 3f
14. Mittermeir R., Informatik: Ein Fach oder ein Gebiet, Schulinformatik in Österreich, Ueberreuter, Wien 2003, p. 5f

15. Micheuz P., Tu felix Austria informatica?, Schulinformatik in Österreich, Ueberreuter, Wien 2003
16. Micheuz P., Informatics and Standards at an Early Stage, Informatics and Student Assessment, GI Lecture Notes, 2004
17. Rechenberg P, Was ist Informatik?, Hanser, 2000
18. Schwill A., Fundamentale Ideen der Informatik, Zentralblatt für Didaktik der Mathematik
19. Humbert L., Zur wissenschaftlichen Fundierung der Schulinformatik, 2003, Siegen, Univ., Diss., 2003
20. GI Empfehlungen, 2000, LOG IN 2/00, Informatik-Spektrum 23 (2000)

# Informatics *Versus* Information Technology – How Much Informatics Is Needed to Use Information Technology – A School Perspective

Maciej M. Syslo[1] and Anna Beata Kwiatkowska[2]

[1] Institute of Computer Science, University of Wroclaw
Przesmyckiego 20, 51-151 Wroclaw, Poland
syslo@ii.uni.wroc.pl
[2] Faculty of Mathematics and Informatics, Nicolaus Copernicus University
Chopin str. 12/18, 87-100 Torun, Poland
abak@uni.torun.pl

**Abstract.** We discuss the role of computers and informatics in school education in Poland; 'informatics' generally stands for 'computer science'. Although, our investigations are based on the situation in Polish schools, the conclusions may apply to other countries. The main attention is paid here to didactical approaches in teaching and learning informatics and its applications with the emphasis on preparation for living and lifelong learning in the information society (knowledge-based society). In recent years one can observe many changes in schools regarding the role of computers and informatics education. On the other hand we still have to address fundamental questions:

1. How to teach a changing discipline and how to keep track of developments in the field of informatics and its applications?
2. What to teach, in particular to what extent one should learn a discipline (informatics) to be able to use its applications (information technology)?
3. How to prepare teachers of informatics, IT and other subjects (but equipped with IT) for their new role of advisers to students?

In answering these and other questions we discuss some of the solutions we proposed and which have been introduced to Polish schools and to the system of teacher training. In particular, we focus our attention on the didactical approach to teaching IT-relevant subjects and the integration of IT with other subjects and to teaching informatics (as a process of designing a computer solution of a problem). With regard to teacher preparation, we present the preparation standards and discuss the role of school IT co-ordinators.

We plan to demonstrate also an **e-IT-book**, an implementation of a new approach to teaching and learning of new technology with the help of technology.

## 1   Technology in Education

### 1.1   Computers in Education

The development of educational technology closely follows the development of technical equipment. In the case of computers, they were introduced to education in the sixties of the last century. In Poland, first regular classes on informatics were

R.T. Mittermeir (Ed.): ISSEP 2005, LNCS 3422, pp. 178–188, 2005.

organized in two secondary schools in Wroclaw in mid sixties, just 'a day after' the first mainframe computer (Elliott 803, made in the UK) was installed in the country. The main topics were algorithms and programming in Algol. The approach was machine oriented: electronic data processing and computer calculations according to mathematical and engineering formulas.

The official history of computers in Polish schools started in 1985 in the beginning of personal computer era with the first official curriculum proposed by the Polish Computer Society. For about 10 years (micro) computers appeared mainly in teaching informatics as a separate subject and only occasionally they were used as a teaching aid. The main turning point appeared with the development of user-friendly human-computer interfaces, which support user's approach to computer use. Then the Internet became popular and came to schools and since then it has been the main factor which influences the way technology is applied in and integrated with education.

In the mid 90', a big struggle has begun among the education policy makers in Poland to accept the term 'information technology' for 'informatics for all students' as the combination of informatics technology with other related technologies (such as communication technology) and their applications in education and society, and human aspects. Today 'information technology' is widely used in our education system in the same meaning as 'information and communication technology' is used in other countries.

In 1997 in Poland, a national initiative, called the **Education Reform**, has been launched according which schools should be oriented towards across-curriculum integration of computers, information technology, and the Internet with learning and teaching of various subjects. Today one of the main goals of our education system is to prepare all students to actively live in the information, knowledge-based society.

## 1.2  IT in the Education System in Poland

Formal education starts in Poland at the age of 7 (from 2004 it will be moved down to 6). The formal school system at primary and secondary levels consists now of three stages:

- primary school – 1-6 grades (age 7 to 13);
- middle school (in Polish: gimnazjum) – 7-9 grades (age 13 to 16);
- high school – 10-12 grades (to 13 in certain vocational schools) – (age 16 to 19).

Information technology (IT) as a separate subject is taught in[1]:

- 4-6 grades of primary school, for at least 2 hours per week for one year;
- middle school, for at least 2 hours per week for one year;
- high school, for at least 2 hours per week for one year;

Moreover, in high schools students may choose informatics as a subject of specialization and take an external final examination (matura in Polish) in that subject.

---

[1]  In primary and middle schools the subject is still called informatics, but it will be changed for information technology in two to three years, since its curriculum is in fact on how to use information technology across the curriculum in different subjects and applications.

The national project "Internet laboratory in every middle school" initiated in 1998 put a solid technical basis for IT education in middle schools in Poland. Today all middle schools are equipped with at least 10 PCs and additional equipment. In 2001, a similar project was launched "Internet laboratory in every high school" with 15 PCs for computer laboratory and 5 PCs for a multimedia laboratory connected with a school library.

The EU eLearning initiative [3] has set the target that by 2003 all students leaving the school system (formal education) should be digitally literate. In Poland, this target has been met by all students leaving middle school (when they are 16 of age) since 2002 and will be met by graduates from high schools beginning in 2005.

## 2   Informatics *Versus* Information Technology – A School Perspective

As already mentioned, the term 'informatics' is used in the sense of computer science and the term 'information technology' has been recently accepted in education in the sense of applications of informatics. For the educational purpose one may assume that informatics deals with producing new products related to computers (hardware, software, ideas, theories, etc.) and IT is on applying and using informatics (computer related) products.

### 2.1   The Era of Informatics

Informatics (in fact, elements of informatics – EI) was in Poland a part of the curriculum for more than fifteen years (1985 – 2002). It has been taught in elementary schools (1-8 – mainly during the last two years) and in high schools (9-12 – for one, two, three and even four years).

There were three EI curricula approved by the Ministry of Education. The one proposed by the team led by the first author had a very general structure and consisted of a number of modules which could be used to design an instruction plan for teaching EI from one up to four years with the emphasis on different aspects of informatics, e.g. problem solving, algorithmics, application software.

There was also a textbook published (first edition appeared in 1988). It is perhaps interesting to mention that this textbook had a new, unchanged edition every year (two in 1995) and more than 100 000 copies have been sold. It is unusual for a book on informatics to remain unchanged on the market for so long. It was mainly due to the approach adopted in the book. Computers and software tools were not described in full details but only with respect to the main theme (problem) of the presentation and discussion. Therefore, the content of the textbook was universal although there were some key components of the contemporary IT missed, especially related to computer networks and computer supported communication, which have entered schools recently. Let us list chapters of that textbook: history of computers and informatics, how computers are designed and how they work (operating systems), playing and learning (turtle graphics – Logo), from problems to programs (elements of programming in Pascal), designing an own directory (data base), calculations in mathematics (numerical methods), computing faster – efficiency of algorithms (elements of algorithmics), writing with no pencil and paper (text editing), easy and effective managing of a small business (spreadsheet).

There was also a package of educational software designed and produced to help the teachers of Elements of Informatics in the main subject areas: a model of computer and computations, operating system, programming in Pascal, designing and running algorithms, numerical computations, statistical analysis of experimental data. The Ministry of Education sent the package to high schools and to teachers' colleges.

In recent years one can observe a growing awareness among teachers that the use of computers in schools cannot be limited to a separate subject. It is recognized however that when there were only few computers in a school and there was only one teacher who knew how to operate them, the separate subject and a computer laboratory in one room guaranteed the most effective use of technology. Today however, most of the teachers are interested in using computers in their classrooms.

## 2.2  Information Technology and Informatics

As a part of the Education Reform, **the education standards** for the main subjects in elementary and high schools have been published in 1997. The main part of the standards consists of the list of education goals (tasks) which are to be realized and met by schools – schools are responsible for supporting and helping students in their cognitive and creative activities, learning, and self-development. In consequence, students should become competent in many areas. For instance, they should: *successfully communicate and use new communication technology for that purpose; search, sort, organize, and use information from different sources; use different information technology and media with competence and responsibility.* With respect to informatics education the main education goal is formulated as follows:

> **to guarantee students the possibility of using information and communication technology, and to prepare them to live in the information society.**

Information technology (IT) is now taught as a separate subject 2 hours a week for one year in all types of schools. Moreover, in high schools students may choose informatics as an optional subject and take an external final examination (matura in Polish) in that subject.

The team led by the first author has published curricula, textbooks and guidebooks for all types of informatics and information technology subjects in schools. Moreover, a book on using computers and information technology in ten other subjects in gimnazjum and two elementary books on algorithmics have been also published.

## 2.3  IT in the Education Standards

Using IT may effectively support achieving several education goals by schools and competences by students. We briefly review such possibilities.

In primary schools students are supposed to develop a competence in using different sources of information and to use IT in collecting, storing and processing information. Internet is an example of a source of information, other than books, where students can search, store and process information.

In gimnazjum and in high schools there are many opportunities for students to use IT and Internet. For instance, students should be prepared to individually integrate knowledge about the past learnt from different sources of information (history); they should have an opportunity to use different media and techniques for communication; they should learn and have a chance to use educational software, computer networks, electronic mail, Internet, and data bases. The following competences appear in different education areas such as history, physics, geography: use of different techniques for collecting, selecting, storing, processing and interpreting information, critical use of information about public and social life, use of media in personal search for information, use of IT to collect, process and analyze data from experiments, collect and interpret information, e.g. coming from satellite pictures, Internet, and GIS systems.

Moreover in high schools students are supposed to be able to use IT tools and Internet in almost all education areas, and mainly to use libraries with electronic sources of information, video-libraries, computer programs and other information bases. They should be prepared to use a library as a centre for global information.

Social aspects of information age: information as a product and a source of power, global village, and technopol are also considered.

Moreover, the following topics are discussed: multimedia; local and wide area computer networks; searching for information in wide area networks; communication via computer network; preparing presentations with the help of IT tools; creating documents which are accessible in Internet.

Internet is considered as one of the most important elements of IT and of its integration with learning and teaching. It may be both, a subject of instruction and a tool for: information retrieval, global communication, problem solving and decision making in almost all school subjects and off-class activities.

## 2.4  Methodology of Changes

After computers were introduced to schools, they themselves together with networks have been the main IT topics of instruction. More important, however, is to be able to use a computer as an educational aid in all areas of learning and teaching. With the help of methods and tools of IT, old and traditional teaching material can be enhanced and new topics and skills, which otherwise cannot be learnt and taught, can be introduced and added.

The introduction of computers to schools in the 80's induced high expectations for improving education. Today, however, those expectations have not yet been fulfilled – it is argued that this is mainly due to unrealistic assumptions about learning as a passive process of information absorption. It is believed that to improve the results of learning **computers should be embedded** in, instead of added only to, learning environments as tools that elicit and support in students active processes of knowledge construction and skill development.

Access to information, especially through a network, is not sufficient to enhance learning and teaching. The amount of information is growing in exponential rate. Therefore it is necessary to teach how to critically evaluate its contents. Learning does not simply mean reading and watching, it should proceed through doing: performing tasks and solving problems. To properly operate information, one has to master several skills, e.g., building an information structure, evaluation of contents of information, information search and retrieval, information processing and presentation. Education should give students knowledge and skills that will enable them to find the proper information they need.

Working with information, students should be aware of social, ethical and legal aspects of unrestricted access to information. It applies mainly to personal data, collected and processed in computers for different purposes. Advantages and disadvantages of computers and computer networks in education have not been recognized completely. Usually, teachers and educators talk about their positive aspects and influence on learning and teaching. One has to take into account also that school is responsible for preparing students for the years to come when they leave school, join society, and are expected to make decisions on their own.

### 2.5 A Model for IT Development

In developing a curriculum for IT and informatics education it is very useful to have a model for IT development. Such a model has been presented in the UNECSO Curriculum [8][2]. The model is not a curriculum but provides a framework which shows the interrelationship of various components within a system and aids understanding by all parties involved in education: students, parents, teachers, educational administrators and policy-makers.

The model of IT development at the school level [8] consists of four stages: emerging, applying, infusing (integrating) and transforming. It describes also stages of teaching and learning and can be applied to learning and using IT (by students and also by teachers), teaching IT and teaching with the help of IT. The model can also help to understand why students, teachers, schools and other users of IT have to follow a similar route of IT development in their personal and professional life. For instance, in the case of preparation of teachers, they first have to learn about computers (emerging stage) to be able to use them in their subjects (applying stage), and then they begin to integrate IT with other teaching areas (infusing stage) and finally (in fact, after many years) school becomes ready for transforming its role in the community and society.

We successfully use the UNESCO model in designing curricula for schools and teacher preparation courses.

### 2.6 IT *Versus* Informatics Education

Many people assume that anything related to computers belongs to informatics. In education it is quite popular to use 'informatics' as a name for a subject and classes which take place in a computer laboratory regardless of what students are learning and doing (in fact, quite often they are playing computer games and surfing the web). It happened also in our education system: informatics is the subject in primary and middle schools although the curriculum is in fact on how to use information technology across curriculum in different subjects and applications.

---

[2] In fact, the first author has published a similar model, also consisting of four stages, in 1999 as a part of the project [4].

Fortunately all parties have recently accepted the term 'information technology' in our education system as the name for applications of informatics and its use in other disciplines and in every day life.

In our project on informatics and IT in education (see [4]) we assume that informatics deals with producing 'new products' related to computers (hardware, software, ideas, theories, etc.) and IT is on applying and using 'informatics (computer related) products'. Although this distinction does define neither informatics nor IT, it is very useful in describing methodology of learning and teaching both subjects.

In our approach of teaching and using information technology [4] we convince a learner to elaborate her or his style of working with information. Application software has usually several options, which support a user in improving a style (e.g. styles, templates, wizards, etc.). Elements of style are also very welcome when working with information on the Internet, in searching, publishing and communicating on the net.

In teaching informatics we follow a traditional way of producing a 'computer product', which consists of the three main stages:

- define a problem (i.e. its specification) and design its solution (algorithm) – this stage supports an algorithmic thinking;
- build a computer solution (program) of the problem – it is a place for working on programming style;
- test and evaluate the computer solution – also testing the correctness of the solution.

This approach and methodology can be applied to many sorts of problems in informatics, also at the high school level, e.g. in: solving mathematical problems, designing and producing a data base, designing and writing a web page, designing and producing a multimedia presentation.

## 3   Teacher Preparation and Training

With regard to the level of competences in IT, all teachers in schools in Poland fall into the following categories:

- teachers of separate informatics subjects (under different names: informatics, information technology, computerisation, etc.);
- teachers of all other subjects, who use and integrate IT with different areas of education;
- school IT co-ordinators.

*The Standards for Information Technology and Informatics in Teacher Preparation* [6] determine what teachers in different groups should know about and be able to do with the information technology (and informatics).

A position (function) of **school IT co-ordinator** was introduced to schools in Poland by the first author in 1998. This IT co-ordinator is supposed to be a teacher of a separate subject on IT or informatics and moreover he or she:

- leads continuous self-learning of IT of all teachers in the school; therefore a school IT co-ordinator is responsible for building professional learning of IT into the workplace (school);

- guides other teachers how to introduce IT to particular subjects and then integrate the technology with different subjects; in the beginning he/she may even help other teachers with the technology in the classroom;
- promotes and co-ordinates all changes in the school which involve IT and its use in education and school management.

A classroom as a working place contributes only a little to teachers' learning, so teachers have to find an extra time for their personal development. On the other hand, learning should happen locally. With respect to technology, school IT co-ordinators are to help other teachers in everyday working and learning in schools.

Based on the standards [6], two types of in-service training courses have been designed for:

- school IT co-ordinators;
- teachers of other subjects on how to use and integrate IT with different areas of education.

It is perhaps worthwhile to mention that 30% of course time teachers attending these courses spend working in their schools in cooperation with other teachers and with school IT co-ordinators.

Higher (tertiary) education institutions are major resources for teachers' professional development. They offer post-graduate in-service courses and training to different interest groups of teachers, in IT and in other subjects. The standards [5] serve as guidelines for accreditation of such courses and are used by the National Accreditation Board of Higher Education Institutions for that purpose (the first author is a member of the Board).

## 4 School as a Lifelong Learning Institution

The transformation to the knowledge-based society is today very high on the political agenda. The society expects from citizens new knowledge, skills and competences and to be active – self-motivated to pursue own personal and professional development throughout life. Lifelong learning is the most important and promising way to empower citizens to meet these demands. According to EU Memoranda (see [9], and also [7] and [3]), **lifelong learning** is defined as *all learning activity undertaken throughout life, with the aim of improving knowledge, skills and competences, within a personal, civic, social and/or employment-related perspective*. Therefore, lifelong learning is not limited to economic outlook and to learning opportunities for adults only. In the implementation, main emphasis is put on the centrality of learner, equal opportunity, and learning needs. Such approach to teaching and learning requires all education institutions to become more learner-oriented than program (or curriculum or institution)-centred.

Lifelong learning places new demands on all types of learning activities and educational institutions, in particular on schools. Information technology plays an important role in lifelong learning due to its great potential for innovation in learning and in teaching methods, educational tools and environments. We refer the reader to [7] where we discuss a new role of school and information technology in designing a lifelong learning strategy for schools, teachers and individual citizens.

It is still not obvious to students and to teachers in schools, that lifelong learning starts at the very beginning of formal education in primary schools and that tertiary education, learning at a workplace, and adult education are just next stages of lifelong learning, based on the foundation laid down at the beginning of education.

In the rest of this section we shortly comment on the situation of students and teachers in our schools with regard to lifelong learning.

## 4.1 Students

How to adopt changes brought especially by rapid development of IT and how to make sense and use of the vast amount of information available in the net – two main items on the list of what students should learn in school with regard to lifelong learning, are included in the IT curriculum for different levels of education in Polish schools. Actually, all students have separate classes on IT in primary, middle (gimnazjum) and high schools, so they learn how to adapt to changes in the technology for 9 years of formal school education.

Moreover in high schools, lessons on IT are related to subjects chosen by students as their specialization and one of the curriculum goals is to have students prepare their own personal IT environments which then they use in continuing education.

## 4.2 Teachers

The role of schoolteachers with regard to lifelong learning is twofold:

- they are lifelong learners themselves to develop their own professional knowledge;
- they should develop their students as lifelong learners.

These two fields of activities need different skills and competencies. To be prepared themselves for lifelong learning and to promote lifelong learning to students teachers should:

- be pedagogically literate in lifelong learning and know its role in changing the learning environment;
- know how to promote and integrate innovations in learning;
- be competent in using IT to support and manage the learning process.

Moreover, in learner-centred environments, teachers become guides, mentors, and mediators, who mainly help and support learners.

In understanding and using IT in teaching and learning, and in education in general, schools, teachers, and students go through four stages (see [9]): first they discover general functions and use of IT tools (emerging stage), second they learn how to use IT in different subjects (applying stage), then they learn how to recognise situations in which IT could be helpful in solving (real world) problems and how to choose appropriate methods and tools of IT (integrating stage), and finally IT becomes integral part of the professional practice in school (transformation stage). These stages are very important to teachers' personal preparation and professional practice with the use of IT: first they become IT literate (awareness stage), second, they begin to apply IT in their subjects, then different teachers begin to integrate and overlap different subjects, and finally they are able to design lessons on larger real-world projects using IT tools, methods, resources.

Regarding technology, the optimal vision of education is to combine best practice of human and machine (e-learning) teaching and providing access to non-local instruction and resources.

## 5 Other Activities

1. In 2000, **Association of IT Teachers** (AITT) (see [2]) has been founded by a group of school IT co-ordinators. The Association:

- by removing or diminishing geographical and psychological barriers, brings learners closer together at local conferences and workshops, organized all over the country in local communities or in schools;
- contributes to organization of local learning centres for students and teachers;
- promotes continuous education, in particular lifelong learning of teachers,
- promotes examples of good practice from classrooms in other classrooms;
- helps in providing access to IT for disabled students in their homes; in general, puts special emphasis on special education.

2. **Post-graduate in-service courses** (350 hours of instruction) **for school IT co-ordinators** are organized by the University of Wrocław.
3. **Educational Forum for Information Society** was founded in 2003 to co-ordinate and organize continuous in-service training in IT for teachers from the region of Lower Silesia. The Forum will provide infrastructure of access to lifelong learning of teachers and will prepare projects for structural grant from the EU.
4. **Conference "Informatics in School".** Institute of Computer Science, University of Wroclaw, in cooperation with the Ministry of Education, is the main organizer of the annual national Conference „Informatyka w Szkole" (Informatics in Schools). In 2004, more than 500 participants from elementary and high schools, universities, hardware and software companies attended the 20th Conference. Among the main speakers at these conferences were in past: Alain Bron (Switzerland), Ian Carter (UK), Margaret Cox (UK), Eric de Corte (Belgium), Peter Gorny (Germany), Ivan Kalas (The Slovak Republic), Angela McFarlane (UK), Raymond Morel (Switzerland), Bojidar and Evgenia Sendov (Bulgaria).
5. International events to be held in Poland in 2005: EUROLOGO and IOI.

## References

1. *A Model Curriculum for K-12 Computer Science*, ACM, 2004.
2. Association of IT Teachers (AITT – pol. Stowarzyszenie Nauczycieli Technologii Informacyjnej – SNTI), http://www.snti.pl/.
3. Commission of the European Communities, *eLearning – designing tomorrow's education,* Brussels, SEC (2000) 318 final.
4. Syslo M.M. (ed.), *Meeting and Learning with Computers*, WSiP (Publisher Company), Warsaw 1998-2003, http://www.wsip.com.pl/serwisy/ti/. Project on informatics and IT in education addressed to all levels of education, to students and to teachers.

5. Syslo M.M., From elements of informatics to information technology across the curriculum: the Polish approach, *Int. J. Cont. Engineering Education and Lifelong Learning* 11(2001), 526-533,
6. Syslo M.M. (ed.), *Standards for Information Technology and Informatics in Teacher Preparation*, presented to the Ministry of Education and Sport in Poland, Warsaw 2003.
7. Syslo M.M., Schools as Lifelong Learning Institutions and the Role of Information Technology, in: van Weert T.J., Kendall M., *Lifelong Learning in the Digital Age*, Kluwer Academic Publishers, Dordrecht 2004, pp. 99-110.
8. UNESCO, *Information and Communication Technology in Education. A Curriculum for Schools and Programme of Teacher Development*, Paris 2002.
9. van Weert T.J., Kendall M., *Lifelong Learning in the Digital Age*, Kluwer Academic Publishers, Dordrecht 2004.

# Standard Software as Microworld?

Peter K. Antonitsch

Universität Klagenfurt, Austria
Institut für Informatiksysteme
Peter.Antonitsch@uni-klu.ac.at

**Abstract.** Traditionally programming is considered to be a core content of informatics education. Just as traditional is the discussion of how to teach programming at school. One major aspect seems to be the choice of a suitable software tool allowing to focus on the basic concepts and avoiding tool-specific overhead at the same time. Therefore, special learning environments (so called microworlds) have been developed, designed to reduce the complexity learners are confronted with. But – in most cases – these microworlds are a sort of isolated solution and call for a shift to "real" programming environments later on. The contrary approach is to downsize professional programming or (to be more general) software environments to the needs of the learner, which appears to be almost impossible due to the complexity of current software. This paper discusses how this might be achieved though by concentrating on programmable spread-sheet software. It points at possible didactic and methodical benefits by teaching programming this way and presents a list of criteria that can be helpful in deciding the relevance of software-tools for informatics classes.

## 1 Microworlds

A "microworld" is defined as a learning environment that allows to get in touch with programming basics by concentrating on the underlying concepts. Criteria that characterize such environments are listed in [1] and [2]:

According to Papert, a microworld should allow learners to enter an "active and self-determined process, where body knowledge can be used to communicate with and to take control over the computer by means of a program. Learners should be able to define, create and combine modules by making use of nothing more than the elementary concepts of branching and iteration. In this way they can become "architects of their own intellectual structures". To achieve this, the learning environment must have a clear and transparent structure and it must allow to tie up to the "personal knowledge of the learners".

Reichert, Nievergelt and Hartmann refer to Brusilovsky et al. ([3]) and du Boulay et al. ([4]) when they expect from microworlds:

- reduction of complexity, i.e. the "complex machine computer" must be substituted by a conceptually simpler machine;

R.T. Mittermeir (Ed.): ISSEP 2005, LNCS 3422, pp. 189–197, 2005.

- hiding of complexity, i.e. even with a conceptually simpler machine, the program-mer does not have to understand how the machine works internally (but he must understand the meaning of the actions performed);
- visualisation of program runs to clarify the semantics and structure of the program;
- small scope of the programming language and a simple programming environment;
- the possibility to pose "everyday problems" that are easy to explain and easy to understand, that stimulate problem solving activities, and where the solution is felt to be within reach.

## 2   Reflection: The Role of Programming

The criteria just mentioned refer to environments for learning how to program. But can these criteria be transferred to more general software environments that are used in (informatics) classes? Does programming boast such a general-educative core, that concepts for programming classes can be generalized and modified to concepts suitable for learning activities with other (whatever?) software?

According to S. Schubert programming is "problem solving – i.e. modelling and structuring – by making use of the principles and methods of informatics", whereby "the programming language has to be kept in the background" ([5]). Yet modelling and structuring are activities that are essential whenever it comes to comprehend the so called "real world" (see e.g. the considerations in [6]). To change the viewpoint: Programming stands for structured decomposition and recomposition (when programs consist of modules and corresponding interfaces), for formalization (when the con-ceptual solution of the problem is translated into executable code) and for automation (when the program code is executed by "a machine"), which are the three fundamen-tal concepts of informatics, that should be the underlying subject in any informatics course (referring to [7] and A. Schwill in [5]).

I would like to stress that I do not presume to assign a universal educative core to programming. But I see programming as a representative for many of the principles that must be part of informatics education in order to prepare the learners for an increasingly information-centred world. From this perspective the criteria I mentioned beforehand can be seen as guidelines for software environments that are rather learner-centred than computer- or application-centred. Therefore, I propose to aggregate and restructure the list of criteria mentioned above. This aggregation yields (see [8]):

- **Scalability** as aggregation of "reduction and hiding of complexity" and the de-mand for a learning environment that is transparent and easy to survey (referring to "small scope of the programming language" and "simple programming environ-ment")
- **Transferability**, accentuating the implicit assumption that basic concepts learned in microworlds can be applied in "professional programming environments" quite easily.
- **Visualisation** (as stated before).

Because these criteria were defined for programming, I will demonstrate their applicability to a "hybrid" system, i.e. a standard software-system with an underlying programming environment. Besides, this points at the necessity to understand basic programming structures even when it is only up to user-friendly adaption of ready-to-use software.

# 3  Example: Spread-Sheet Programs

Spread-sheet systems with an (additional) underlying programming environment are quite suitable for comparison with microworlds, because learners can either refer to past experience with environments like those (e.g. working with relative and absolute cell addressing as a first step towards automation) or are at least used to working with tables. Therefore, the structure of the environment should be familiar and it should be easy to tie up to the personal knowledge of the learners. Furthermore, the tables provide a given structure to the input area, the output area and the representation area, which helps to scale complexity and to visualize program runs.

Without giving prominence to specific software, the following considerations refer to Microsoft Excel with Visual Basic for Applications (short: VBA) as an underlying programming environment, simply because this software can be found in Austrian schools quite often. But it should be mentioned, that there exist (almost) as powerful programming environments supporting open-source spread-sheet programs. Thus the following considerations apply to these programs as well.

## 3.1  Structural Scalability

Frequently, software tools possess far too much functionality to be suitable for learning purposes. Structural scalability is given, if this overwhelming functionality can be tailored to the learner's needs or if the structure of the software can be used to hide certain aspects of the posed problems. In either case learners can concentrate on the intended learning objective more easily. With Excel VBA structural scalability can be found (at least) with regard to input, output and the data structure "array".

Input and output can be managed via table cells (just like when working with the accompanied spread-sheet program), by means of predefined I-/O-GUIs or rather by defining input- and output-forms oneself. This helps to concentrate on the structure of the program (control and data structure) because the effort for input and output can be kept reasonably small initially (see the following code for input and output via table cells and Fig 1 alike):

```
Private Sub CommandButton1_Click()
  Rem Declaration of variables
  Dim value_1 As Integer
  Dim value_2 As Integer
  Dim result As Integer
  Rem input
  value_1 = Cells(2, 2)
  value_2 = Cells(4, 2)
  Rem processing
  result = value_1 + value_2 'any operation  Rem output
  Cells(6, 2) = result
End Sub
```

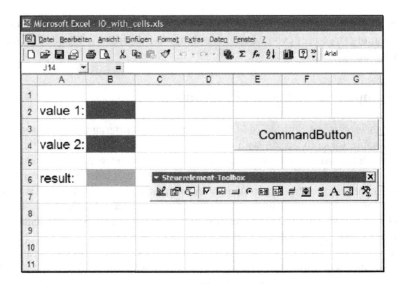

**Fig. 1.** Input and output using table cells (input and output areas are highlighted by shading)

Very often the learning of program structures is made difficult because control and data structures should be learned at the same time. The advantage of the control structure "iteration" can be sensed thoroughly only in the context of the data structure "array" (and vice versa). Therefore, learners have to understand two rather abstract concepts simultaneously to make the best of it. But the structure of spread-sheets allows the "simulation" of arrays so that learners can solely concentrate on iterations at first and deal with arrays afterwards (see Fig. 2).

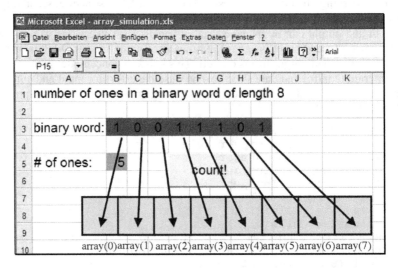

**Fig. 2.** Simulation of a one-dimensional array as section of a table row. This allows to focus on control structures without having to deal with abstract data structures at the same time

## 3.2 Methodical Scalability

A software tool shall be methodically scalable, if it encourages the use of different learning (!) methods when dealing with a certain topic. As table-like structures are quite common in every-day life, it is not too hard to create a "real-life situation" when using a spread-sheet environment, even if the posed problem is rather simple and seems to have nothing to do with real life at first glance (see Fig. 3). Moreover, the creation of a physical representation of the problem facilitates

- understanding of the problem structure (to be understood as a process of abstraction),
- modelling of the problem structure (due to sensual perception),
- translation (coding) of the solution to the problem into a programming language (to be understood as a process of further abstraction and automation) and
- to work with different forms of social interaction between the learners while the teacher might step aside and merely watch the learners' analysis of the problem.

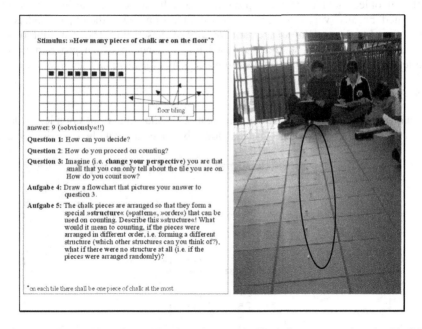

**Fig. 3.** Methodical scaling of a problem by using a table-like infrastructure of a school building (the position of the chalks is marked for better visibility)

## 3.3 Curricular Scalability

Finally, I speak of curricular scalability, if a software tool can be (re-) used in different (consecutive) informatics lessons, thus helping to explain different subject-matters in the field of informatics. This is an important aspect, as it takes time to get familiar with any new software. But time is a precious good, especially when talking about informatics education. Since programmable standard-software of the discussed kind can be used for application-oriented problems and for problems that call for programming activities alike, curricular scalability seems to be a natural fact, as long as the topics, the corresponding methods, and the (adequate) tools are chosen carefully. That is why I omit a detailed description of curricular scalability when working with spread-sheet environments.

### 3.4 Transferability

By restriction to the paradigm of procedural (and – to some extent – object oriented) programming, the basic control structures "sequence", "branching", and "iteration", as well as the data structure "array" can be found in any imperative programming language. Therefore the concepts that have been learned with one of these languages can be transferred to any other related language (see Fig. 5). This applies likewise to "classic" microworlds! But the programming environment VBA is available for all application programs of the Microsoft Office family, which means that the basic program structures that have been learned with Excel VBA can be applied to a variety of real-life problems. Furthermore, this special transferability permits insight into the different object-models of these programs, an advantage that hardly can be over-estimated, because very often only profound understanding of the object models leads to profound understanding of the functionality of these programs. Just think of serial letters, where the steps to create a serial letter change between program versions, while the underlying database and word processing objects remain the same.

### 3.5 Visualisation

Visualisation has to support learners in creating mental images of complex structures or abstract processes. But visualisations become a real benefit for learning

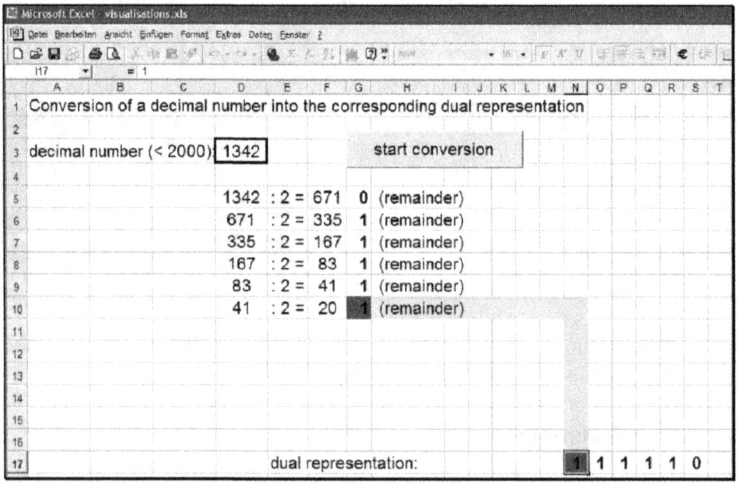

**Fig. 4.** Visualisation of the algorithm to convert a decimal number into its dual representation. The basic concept is to arrange the remainders of division by two in reverse order, which is emphasized by a "running bar". A slight modification of this visualisation can guide learners to reach a pre-concept of the data structure stack, where items are piled one upon the other and can be taken away only from the top

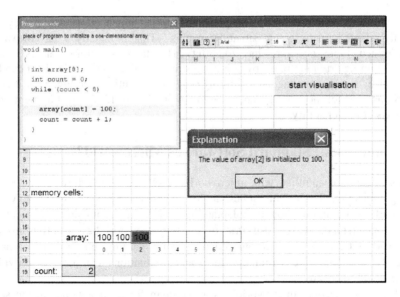

**Fig. 5.** Visualisation of memory management during the execution of a simple program, where table cells serve as a model for storage cells. The program code is displayed in a form (that has to be designed by the programmer) and the actual line of code is highlighted by a shaded bar. This and the display of an "explanation window" make it easy to understand the semantics of the program, the only purpose of which is to initialize an array with certain values. Notably the program is coded in C, which points at the transferability of the visualized concept

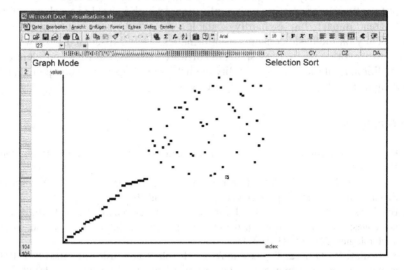

**Fig. 6.** Raster graphic simulated by the table structure of a spread-sheet map (note that height and width of cells are set to a small value within the graphics region!). The graphic visualizes the process of sorting the values stored an array using the selection-sort algorithm. By creating (animated) plots of the values over the (current) index, each sorting process reveals a specific "sorting-pattern"

and teaching only if they can be prepared without much effort and if they can be easily adapted to the actual situation in class. That is exactly what software with predefined table structure has to offer. The table structure can be used for programming "running bars" by colouring rows or columns (see Fig. 4), it can help to visualize "memory management" during program execution (see Fig. 5) or it even can serve as a model for raster graphic (see Fig. 6 and [5], p. 137f) – just to mention a few aspects of its versatility.

## 4    Conclusion: Standard Software as Microworld?

Those who are familiar with microworlds like the "Logo turtle" or "Kara, the programmable lady bird" might hesitate to call spread-sheet systems "microworlds" in spite of my attempt to show the adaptability of these environments. This scepticism is quite understandable because first of all a microworld has to offer an *optimal* environment for *special* learning situations when learning how to write a program. Clearly, an *optimal* environment for *special* situations can not be provided by "*universal*" software.

But if we accept "microworld" as a synonym for an adaptable (in the sense of scalable) "learning-cosmos", that is consistent to learners, I believe that scalability, transferability and visualisation are applicable concepts that should enable teachers to examine existing software with respect to its usability in class. This might be an important step to provide optimized learning environments on the basis of professional tools and to use their (increased) didactical and methodical potential.

Some sceptics may be not sufficiently convinced by these arguments. They may point to software for creating web-applications, which is used in teaching informatics with great impact, but is hardly scalable. To avoid such arguments, I focussed specifically on the basic concepts of informatics, when I discussed what we can learn from microworlds when using standard software systems, but I am confident that with the additional criterion of applicability the list of concepts can be completed and made applicable even for "advanced" software systems.

## References

1. Papert S.: Mindstorms. Children, Computer and Powerful Ideas. Basic Books Inc.; New York (1980)
2. R. Reichert R., Nievergelt J., Hartmann W.: Programmieren mit Kara. Ein spielerischer Zugang zur Informatik. Springer Verlag; Berlin, Heidelberg (2004)
3. Brusilovsky, P., Calabrese, E., Hvorecky J., Kouchnirenko, A., and Miller P.: Mini-languages: A way to learn programming principles. In: Education and Information Technologies, 2(1): 65-83 (1997)
4. du Boulay, B., O'Shea, T., and Monk, J.: The black box inside the glass box: Presenting computing concepts to novices. In: International Journal of Human-Computer Studies 51(2): 265-277 (1999)
5. Hubwieser P.: Didaktik der Informatik. Grundlagen, Konzepte, Beispiele. Springer Verlag; Berlin, Heidelberg (2000)

6. Antonitsch P.: Überlegungen zum Erreichen eines Minimalstandards im Programmierunterricht. In: CD Austria 5/2004, Sonderheft des bm:bwk zum Thema "Standards in der Schulinformatik" (2004)
7. Baumann R.: Didaktik der Informatik. Ernst Klett Verlag; Stuttgart, 2., vollständig neu bearbeitete Auflage (1996)
8. Antonitsch P.: Skalierbarkeit - Übertragbarkeit - Visualisierung. Gedanken zur Unterrichtsrelevanz von Software-Werkzeugen. Unpublished handout (in German) to a lecture held at "Pädagogisches Institut des Bundes in Kärnten" (March 2004)

# The Future Is Mobile – Education Meets Mobile Communication

Werner Wiedermann

Strategic Projects / Technology Relations,
Mobilkom Austria AG & Co KG,
Obere Donaustrasse 29,
A-1020 Wien, Austria
w.wiedermann@mobilkom.at

**Abstract.** More than three million Austrians make their calls with A1. Approximately 42 percent of all Austrian mobile phone users trust in the market leader in mobile communications.

Our large market shares in attractive customer-segments offer great potential for mobile data services. The world's first GPRS network and the first nation-wide UMTS network in Europe show that mobilkom austria is well prepared for the future of mobile communication.

## 1 Communication Moves the World

Within a single decade, mobile telephony has developed into one of the most successful innovations of the last 50 years - comparable to the success of the PC. In Austria alone, 5.5 million people make calls by mobile phone - placing Austrians among the mobile phone's biggest fans.

A leader in innovations like mobilkom austria sets the pace for changes in the market itself - and the mobile Internet is the future. We are only at the beginning of this era, where the mobile phone is fast becoming a 'universal' tool, capable of processing language as well as complex digital data.

In order to guarantee our customers a first class mobile network and more security, new technologies and a comprehensive technological infrastructure are necessary. In October 2002, mobilkom austria took the most important step toward that future by becoming the first European network operator to launch a UMTS[1] network.

For the Austrians, the mobile phone has become an indispensable everyday tool. This is confirmed in a recent study by the Fessel-GfK Institute, commissioned by mobilkom austria. The mobile phone has become an everyday object. In total, every household of Austrian mobile phone users has an average of 2.6 mobiles; we currently have a penetration rate of nearly 92%. Since owning their mobiles 52% of Austrians also make more calls. Nevertheless the trend is moving in a different direction: mobile phones increasingly switched off or muted.

---

[1] Standing for "Universal Mobile Telecommunications System", framework for third generation (3G) mobile networks, offering transmission rates up to 2 Mbit/s.

R.T. Mittermeir (Ed.): ISSEP 2005, LNCS 3422, pp. 198–201, 2005.

Thanks to the mobile phone, young mobile phone users become more spontaneous and arrange to meet more often on short notice. They benefit especially from their mobiles. But also senior citizens have been able to intensify their social contacts. This study by the Fessel-GfK Institute also allowed us to identify five types of mobile phone users.

A company truly willing to take direct social responsibility, even against the backdrop of a 'globalized' economy, cannot ignore subjects such as the 'digital divide' or the 'social divide'. On the contrary, mobilkom austria is actively seeking to address those issues, in constant dialogue with the scientific world as well as with 'the man and the woman on the street'. For us, the focus is still on the individual, not on technology.

A quote often heard in reference to information technology tells us that "inventing the future is the best way to predict it". Valdemar Poulsen must have had this in mind when, in 1899, he was applying for a patent on the world's first answering machine - undoubtedly a brilliant invention, yet during Poulsen's lifetime a rather redundant one. Only 70 years later would there be a growing demand for this "functionality" in society. With his invention, Poulsen was far ahead of his times; too far. Few patents and inventions actually manage to become innovations in a true sense; technical innovations will only be accepted if they are useful and needed.

The vision of digitally interlinking various electrical devices such as computers, mobile phones, car radios or even refrigerators goes back at least 15 years, with roots that reach back even further. Yet only now, with the mobile Internet and UMTS, do we finally seem ready to take the first step towards realizing this vision.

## 2 Market Leadership as Responsibility

Social commitment and education sponsoring, safety and the environment are very important to mobilkom austria. As Austria's leader both on the market and in innovations, we want to live up to our social responsibility as a role model. mobilkom austria's commitment is based on the concept of partnership and know-how transfer - in these cooperative efforts, the emphasis is not on the sponsoring, but on the projects carried out together. Besides the social aspects, the subject of "the future of society" is also at the heart of these activities.

Trends develop in the blink of an eye; the digital, internetworking world is transforming everyone's life, business and private and education life. What role do we play in this? While we can't see into the future, we can prepare ourselves for it.

Today's students, however, are sure not only to experience but also to shape the future. We want to let their creativity and their vitality inspire us, while at the same time making it possible for them to research and develop under ideal circumstances - and encouraging them to ask questions.

Education and Training is not limited to locations any more. Distance based learning has changed: from satellite-based distribution in the past to two-way interactive videoconferencing to today's online courses. With MOBILE BROAD BAND, mobilkom austria now combines the advantages of high-speed data transmission with the advantages of complete mobility. Whether you are a teacher who would liked to be online with your students – for example off school on a seminar - or as a student who needs to be connected with the online training programs of his master class: with MOBILE BROADBAND, no one has to do without the comfort of broadband transmission while on the go. Attractive packages in combination with easy to use hardware and set-up procedures ensure "plug & play" utilization and access speed like in home environment. Browsing, serving and even downloading of large files on the move is no problem any more and even makes it easier and more convenient to communicate – for teachers and students. Broadband transmission is based on UMTS PLUS®. With UMTS PLUS® seamless 3G service is offered in combination of UMTS and EDGE[2] . Together with WLAN[3] hotspots mobilkom austria opens the door to a new dimension of speed in mobile communication. There is no limitation to content for mobile learning, telecommunication services and new media projects. Any kind of materials, like charts, drawings, pictures, text and videos can be easily sent and received. In combination with multimedia mobile phones mobile learning has come alive and offers the possibility to study even on the way to school or while waiting for somebody. Through advances in educational technology in combination with mobile communication we can gain success of innovative new approaches to learning. Today education for students, livelong learning or even off-the-job training and can be easily integrated in every days life.

Enhanced e-learning technologies also changed our internal training strategies. For an outstanding company like mobilkom austria market oriented education and additional trainings are based on strategic goals to prosper successful in a dynamic and competitive market. Our employees will be individually prepared to meet the major demands of our business and are very pleased to deal with all the individual and different skills of our staff. Everybody knows the situation: You are dealing with new software tools but having no time to attend a training course. What can you do? You can ask your colleague, you can struggle through senseless texts within the help menus, you challenge it more or less intuitive or you do overtime to understand the problem. But we have an alternative solution: Our e-learning centre and our internal Employee-Self-Service-Tool "EASY" offers access to computer based trainings at anytime and via mobile remote access from anywhere. The employees themselves have the opportunity to control timing and location – even at home - of their individual training lessons themselves. And even more: the possibility to transfer know-how and to access information via these new technologies gives us competitive advantages and a fast and competent acting.

To make the technology behind mobile phones transparent, mobilkom austria also has been the initiator of an unique project called "Kinderuni Wien". The aim of this activity is to make the technology behind mobile phones understandable to children. The kids will be able to examine pioneering mobile phones or test new technologies such as multimedia messaging.

---

[2] "Enhanced Data Rates for Global Evolution" boosts data transfer rates and volumes on existing GSM/GPRS networks.

[3] "Wireless Local Area Network" for high speed accessing the internet or corporate intranet.

Mobilkom austria also offers platforms to encourage the exchange of ideas between scientists, teachers, parents and business on the subject of children/kids/students and new technologies. ROUNDABOUT KIDS is a series of discussions taking place regularly since a few years, which examines subjects such as transformation of reading and writing among children or their understanding of technology. In co-operation with ZOOM Children's Museum located in Vienna mobilkom austria hosted the first European "Network Kids" symposium.

It's all about skills - innovative technology, creative students, and clear solutions to the most complicated technical problems – that's why mobilkom austria is active in the field of education as well.

# Author Index

# Lecture Notes in Computer Science

For information about Vols. 1–3331

please contact your bookseller or Springer

Vol. 3378: J. Kilian (Ed.), Theory of Cryptography. XII, 621 pages. 2005.

Vol. 3377: B. Goethals, A. Siebes (Eds.), Knowledge Discovery in Inductive Databases. VII, 190 pages. 2005.

Vol. 3376: A. Menezes (Ed.), Topics in Cryptology – CT-RSA 2005. X, 385 pages. 2005.

Vol. 3375: M.A. Marsan, G. Bianchi, M. Listanti, M. Meo (Eds.), Quality of Service in Multiservice IP Networks. XIII, 656 pages. 2005.

Vol. 3374: D. Weyns, H.V.D. Parunak, F. Michel (Eds.), Environments for Multi-Agent Systems. X, 279 pages. 2005. (Subseries LNAI).

Vol. 3372: C. Bussler, V. Tannen, I. Fundulaki (Eds.), Semantic Web and Databases. X, 227 pages. 2005.

Vol. 3371: M.W. Barley, N. Kasabov (Eds.), Intelligent Agents and Multi-Agent Systems. X, 329 pages. 2005. (Subseries LNAI).

Vol. 3370: A. Konagaya, K. Satou (Eds.), Grid Computing in Life Science. X, 188 pages. 2005. (Subseries LNBI).

Vol. 3369: V.R. Benjamins, P. Casanovas, J. Breuker, A. Gangemi (Eds.), Law and the Semantic Web. XII, 249 pages. 2005. (Subseries LNAI).

Vol. 3368: L. Paletta, J.K. Tsotsos, E. Rome, G.W. Humphreys (Eds.), Attention and Performance in Computational Vision. VIII, 231 pages. 2005.

Vol. 3367: W.S. Ng, B.C. Ooi, A. Ouksel, C. Sartori (Eds.), Databases, Information Systems, and Peer-to-Peer Computing. X, 231 pages. 2005.

Vol. 3366: I. Rahwan, P. Moraitis, C. Reed (Eds.), Argumentation in Multi-Agent Systems. XII, 263 pages. 2005. (Subseries LNAI).

Vol. 3365: G. Mauri, G. Păun, M.J. Pérez-Jiménez, G. Rozenberg, A. Salomaa (Eds.), Membrane Computing. IX, 415 pages. 2005.

Vol. 3363: T. Eiter, L. Libkin (Eds.), Database Theory - ICDT 2005. XI, 413 pages. 2004.

Vol. 3362: G. Barthe, L. Burdy, M. Huisman, J.-L. Lanet, T. Muntean (Eds.), Construction and Analysis of Safe, Secure, and Interoperable Smart Devices. IX, 257 pages. 2005.

Vol. 3361: S. Bengio, H. Bourlard (Eds.), Machine Learning for Multimodal Interaction. XII, 362 pages. 2005.

Vol. 3360: S. Spaccapietra, E. Bertino, S. Jajodia, R. King, D. McLeod, M.E. Orlowska, L. Strous (Eds.), Journal on Data Semantics II. XI, 223 pages. 2005.

Vol. 3359: G. Grieser, Y. Tanaka (Eds.), Intuitive Human Interfaces for Organizing and Accessing Intellectual Assets. XIV, 257 pages. 2005. (Subseries LNAI).

Vol. 3358: J. Cao, L.T. Yang, M. Guo, F. Lau (Eds.), Parallel and Distributed Processing and Applications. XXIV, 1058 pages. 2004.

Vol. 3357: H. Handschuh, M.A. Hasan (Eds.), Selected Areas in Cryptography. XI, 354 pages. 2004.

Vol. 3356: G. Das, V.P. Gulati (Eds.), Intelligent Information Technology. XII, 428 pages. 2004.

Vol. 3355: R. Murray-Smith, R. Shorten (Eds.), Switching and Learning in Feedback Systems. X, 343 pages. 2005.

Vol. 3354: M. Margenstern (Ed.), Machines, Computations, and Universality. VIII, 329 pages. 2005.

Vol. 3353: J. Hromkovič, M. Nagl, B. Westfechtel (Eds.), Graph-Theoretic Concepts in Computer Science. XI, 404 pages. 2004.

Vol. 3352: C. Blundo, S. Cimato (Eds.), Security in Communication Networks. XI, 381 pages. 2005.

Vol. 3351: G. Persiano, R. Solis-Oba (Eds.), Approximation and Online Algorithms. VIII, 295 pages. 2005.

Vol. 3350: M. Hermenegildo, D. Cabeza (Eds.), Practical Aspects of Declarative Languages. VIII, 269 pages. 2005.

Vol. 3349: B.M. Chapman (Ed.), Shared Memory Parallel Programming with Open MP. X, 149 pages. 2005.

Vol. 3348: A. Canteaut, K. Viswanathan (Eds.), Progress in Cryptology - INDOCRYPT 2004. XIV, 431 pages. 2004.

Vol. 3347: R.K. Ghosh, H. Mohanty (Eds.), Distributed Computing and Internet Technology. XX, 472 pages. 2004.

Vol. 3346: R.H. Bordini, M. Dastani, J. Dix, A.E.F. Seghrouchni (Eds.), Programming Multi-Agent Systems. XIV, 249 pages. 2005. (Subseries LNAI).

Vol. 3345: Y. Cai (Ed.), Ambient Intelligence for Scientific Discovery. XII, 311 pages. 2005. (Subseries LNAI).

Vol. 3344: J. Malenfant, B.M. Østvold (Eds.), Object-Oriented Technology. ECOOP 2004 Workshop Reader. VIII, 215 pages. 2005.

Vol. 3343: C. Freksa, M. Knauff, B. Krieg-Brückner, B. Nebel, T. Barkowsky (Eds.), Spatial Cognition IV. Reasoning, Action, and Interaction. XIII, 519 pages. 2005. (Subseries LNAI).

Vol. 3342: E. Şahin, W.M. Spears (Eds.), Swarm Robotics. IX, 175 pages. 2005.

Vol. 3341: R. Fleischer, G. Trippen (Eds.), Algorithms and Computation. XVII, 935 pages. 2004.

Vol. 3340: C.S. Calude, E. Calude, M.J. Dinneen (Eds.), Developments in Language Theory. XI, 431 pages. 2004.

Vol. 3339: G.I. Webb, X. Yu (Eds.), AI 2004: Advances in Artificial Intelligence. XXII, 1272 pages. 2004. (Subseries LNAI).

Vol. 3338: S.Z. Li, J. Lai, T. Tan, G. Feng, Y. Wang (Eds.), Advances in Biometric Person Authentication. XVIII, 699 pages. 2004.

Vol. 3337: J.M. Barreiro, F. Martin-Sanchez, V. Maojo, F. Sanz (Eds.), Biological and Medical Data Analysis. XI, 508 pages. 2004.

Vol. 3336: D. Karagiannis, U. Reimer (Eds.), Practical Aspects of Knowledge Management. X, 523 pages. 2004. (Subseries LNAI).

Vol. 3335: M. Malek, M. Reitenspieß, J. Kaiser (Eds.), Service Availability. X, 213 pages. 2005.

Vol. 3334: Z. Chen, H. Chen, Q. Miao, Y. Fu, E. Fox, E.-p. Lim (Eds.), Digital Libraries: International Collaboration and Cross-Fertilization. XX, 690 pages. 2004.

Vol. 3333: K. Aizawa, Y. Nakamura, S. Satoh (Eds.), Advances in Multimedia Information Processing - PCM 2004, Part III. XXXV, 785 pages. 2004.

Vol. 3332: K. Aizawa, Y. Nakamura, S. Satoh (Eds.), Advances in Multimedia Information Processing - PCM 2004, Part II. XXXVI, 1051 pages. 2004.